Drum Roll

by the same author

PERCUSSION INSTRUMENTS AND THEIR HISTORY

ORCHESTRAL PERCUSSION TECHNIQUE

(Oxford)

drawing by Richard Cole

Drum Roll

A Professional Adventure
from the Circus to the Concert Hall

JAMES BLADES

Jenny.

With my signature comes
my best wishes.

James Blades.

Cheam 8/4/79.

FABER AND FABER
3 Queen Square
London

First published in 1977
by Faber and Faber Limited
3 Queen Square London WC1
Printed in Great Britain by
The Bowering Press Ltd
Plymouth
All rights reserved

British Library Cataloguing in Publication Data

Blades, James
   Drum roll.
  1. Blades, James 2. Musicians—Biography
  I. Title
  789'.01'0924   ML419.B/

  ISBN 0–571–10107–0

In memory of those
who brought me up by hand, my brother Cecil, and
my friend Arthur Langford,
who always said that I had a tale to tell

Preface

'It sounds very funny to hear me say *spirit*. But *drumming is spirit*.
You have got to have that in your body, in your soul. . . . And it can't
be an evil spirit. If you're evil, you're going to drum evil, and if you
drum evil, you're going to put evil in somebody else's mind. What kind
of a band have you got then? Nothing but an evil spirit band. And
God help a bad spirit band. . . . So you've got to keep a spirit up. A
drummer's place is to help the other fellow, not make him play himself
to death. Without a drummer that knows how to *help*, there's no
band.' I was reminded of these words of Baby Dodds, supreme among
New Orleans drummers, as I read James Blades's autobiographical
book, for, given the vast difference between the two men's environ-
ments, Dodds's words are pertinent to Blades's greatness as well as to
his own. Baby Dodds was born into the squalor and luxury, the
violence and ecstasy, of old-time New Orleans, and the bands that
rode on the beat of his 'good spirit' made a music that was life-affirming
no less in plumbing the depths than in scaling the heights of 'un-
accommodated man'. Though in Blades's world there was no wail of
'low-down dirty blues', his early life was hard, and the stalwart Peterborough folk that sired him had their own kind of rock-bottom reality.
Down to earth you could certainly call them, even though their earth
was less grubbily ripe than that of New Orleans. From them young
Jimmy imbibed a zest for living which he translated into corporeal
action, asserting, on whatever *ad hoc* percussion instruments came
his way or could be magicked out of junk, a pride in being human,
measuring out time without fear or favour.

Blades's progress has been gladiatorial: from outhouse to Sunday
parlour, from home to school, from school to itinerant gig in dance-
hall or on parade. Jimmy's first professional job, ill and irregularly
paid, was in a circus tent; from which he graduated to flea-pit cinema
or theatre; hence to the Regal, Majestic or Metropolitan; hence to
London theatres, cinemas and the posher hotels. London led to the big
time: film and recording sessions, the leading symphony orchestras,
a long association with the English Opera Group, an O.B.E., world
travel, international honours. Taking off puckishly from the top rung

A*

ix

of the ladder, Jimmy airily danced into three new activities! He became a highly esteemed teacher at London's centres of musical Establishment – institutions which had played no part in his own arduous training; he became a popularising lecturer to schools and music clubs, achieving a triumph that owed as much to wit and character as to professionally percussive expertise; and he became an author and scholar, producing an immense, admirably written book on the nature and history of percussion instruments which is, and is likely to remain, definitive.

What's most remarkable, indeed well-nigh incredible, is that Jimmy has pursued, and still pursues, all these activities collaterally. He views his 'progress' in the technical sense as movement in time and space, not as an ascent from depths to heights. He has shown fantastic ingenuity and imagination in devising sonorities for the operas of his friend and colleague, Benjamin Britten; he has performed prodigies of virtuosity in playing 'advanced' percussion parts from Bartók's superb sonata onwards. Yet throughout this book he speaks with no less respect, as well as affection, of men and music from the more commercial fields in which he has operated : his tributes to Charlie Kunz or Louis Levy, for instance, sound no less heartfelt than his homage to Britten, nor does he imply that they belong to distinct and irreconcilable worlds. So in reading this book we experience a marvellous refreshment in the contemplation of a life lived whole, the parts interdependent, mutually supportive. Though one might say that such a sense of happiness, of a life fulfilled, stems from an Edenic innocence, this is far from being a heartless or mindless euphoria. Jimmy has lived through two world wars, has sustained the loss of a first and deeply loved wife, and hints at phases of darkness and depression, even at momentary failures of nerve, in his professional life. No more than hints are necessary, however, for since drumming has been for him as for Baby Dodds an affirmation of spirit and an act of love, it has enabled him to 'help' himself no less than the 'band'. Ebullience as well as endurance springs electrically from his diminutive body; it's not fortuitous that of the many tributes paid to him by his legions of admirers none rings truer than that of a child at a Sussex primary school.

> 'The instruments are nothing
> Without your magic touch,
> So, sir, please come to us again,
> We've loved you very much.'

WILFRID MELLERS

Foreword

In one of his inimitable broadcasts Alistair Cooke said: 'What people most want to know about people is how they got where they are today.' In the case of a professional musician people are also interested in discovering why a player chose to be such, and what prompted him to choose his particular instrument. For my part, I am afraid I can lay no claim to any classical masterpiece giving me my early inspiration and urge to make music. No, possibly it was the sound of a sweet voice: my mother's, or the little bird who sang in the hollyhock near our living room window, or Grandad's melodion, or Uncle George's gramophone, or Playford's mouth-organ; and in due course Jim Pack's big bass drum. The big drum may have led me to the circus, and my mother's tuneful voice may have been responsible for the concert hall. To climb the professional ladder is no easy matter, and if I can lay no claim to the top of this ladder, I can state without fear of contradiction that I started on the bottom rung.

My fifty years of 'percussing' have been an adventure. Not by any means the type of adventure I dreamed of as a child or a boy, like driving an express train through the night, or going to distant shores to build bridges over rivers such as the Zambesi; but nevertheless an adventure, during which I have been spurred on by the help of many friends and the memory of people who fought a much harder battle than I have done, so – thanks to the invaluable assistance of my wife Joan and my friend John Lingard who (as in my earlier excursions into literature) have given me unstinted support, and to Patricia Herrmann for her editorial assistance – here is my story.

J. BLADES

Cheam, 31st December 1976

Contents

Illustrations

❧ 1 ❧

Early Days

In the early hours of 9th September 1901, my father, Thomas Weston Blades, a journeyman tailor of 166, Star Road, Peterborough, was presented with his first son. In later years my father informed me that I arrived unexpectedly in the region of 2 a.m. – a most inconvenient time, for the deliverer of babies in our road, a lady who lived at the far end of our yard, had to be hastily awakened to perform the necessary ritual. For this inconvenience which was completely out of my control I apologise to the lady whose nocturnal slumbers were so rudely disturbed; she was a great 'artist', and had, it was said, on more than one occasion left the washtub and delivered a 'brat' with the soapsuds still on her hands.

After a lapse of time (governed to some extent by the prevailing birth rate in the parish) I was christened James after my mother's favourite brother who had recently died, supposedly through having slept in a damp bed and catching double pneumonia. According to family history I behaved quite well at the font in St. Mary's Church, only whimpering a little as I was figuratively immersed in the water of Jordan. I have no recollection of a swell christening party, or receiving a vast number of silver spoons and such like. In fact from all accounts I was not born with a silver spoon in my mouth, and the addition to the Blades family was not likely to improve prevailing conditions. My father was on short time at work, and my mother (who was in a poor state of health) was having to look after her parents who were living with us. My grandfather (a farm worker) was laid up – a horse whose bruised fetlock he was dressing having kicked out his eye – and Grandmam was a permanent invalid almost confined to her couch. Added to this the whole of the house was thoroughly downcast over the death of my Uncle James, and the further sad news that Mam's soldier brother, Gadsby,[1] had died from cholera while serving with his regiment in India. So it can be said that whilst I was completely unaware of prevailing conditions, the close of the year 1901 was sad and anxious for all those around me. Information concerning my earliest years was given to

[1] Grandmam Close's maiden name.

1

me at a later date by my mother and my cousin Lily, who was living with us to relieve the distress in her home in London. Lily – who was always known as 'our Lil' – became my supreme adviser and confidante.

From my informants I learned that Grandmam and Grandad Close, who lived with us – or to be more correct as the rent book was in Grandad's name, we with them – were my mother's parents and that they had recently moved to Peterborough from Longthorpe. Longthorpe, a village two miles from Peterborough, was my mother's birthplace. In the little church was the record of her baptism as Catherine Close, and in the churchyard lay five of her brothers and sisters who had died in infancy. The reason for Grandad's coming to town was that two of Mam's brothers were now working 'on the Line' – as the Great Northern Railway was known in Peterborough. These young men were soon to be known to me as Uncle David and Uncle Dick. Auntie Lizzie, my mother's eldest sister and 'our Lil's' mother, was living in London. Auntie Fanny (the ninth child and given to prophecy), had recently married and gone to live 'up North' – near to Manchester. The only unmarried member of Mam's family was my Auntie Lydia. Auntie Liddy, who was in service, was 'keeping company' with a young carpenter named George Cox, whose eventual entry into our family circle presented it with my redoubtable Uncle George.

My mother's side of the family was well endowed with relations, but of my father's parents I know little. My paternal grandfather had been something of a character. His occupation – when he had one – was in some way connected with horses and race courses. His passion for the turf resulted in my father being rendered completely homeless when quite a small boy and, according to Dad, the workhouse was only averted through the kindness of an aunt and uncle who gave him a home. An interesting home it proved to be, for Uncle Fred Strickson owned a small music shop, and with his brother 'Ness' ran the only dance orchestra that functioned in Peterborough and district at that time. It was known as 'Strickson's String Band'. One of their engagements took the form of a weekly dancing class, and Dad, in addition to his work as an apprentice to the tailoring, helped a bit at the dancing class by being on the door – which turned out to be very lucky for him (and me) because it was here that he met my mother, who was in service at Thorpe Hall. There were few other relations on Dad's side. He had one brother some years his senior who was a coachman to some titled people in Yorkshire, and though he inherited his father's love of horses, my uncle confined himself to driving them at a trot whilst seated comfortably on a leather cushion and wearing a top hat.

To the best of my knowledge there were only two other people to whom my father could claim relationship. One was his Auntie Polly: a sweet character who was kindness itself. The other relative on Dad's side I never met as he died before I was born. He was an elusive character who, it was said, worked and slept in stables, and rejoiced under the nickname of 'Codger'. Codger Blades was always said to be on the verge of winning a fortune but never did, and lost what little he had in the process. There is no doubt that the disasters in his family caused by the lure of gambling had a great influence upon my father for he never had the slightest inclination to try his luck on this or that.[2] As to putting such a thing as a house in jeopardy, this to him would have been unthinkable, particularly such a nice house as the one in which I was born.

Our House

It was a wonderful house, right at the end of the row, and with all the luxury of six rooms, three up and three down. Some of the rooms may have been on the small size, but what matter, for they were all the cosier in the winter. The front room downstairs housed the best furniture, consisting of one easy chair, four rather high-backed chairs and a couch. In one corner stood a small table bearing the family Bible and portrait album, together with one or two small ornaments in the way of souvenirs from seaside places which no one in our family had ever visited. On the mantelpiece stood a coloured glass ornament with three funnel-shaped receptacles for holding flowers. A complete tour of our art gallery included a number of family portraits all of which seemed to stare at me when they weren't looking at each other. In the far corner of the room was a small bookshelf with a single row of books. Dad's library was not vast, but was nevertheless interesting, even if the literature was a trifle heavy for general reading. On the lighter side were *The Last Days of Pompeii*, Darwin's *Origin of Species* and Boswell's *Johnson*. My father's interest in religious matters was reflected in *Why We Are Churchmen*, and his desire to become better educated in two hefty volumes of *Oxford House Papers*.

The front door of our house opened almost directly onto the pavement. It was used only on special occasions such as Christmas Day or Bank Holidays (and of course funerals), and then only to let

[2] And neither have I.

3

out the visitors, who came in by the back door to make sure that their boots were well wiped. On the rare occasions that the front door was opened it made a terrible creak, and opened with a jolt that used to set the flap of the iron letterbox swinging. To close the door was almost as difficult a task as opening it, and when it was eventually locked and bolted there was the ritual of putting back the 'roly-poly' to keep out the draught and to draw the curtains on the pole which, if done in one swoop, made a sound like a shake on a tambourine; a sound which much later I was to know well.

Directly above the front room was a room equally hallowed and strictly taboo: Grandad's and Grandmam's bedroom. Here, in addition to the huge bedstead with its brass posts, was Grandad's coffer and the night commode. In the corner near the window stood a fairly large chair for Grandmam, Grandad using the night commode with the lid down for his chair. Above the small fireplace was the mantelpiece (in iron), used for such things as the candlestick, Grandad's Bible, and the little wooden stand on which he hung his silver watch: a treasured possession which he wound every evening with great care and deliberation with a little key that hung on the end of his watch chain.

Each night before getting into bed Grandad read, slowly and aloud, a few verses from the Good Book. No one was allowed to touch Grandad's Bible, or for that matter to look into his coffer or the little closet in the corner of the bedroom. The coffer was a real antique, having been in Grandad's family as long as he could remember. In this grim oak chest Grandad kept his change of thick underwear and his Sunday clothes all pungent with the smell of mothballs. His one suit was said to be nearly as old as he was and it lasted him until his death. I imagined the closet in the corner of the room to be some sort of treasure island, but our Lil assured me that it was no such thing and only contained a few picture frames and cardboard boxes, and Grandad's melodion; an instrument I was to become acquainted with – on some occasions I confess surreptitiously.

At the top of the stairs (with high rise and narrow tread and banister on the wrong side) the landing led to the middle bedroom where Dad and Mam slept, and I had a small bed in the corner next to the wash-stand. Over my bed hung a painting of a lady with long hair taking refuge on a rock from the huge waves which lashed around her. At the bottom of the picture was a verse of *Rock of Ages*, which Lil told me was one of my mother's favourite hymns, and that she often used it as my lullaby. Adjoining the middle bedroom and down a rather dangerous step was the room where Lil slept. This eventually became the room I shared for several years with my brother Tom. It was a cosy little room with a window at the side of the bed from which there was a wonderful view of the next-door neighbour's backyard and the place where Charlie Ingamells kept his racing pigeons: absorbing and interesting to small boys.

The middle room downstairs was known as the living room. Grandad's chair was to the left of the fireplace and Grandmam's to the right. Her couch was placed under the window to give her a view of the garden. Our clock, the family wedding present to Mam and Dad, was wound up with a large key every Sunday morning. Dad was the official winder, and it was also his job to see that the egg cup inside the clock had some paraffin in it, as Grandad said the fumes kept the works oiled.

We had a coal fire in a shiny black fireplace with a built-in oven and a small boiler (with a brass tap) for hot water. In the fireplace was Grandad's spittoon, which Lil had to clean out and fill with fresh sawdust every morning when she cleaned the grate and lit the fire. In one corner of the living room and under the stairs was a whitewashed pantry with its tiled floor. In the opposite corner of the room, by the fireplace and next to the boiler with the little brass tap, lay the sideboard with the toy cupboard underneath where I used to hide when Lil played hide and seek with me. My favourite toy I well remember was a sailor in a blue suit who did a little dance when he was wound up. This toy came from the big house where my Aunt Liddy was in service. Her mistress also sent me a walking stick with little pearls in the knobbed handle, and a sailor's suit with a hat, and a wooden whistle on a piece of plaited white silk cord.

The remaining room in our house was a multi-purpose room, serving as a back room, scullery and wash-house. The laundry equipment comprised a copper with a little fireplace underneath, a mangle, a clotheshorse and a wooden table. In the corner was a shallow biscuit-coloured stone sink used for face-washing, washing-up and sundry other purposes. It had the luxury of a cold water tap, and a pump which only worked in wet weather. The copper, with its removable wooden top that resembled a Roman shield, was a constant source of interest to me as a child, possibly due to the bubbling sounds and the steam on washday. The kettledrum shape of the iron cauldron never suggested anything to me in the way of a musical instrument, though I was to sit behind many similarly-shaped objects in copper in the course of time.

The back door led to the back yard, garden, coal shed, a place for the kindling and last, but by no means least in importance, the 'double-u'. The 'W' was rather small, very plain, but very clean with its carefully scrubbed wooden seat on which stood a little box filled with squares of newspaper carefully cut from the local paper : our one other paper, Dad's *Church Family Newspaper*, was excluded as it was not the type of literature to be cut up for potty paper. It was great fun in the 'W', when you could get in, for it was Grandad's monopoly – which reminds me of the many times my brothers and I waited outside holding our tummies and saying, 'Have you nearly finished Grandad?' Once inside (when I was old enough to be left on my own) I amused myself by looking at the papers to find pictures and got excited if a photograph of a horse or dog turned up; and then came the thrill of being held up to pull the chain which made a noise like Niagara Falls. If it was fine weather, this event was followed by a trip down the garden as far as the pigsty to give the pig a little poke with a stick to make him grunt. But perhaps on the way back to the house there was a confession to make : I hadn't been anywhere properly when I was in the 'W' ! Then out would come the little saucer and the spoon which had lost its silver plating, and a frightful powder called liquorice powder. Into the kitchen and over the sink for the mixing, and then the administration with Mam always saying the same thing : 'Head back, open your mouth and down it goes before you can say Jack Robinson.' If instead of your tummy being stubborn you had what Dad called 'the back door trot', then you were regaled with a spoonful of sugar to which had been added a sprinkling of diarrhoea drops, and then that mysterious Jack Robinson would crop up again, possibly to see that 'it all went down' !

My Earliest Recollections

The first recorded event to follow my baptismal entry in the parish and other official registers was being photographed on the occasion of my first birthday. This incident I cannot remember, but I *can* recall when little more than a year older being wheeled in a high pram to the shops on shopping day, which in our family was Friday. For this I was spruced up after dinner, settled in my pram in company with the shopping basket, and was taken by Mam and Lil to the most important port of call – Manley's grocer's shop where it was said you could get anything from a packet of pins to a side of bacon. Once at Manley's, I was taken out of my pram and helped down the steep step into the shop: a shop crammed with pickles, jams, corn plasters, cheeses, candles, cough mixture, and such things as bottles of rubbing oils; all to delight the eye and the nose, for such a delightful smell as Manley's shop there has never been. And probably never a more kindly man nor one better fitted to keep a shop in this poor slum district known as 'Bungit' (Boongate), where half the residents owed a little something which would go on next week's bill and hope for the best. Such things as short weeks and owing a bit were beyond my comprehension at this time, but there is no doubt that Mr. Manley occasionally forgot to put a bit on the slate for the Blades family as he frequently did for other people. One thing Mr. Manley never did forget, and that was to give me a fig biscuit. The taste of that soft juicy biscuit I have never forgotten; in fact the very sight of a fig biscuit transports me immediately to a grocer's shop.

Our next call in town was Narrow Street: a busy shopping street which in my young days really lived up to its name as a couple of men could almost have shaken hands from opposite pavements. In Narrow Street Mam made an occasional purchase, and I have a dim recollection of a shop which sold plain cake; a smaller shop where tea was sold, and Stickleback's photographer's shop which specialised in children's photographs. It was a tiny place, noted for tiny photographs – twelve for sixpence. The day I had my photograph taken there must have been quite an occasion. Face wash, sailor's hat and little coat with the shiny buttons, and no getting out at Manley's in case I creased the ribbon on my hat.

Friday afternoon trips to Mr. Manley and Narrow Street concluded with the trek home by way of Long Causeway to see what was in the window of Duddington's toy shop. Then into Midgate to call at Mr. Tebbs the butcher for the Sunday beef. With this, Mr. Tebbs always gave Mam a few bones to make some extra gravy, and a piece of suet to help with the making of such things as dumplings and suet pudding. Once out of Mr. Tebbs's shop it was straight home for tea. After tea was bath time, all very comfortable in front of the fire in a little zinc bath screened from the world and the draught from under the kitchen door and the nearby fens by the clotheshorse draped with anything that needed airing.

So life went along happily for me and in a steadily-expanding family circle. I now had a little brother, Tom, and a great friend in Uncle George who had married Auntie Liddy. My first recollection of brother Tom was sharing my fig biscuit with him every Friday. By this time I had vacated the pram in Tom's favour and was able to go up and down the steps at Manley's shop as quickly as Lil. Of Uncle George I have clear memories of sitting on his knee and admiring the football medal on his watch chain, and the (five shilling) Ingersoll watch he would put to my ear and with which he taught me to tell the time; a sure sign of my growing up, which was certainly the case as I was every bit of four years old and all set for my first day at school.

No extensive arrangements were necessary regarding my school wardrobe: Bishop's Road Infants' School was a modest establishment. The walk of a mile admittedly from home to school, but no fear of traffic congestion or the need of a warden to cross the road in those days. The only thing on wheels was an occasional farm cart or a tradesman's van, or perhaps a pony and trap with its pleasant 'clippidy-clop' and jingling (a sound I was to reproduce on many occasions in later years). Lessons took place in a long room in which we were also taught to sing simple hymns and songs when our teacher, Miss Hillam, played the piano: a new and absorbing sound to me.

A sound of another kind remains with me: that of a wooden whistle, and what is more blown by me. This whistle and the little walking stick with pearls in the handle were the greatest treasures of my childhood. The whistle which was my particular favourite was carried almost constantly round my neck suspended by its length of strong white cord. I never went to school without my whistle, if only for one reason: on the way home to dinner I usually played a train game. I started myself off with a blow on the whistle and then chuffed away at a furious pace with my arms acting as pistons[3], and in next to no time I was at the corner near our house where I would pause for enough breath to blow two long blasts on my whistle. These were to warn Mam that I was nearly home and to have the dinner ready. My first question to Mam was always, 'Did you hear the whistle?' Before chuffing myself back to school I probably gave Lil instructions to 'meet me out' and reminded Mam to listen for the whistle at tea-time and to be ready for me. This was by no means an easy matter for her, for as well as looking after Grandmam and my brother Tom (who was getting to be a bit of a handful), another brother (Chris) had come along, and he was teething.

Fortunately, when one is in the region of six, the cares of existence

[3] I little thought that an imitation of a 'puffer' train (with whistles and wire brushes) would prove a furore in my lecture-recitals on orchestral percussion.

are rarely magnified, though I was not completely unaware of the fact that life at 166, Star Road, was not without sadness and anxiety. My father earned on an average twelve shillings a week. He allowed himself twopence per week pocket money: a penny for the collection on Sundays[4] and a penny for Mrs. Knight who laundered his Sunday collar and cuffs as Mam had no time (nor facilities) for these extras. If trade was good Dad allowed himself an extra penny which was spent on sweets on Saturday night. He always bought the same thing as they were the best value: goody-fishes, four different flavours for a penny. Grandad's earnings amounted to about ten shillings a week.[5] A shilling or so of this was spent on Grandmam's medicine; his very occasional glass of beer; half-an-ounce of thick twist tobacco, and when required a new clay pipe. He rarely spent money on matches as he lit his pipe from the fire with little rolls of paper (spills) which he made as he sat in his armchair smoking his evening 'pipe-o-baccy', and whilst aiming his spittle into the spittoon with the precision of a darts champion. Grandad continued to work at the farm in Longthorpe, which meant that he walked six miles a day, six days a week, summer and winter, leaving home at 5 a.m., and if he was not clear of the subway under the main Great Northern line by 5.30 he was said to be like a bear with a sore head for the rest of the day. Now and again Grandad brought home a field rabbit, and this was a nice change from the mid-week pound of shin of beef (cost 3½d) besides helping Mam with the butcher's bill, and possibly the rent. The most important thing in Mam's weekly budget was the rent, five shillings a week. However carefully my mother managed her housekeeping she was not always able to pay the full rent, and a trifle would have to be left over.

Being poor had an occasional compensation, as for example the tin of salmon for tea on Easter Sunday if the spring trade was good in the tailoring line. Tea on Easter Sunday was an occasion in our house, as was tea on Christmas Day and August Bank Holiday Sunday, for on these days all Grandad's family living in Peterborough came to visit him. About twenty people sat down to tea: twelve grown-ups (and two babies) at the table in the living room, and eight children at a small table in the scullery next to the copper, the top of which Mam had made into a table for the extra crockery (provided by each family). Auntie Liddy always helped with the tea-making, and when everybody was seated Grandad said grace in his deep bass voice, and if in a good mood made his great joke, 'I'm

---

[4] A half-penny morning and evening.
[5] He was getting on for seventy at this time.

9

at home and wish you all was!' Then the tea-drinking and the chatter started, with plenty of the latter in the scullery, or at least in between the mouthfuls of thin bread and butter (not the usual 'doorsteps') dipped into the scrumptious gravy (our portion from the tin of salmon), helped down with some cucumber and cress or lettuce, if in season, from Uncle Dick's allotment. Even the salmon tin was something quite special with its picture of a man fishing in a stream with real mountains behind. Dad felt sure these were the Rockies as the salmon came from Canada where, according to Grandad, the maxim was 'eat what you can, can what you can't.' After the bread and butter and salmon came the Sunday cake which Mam cut with some anxiety in front of her sisters-in-law who had the reputation of being good cooks. But the cake was always wonderful and received high praise from everybody, particularly the younger members, who occasionally invaded the living room in the hope of getting anything going spare, and also to see how Uncle George was getting on, as apart from being a great favourite he usually managed to get his ears boxed by Auntie Liddy for some prank or other at the tea-table. (Dad usually managed to get in one of his perennial stories, such as the tipsy fisherman who, on encountering a scarecrow, said 'It's a damned lie, there never was a fish that length'. His favourite went: Bill had a bill-board;[6] Bill also had a board bill. Now the board bill bored Bill, so Bill sold the bill-board to pay the board bill. Now the board bill no longer bores Bill.) After tea came the washing-up; the privilege of the ladies who welcomed the opportunity of discussing intimate feminine topics whilst the men took a look at Grandad's garden and the pig and the tortoise (if he was to be seen). Whilst we children had a race round the yard or the Common, the men discussed such things as 'taters' and greens, and if it was Easter Sunday they heard about Uncle Dick's allotment and how he had set so many rows of King Edward's or Sharp's Express on Good Friday – as had a few thousand others in accordance with a centuries-old custom. So would end a happy day with the question of making ends meet forgotten, at least for a spell.

Some of Grandad's family were better off than others. For instance, Uncle Harry had a foreman's job on the railway, but with Auntie Liddy things were generally bad, as Uncle George, though a marvellous carpenter, was often out of work months at a time. Day after day he trudged the district with his bag of tools on his back looking for work, and night after night he returned home completely worn out and crestfallen. Often Lil and I went in the evening (when

6 Bill-board : tailor's ironing board.

it was dusk) to Auntie Liddy's with a jug of milk and water (or skim milk from the farm) and half a loaf of bread to make sure that Uncle had some supper, and if it was not too late we stayed a little while to talk. One of my chief delights was to sit on Uncle's knee and chat to him. I was always curious it seems about his pocket-money, the amount of which he never divulged to me. I was also most inquisitive about Uncle's wages, and would ask time and time again how much he earned. Was it five shillings or ten shillings, or perhaps only a shilling? I would venture, and he always promised to tell me one day, or reply as my mother so often did when asked how much anything cost, 'Money and fair words, my boy.'

Occasionally Uncle got a run of work, and with Auntie taking a lodger or two things would pick up for a time. Once Uncle was able to buy a gramophone, a thing he had always wanted. Now here was something: a real gramophone with a large metal horn and cylindrical wax records. At first Uncle had only two records, *Belphegor* and *Under the Double Eagle*, both military marches played by a German military band. To save wearing out the records Uncle played his gramophone only once a week, on Sunday mornings when Auntie was in the back kitchen cooking dinner. Though Sunday was an austere day in our house I was allowed to listen to Uncle's gramophone on alternate Sundays when I went to Auntie Liddy's to dinner. This was a great treat with gramophone music followed by Auntie's hefty helpings of Yorkshire pudding (the thick variety) with thick gravy, and a sweet. Getting to 36 Charles Street in time for the gramophone concert took my attention somewhat from the Chapel service where I went (not always willingly I fear) with Grandad before I was considered old enough to go to Sunday School at the Mission Church. But the Chapel service with its hard seats had its compensations. There was a harmonium and a choir, and I never failed to be intrigued by the 'God be with you's' and 'So be it's' which came gruffly at any point during the service from such senior members of the congregation as Grandad. Once out of Chapel, I went at express speed to Auntie's place and into the holy of holies, the front room with its carefully-covered furniture, and above all the gramophone – an Edison Bell. First Uncle carefully wiped the wax record (with his handkerchief) and placed it on the circular sleeve. Then he reverently wound up the machinery and started the gramophone going. After a bit of scratching and hissing the music came on with a rhythm that nearly knocked you off your feet. I was soon off mine and laid flat on the rug as near as possible to the gramophone horn. Then Uncle and I got to work. He had a

11

pair of drumsticks as he occasionally played in the Volunteers' Band as a side drummer, and whilst he tapped in time on the heel of his boot, I played an imaginary big drum by beating on the rug with my fist. This was tremendous fun, but quite often before we got to the end of the second record in came Auntie and boxed our ears, saying it was Sunday and that dinner was ready. There was no great quantity of meat but there was plenty of fun, but Uncle and I used to get into trouble now and again by beating the rhythm of *Belphegor* or *Under the Double Eagle* on our dinner plates with the Sunday knives and forks.

There were other attractions at Uncle's house, such as games of ring board and listening to Mr. Playford's mouth-organ. Charlie Playford (who was always known as Playford) was Uncle's great friend. He lived just up the yard in exactly the same sort of house as No. 36, and came most evenings to have a talk with Uncle George, while Auntie Liddy went most evenings to have a few words (as a brief chat of about two hours was known) with Mrs. Playford. Once Auntie was clear of 36, Uncle would light his Woodbine, and Playford his Gold Flake cigarette. Playford could afford Gold Flake, for in comparison to Uncle George he was a rich man as he had a regular job with the Gas Company: collecting the money from gas meters. After a smoke and a chat Uncle George and Playford had their game of ring board. After several games it was time for music; not the gramophone, but Playford's mouth-organ. First he tapped the mouth-organ on the palm of his hand, and then got going on such tunes as 'Tommy Atkins', 'The Bluebells of Scotland' and 'Home Sweet Home'. Then came my turn for a blow. Once again the mouth-organ was tapped on Mr. Playford's palm to get out the spittle, and after carefully wiping it on the sleeve of his jacket, the instrument was given to me, and, following Playford's instructions, 'Blow, blow, draw, draw, blow, draw', I performed my repertoire to date: the first phrase of *God Save Our Gracious King* sufficiently well for both Playford and Uncle to applaud, so I made up my mind to save up and have a mouth-organ of my own like Mr. Playford's which he told me cost 6½d from Claypole's shop.

Now anything bought at Claypole's was a bargain. Everybody in Peterborough knew that, and I knew it because I had bought a jew's harp from there. It cost me a penny but it was worth it, and I soon got the knack of playing it. You get wonderful tunes on a jew's harp if you breathe on it properly whilst twanging it. Not everyone recognises the tunes you are playing, but if that's the case they don't know the secret about jew's harps. In Claypole's shop among such things as jew's harps, pianos, harmoniums, violins and tin whistles, there was an array of real mouth-organs from Germany; none of your cheap stuff such as came in shop-made Christmas stockings and which sprained easily. There were vampers, some with double reeds, some with a blowing part each side, and one mark you, with two little bells which you could ting with your finger whilst playing a tune. The problem of course was how to manage the sixpence ha'penny for a steam engine I had my eye on and yet save enough for a mouth-organ. I gave this matter plenty of thought during the summer holiday before my eighth birthday and my going to the big boys' school. It would be a good thing I thought to have a mouth-organ in a big school, and yet I really wanted that steam engine for Christmas. It was not long before an idea came into my head. I could start saving up immediately and this, with anything I might get in the way of money for my birthday might just buy the mouth-organ – a sixpenny-ha'penny vamper. So if I got the mouth-organ by September 9th it would be marvellous for taking to 'big' school, and if I saved my Saturday ha'penny from my birthday to Christmas I could buy the steam engine. This meant the strongest self-denial: no gob stoppers or aniseed balls on Saturday mornings, but the mouth-organ and the steam engine were worth the struggle.

Choosing the mouth-organ was no easy matter. Playford had said that I should decide between a *Dreadnought* and a *Bandmaster*. After much pondering in front of Claypole's shop window, I ventured inside and asked if I could try the *Dreadnought* first and then the *Bandmaster*. This I was allowed to do. I remember that there seemed little difference between them, and after considerable deliberation on my part and what must have seemed like eternity to the shop assistant, the *Dreadnought* with the picture of a battleship on the box became mine. Mr. Playford tried it out for me and agreed that I had done the right thing and had got a bargain. The instrument was carefully wiped and put away in its little box to await my birthday by which time I would be eight and installed in Class I, St. John's School, as Dad had already made arrangements with the headmaster for my going there after the holidays. He had also spoken to Mr. Yarholm, the choirmaster at Eastgate Mission Church, about my joining the choir which sang on Sunday evenings in the little tin church where, for some time, I had been a member of Mr. Harvey's Sunday School class. So, all in all, life ahead looked like being as full and exciting as ever.

2

School Days

The day came for me to go to St. John's – the first Monday in September 1909. My education to date had not called for the use of a satchel. In any case these were a rarity in my young day, the one or two exercise books necessary for homework being carried in a homemade knapsack. Pencils and books were provided at school, and all that was needed to make a start at St. John's on this important Monday morning was a clean face, well-brushed hair and a pocket hankie in the pocket of my cord knickers (which 'whistled' as I walked) and, I remember, my mouth-organ, which Mam said I could take as my birthday only wanted a day or two. I made my way to Albert Place with another 'graduate', my infant school mate and constant companion Charlie Kendrick who lived a few doors away, and a boy named Percy ('Perce') Poole. We arrived at St. John's in time to be shown to the top room for the usual lining up in front of the headmaster, Mr. Adams, who spoke to every new boy before school started. His voice was firm, yet kindly, and his twinkling though discerning eyes took in at a glance such details as the state of each boy's hair, back of the neck, teeth, jacket pockets and boots.

St. John's was a rather fearsome place. It was a double-storied brick building as gaunt inside as it was outside. The door leading into school opened into a room in which were clothes pegs, a few wash basins, and two coarse linen towels on rollers. Near each bowl was a chunk of the strongest smelling amber-coloured carbolic soap I have ever encountered, and over each bowl was a notice: CLEAN-LINESS IS NEXT TO GODLINESS – one of 'Boss' Adams' favourite maxims. Others included: IF A THING IS WORTH DOING AT ALL IT'S WORTH DOING WELL and PUNCTUALITY IS POWER. Two flights of stone steps led to the upper storey. At the top of the first flight was another washing room. Here, in addition to the wash bowls and the same carbolic soap and the rows of clothes pegs, was the school 'china' consisting of a dozen or so white enamel mugs which were housed in a small cupboard over which hung instructions to 'leave this place as you would wish to find it'. The mugs were for the use of the whole school and were used in hot weather by the boys who

14

stayed in for dinner. Among the mugs was one without a handle from which only unsuspecting new boys drank as it was known as 'the fever mug' (due to its dark colour). Hung on the wall above the wash basins beneath a heading 'WHAT WILL HE BECOME?' were two framed series of etchings conveying a grim warning as to what might happen to a boy who failed in his duty to God and mankind. The pictures illustrated the seven ages of man, the upper row showing a robust infant in a baby chair; an industrious schoolboy at his desk; a well-dressed young man in an office; a little-older man with his wife and three children; a gentleman in the prime of life dressed in a frock-coat and top hat; a comfortable portly figure sitting in an easy chair and surrounded by obvious signs of prosperity; and finally, an elderly man in the midst of an admiring family. The lower pictures showed the same healthy baby; followed by an indolent schoolboy; an ill-dressed youth leaving a drinking saloon; a haggard man at a gambling table; a middle-aged man in the hands of the police; an elderly man behind bars; and finally, a ragged old figure begging in the street. Whether this series of pictures was an original idea on the part of Mr. Adams or was issued by the Religious Tract Society, or one of the well-intentioned societies of the era, I cannot say. Above this second washing room was a room of similar size and known as the 'museum'. On the lintel of the doorway was carved: THIS IS A PLACE FOR EVERYTHING AND EVERYTHING IN ITS PLACE; another maxim of the redoubtable Edward E. Adams, Headmaster of St. John's Boys' School; churchwarden of St. John's Church; Worshipful Grand Master and one of the pillars so to speak of the local Masonic Temple; a prominent Oddfellow; a friend of the poor; the first man in Peterborough to ride a bicycle with pneumatic tyres; and the terror of all boys, particularly those who ventured into the class with a dirty neck or a sweet in their mouth.

The first duty of the day at St. John's was assembly, during which we were treated to the equivalent of a news bulletin. Pinned to a blackboard in the centre of the largest classroom was the *Daily Graphic* from which Boss Adams read the headlines, stressing anything of a national character, for he was as keen on instilling patriotism into his boys as he was the use of carbolic soap. After being informed of the state of the country and so forth, all made their way to their respective classrooms. Despite some clever manipulation on the part of 'Curly' Kendrick, Percy Poole and I, we were not seated together. I got placed between a rather pimply boy named Charlie Buttifant – the son of a wholesale confectioner in a small way of business – and a boy with an unfortunate sniffle and no pocket handkerchief who, whatever his name may have been soon became known as 'Sniveller' (I was dubbed 'Grinner'). Charlie Buttifant did not turn out a gold mine as far as sweets were concerned, his father believing in 'selling 'em not eating 'em' and on inspection by our teacher Mr. Brocklebank, Sniveller was found to have fleas under his shirt and a few 'creepers' in his hair. He was eventually de-loused and given a place of honour in a corner with a private desk which, though I felt sorry for him, was a relief to me. In Sniveller's place came a boy named Wild, a delightful boy who over the years developed into a literary character and wrote marvellous essays, although on leaving school he went as an assistant in a pawnbroker's shop.

When dinner-time came I could hardly get home quickly enough to tell Mam what a fine place Albert Place School was going to be. I lost no time in getting back to join in the games in the playground and to be shown (along with Charlie Kendrick and Percy Poole) the short cut to the bathing-place and the muck-heap where you might find a glass marble. The muck-heap was also the place where an occasional scrap took place, and though these were not numerous at St. John's (the Head infused comradeship), they usually attracted an interested audience, particularly if a bit of a bully was likely to get a good hiding. But there was an attraction near the muck-heap which could beat anything that could happen for miles around. On the other side of the nearby river was the fairground and in September it was Bridge Fair Week: an annual event dating back to the fifteenth century and, if my information is correct, started to provide funds for the upkeep of a wooden bridge over the river Nene. Bridge Fair was a place for Lil and me to go after tea, for there was plenty to see and hear without spending a lot. First there was a marvellous view of the fair from the Water Bridge. It was here that one got the full beauty of the cacophony of sound from various fair organs playing in diverse keys and time signatures, to which was added the clanging of booth bells and an occasional whistle from a shining green Great Northern express as it crossed the nearby railway bridge. These strident whistles, together with the clash of booth bells in E flat and D natural with a massive fair organ playing the overture to *William Tell* in the original key (E major), and a neighbouring roundabout with a small pipe organ playing the *Skaters' Waltz* in an indescribable key, created music which (in my opinion) made certain of the avant-garde masterpieces inflicted on the audiences of today sounding positively insipid. What is more, one large organ had some drums and bells in the

front of the pipes, with drumsticks working on the instruments
keeping time with the music, of which I was later reminded when
playing Stravinsky's *Petrouchka* (the intriguing part for bass drum
and cymbals in 'The Blackamoor'). The side shows, with people
outside urging the public to come in and see some wonderful happening or another, or the world's greatest mystery, remained, however,
a mystery to me as they were much too expensive at tuppence a
time. This was a great pity as they all looked sensational, particularly
the one with a black man outside who had a spear and a shield and
did a war dance. It was time to go home long before all the sights
had been seen, and in any case by now, according to Lil, it was
getting dark outside the brilliantly-lighted fairground and there was
the long trudge to Star Road and straight to bed after the basin of
sop (bread, warm water and sugar). I may have dreamed about what
was inside some of the side shows. I certainly did not dream that one
day I would make music of a sort on that very ground and sleep
in a tent like the black man.

Bridge Fair was a favourite topic at school and our teachers heard
of what the boys had been on and what sights they had seen. My
teacher had even more exciting stories to tell particularly as he had
been across the Channel to France. I told them at home about France,
which started Grandad off. He was always against 'furriners' saying
they were a queer lot and that 'you couldn't trust 'em'. He had an intense dislike of 'the Roosians' and 'the Proosians' and neither he nor
his friend Matty Goodley had any time for Kaiser Bill. My father was a
more tolerant man with a longing for universal brotherhood. He was a
member of the Church Missionary Society and the C.E.M.S. (Church
of England Men's Society). He was a lay reader at the Parish Church
where he occasionally read the lessons. As he had not been or-
dained (a life-long disappointment to him) he was not able to preach
in the Parish Church. He was however privileged to give the
sermon in the Mission Church: a humble place built of corrugated
iron, though it boasted a sizeable American organ which was used
for the evening service to which I often went with Dad before I
became a choirboy there.[1] At Sunday School my class was held in
the vestry and the teacher (Mr. Harvey) told us Bible stories. The
evening service in the Mission Church was like most other services
in similar circumstances the world over – with one exception, or
at least one that remains unique in my experience, and one in which
Mr. Yarholm the organist – who incidentally gave me my first close

[1] In the opinion of many, my father's sermons were better than the
parson's.

look at a keyboard – was the central figure. There is no doubt that Mr. Yarholm was fond of music. He was also fond of a glass of beer, preferring the latter it would seem to the church sermon (including my father's). It is possible of course that pumping with the foot pedals and working the knee swells on the Mission Church harmonium was thirsty work. So every Sunday evening as the lights were lowered for the sermon he left the harmonium and walked solemnly down the aisle, out by the back door and across to the Britannia Inn where he partook (it is said) of a certain quantity of Phipps' Best Brew. His return to the church was extremely well timed, for when the verger quietly opened the door at the end of the sermon Mr. Yarholm was always awaiting his cue to enter. The verger, a man of tact, kept the lights lowered until Mr. Yarholm was comfortably seated and the organ stops prepared for the closing hymn.

My father, who was a staunch teetotaller and a member of the Total Abstinence League, may have had mixed feelings regarding Mr. Yarholm. Strong drink and public houses, and particularly Sunday opening, were all sore points with Dad and with Grandad, who was as much against intemperance as my father. Politically they were opposed. Dad was for the Tories and Grandad for the Liberals. They also differed on the question of church and chapel and the manner in which the Old Hundredth should be phrased. But on the question of 'drink' there was complete agreement. Beer in our house was permitted only once a year, when Uncle Harry from Manchester came. He was allowed to drink a small bottle of stout with his dinner. Here was a sight which greatly puzzled and amused my brothers and me who, so constantly hearing of the diabolical consequences arising from the consumption of strong drink, would giggle and nudge each other as Uncle Harry drank his stout (including the froth which he cleaned from his heavy military moustache with his tongue and under lip), fully expecting him to collapse in a heap under the table.

Tom's and my own behaviour at table on these and other occasions was not always as correct as it should have been. One or the other was always being told by Grandad to 'git ye furrader throm him' and at times we were either given or promised a flea in the ear from Dad. My chief offence could have been drumming on my empty plate with my knife and fork at which, when I got them bouncing just like Uncle's drumsticks Grandad would shout, 'Dang the boy, he's at it again' – and then there was trouble, particularly if Grandad hadn't finished his pudding. There was trouble too of another sort if I was caught running a stick along the iron railings near Bishop's Road School. This was a pity as it was great fun making short and long 'rolls' as I raced along. Another good place for making drum rolls was on the palings round Old Frosty's house. Frosty (Mr. Frost) lived on a corner near to Star Road Chapel. What with Charlie Kendrick and the rest of us climbing up his fence to steal his apples, and me performing preludial rolls on his palings, possibly when the old chap was having a nap, I fear Mr. Frost was led a bit of a dog's life. He often got his own back though, for he occasionally surprised us by being ready with his cane, which put an end to my drumming on his palings, at least for a time.

There was, however, drumming on a *real* drum which was attracting me: the sound of the big drum in our Salvation Army Band. Almost every Sunday evening after tea I made my way to Cowgate so that I could march alongside this band as it made its way from the Citadel to the Market Place. The star performer in the band, as far as I was concerned, was the man who played the bass drum. He was an ex-Guards drummer named Jim Pack, a fine tall man, and a tremendous showman on the march with his stick twirling and fancy beating: a pyrotechnic display which so fascinated me that I must have collided with half Peterborough on my journey along Cowgate to the Market Place. But marvellous as the stick twirling was, it was the way Jim Pack played his big drum in the hymns which thrilled me most. I soon knew exactly where to get on the Market Place so as to be near him when the band got into position for the short service before returning to the Citadel. First, he un-strapped the drumsticks from his wrists and then unhooked the big drum from his chest. Then he took off his leopard-skin apron and spread it out on the ground. Finally he tested the big drum – which was a beautiful instrument with white pipe-clayed ropes and the body brightly painted with the Salvation Army crest – before resting it on the leopard-skin. In the hymns Jim played very quietly, with gentle rumbles that sounded like distant thunder, and an occasional crescendo into the last verse which nearly lifted me off my feet. Many a time I was brought back to earth by the Market Place clock chiming a quarter past six, which meant getting away as quickly as possible so as to be in the vestry by the time the five-minute bell started. I cannot call to mind whether or not the big drum was used for collection purposes (penny on the drum) but I feel not, as Jim Pack's bass drum must have been a precious in-strument to him. (I have been constantly reminded of its superb sound when performing or hearing great works in which the orchestral bass drum has a prominent part, as for example in Verdi's *Requiem* or Stravinsky's *The Rite of Spring*.) Jim Pack and his big drum will long be remembered. He is immortalised in a Peterborough cemetery in a unique manner: a pair of crossed drumsticks adorns his headstone. To me he remains a legend and one of my greatest inspirations.[2]

Moving House

The time came to say goodbye to 166, Star Road, which was now getting too small for the Blades and Close families. Our new house, No. 171, had an extra room downstairs and its name, 'Summerfield', carved in stone above the front door. It was certainly worth the extra shilling a week rent, though I must confess that I preferred the view of the fields at the back of No. 166 to that of the gasometer which overlooked the back garden of our new house. Apart from that, however, No. 171, with its own passage and the additional room was a step up the social ladder. Not that we lost touch with our late neighbours – or, to be precise, they with us. One of them (a lady who took in washing) continued to borrow the family knives and forks when she had visitors, or when her own cutlery was on loan to the pawnbrokers, though people around were not always aware of this as the good lady carried the load under her apron – in case of thunder and lightning, she said. Mrs. X was by no means the pawnbroker's only customer. Monday was quite a busy day for him, handing out small sums of money and tickets in return for such things as Sunday clothes, cutlery, and in certain circumstances bed linen. The afternoon of Saturday (pay-day) saw the return, for a weekend visit, of the 'popped' articles or at least the more necessary items.

My grandmother liked the bigger house, but her time in it was short, and it was not long before she lay in her plain wooden coffin in the front room, where we said goodbye to her. It was the custom in my boyhood to walk round the coffin of a loved one, and in parting touch the cold forehead – according to Grandad, to stop bad dreams. Soon after Grandmam's death, Cousin Lil, who was by now quite a young woman, went back to London, to work in a Lyons teashop. I missed her very much, especially on my trips to the Fairground and such jaunts as seeing the expresses rush under Spital Bridge, particularly the *Flying Scot* which Uncle George told me

[2] Don Lusher, one of the world's greatest trombonists, played in the Peterborough Salvation Army Band as a youth.

went through Peterborough North Station so fast that the platform had to be cleared and the shutters pulled down on the newspaper stall. But my time for watching express trains was getting short. I had made up my mind that when I was nine I would get into St. Mary's choir and also to go to work. My ninth birthday came round and with it my tea-party. Birthday tea-parties were modest affairs. Usually Mam made a Sunday cake and let me invite Charlie Kendrick and Perce Poole. Den Leach, another Star 'Roadite', who had disappointed Charlie, Perce and me by going to New Road School, also came along, and with him his cousin Harry Cottom who lived in our yard. Harry was a cripple, who spent most of his day in a wheelchair. He slobbered badly and could barely talk, but he was rarely left out of such things a birthday tea-parties and did his best to join in the fun. After the bread-and-jam came the cake, with stewed plums and custard as an extra. The cake and the plums were beautiful; the only thing to watch was not to get a stone mixed up with a spoonful of custard and swallow it. Curly Kendrick swallowed a plum stone once and had to go straight home and tell his mother. He got into trouble of course, but that was not unusual for him; he was always getting into scrapes, though such things never seemed to worry him. He was a brave boy and would stand up to a lion if need be, and often took a boy's part in a scrap if he thought the odds were uneven. Charlie was the leader of the Star Road Gang and organised the stone fights with Wellington Street Gang, headed by 'Haney' (a boy named Haynes) who, big as he was, never got the better of Charlie. These stone fights were fearsome affairs. Gangs of boys of school age assembled on the road on the Common, a rough track leading to the open country, and took positions near the heaps of granite stones which were used for road building and repairs. The jagged stones were thrown with every intention of damaging the opponent, and at times serious injuries were sustained, resulting in one case in the loss of an eye. Curly Kendrick was certainly the life and soul of any party and he was missed on the occasion he left my tea-party to report the swallowing of the plum stone. The rest of us made do however, and after wrapping up a piece of cake for Diggery Flanders, a poor boy who was always hungry, we had a sing-song with me on the mouth-organ, and after trundling Harry Cottom home had a race round the Common to run down an un-usually large tea.

Having got my birthday over it was high time to think about St. Mary's choir. This proved no problem, and I was made a full chorister and given a surplice. Getting in St. Mary's choir was a lucky thing for me, as I not only got an occasional sixpence for a wedding (and, believe it or not, a shilling for a funeral), but I also got my first real job of work through Mr. Stott, my new choir-master. Mr. Stott owned a large stationers and newspaper shop in Peterborough which his son Harold, who sang tenor in the choir, managed for him. One of the choirboys worked at Stott's as a paper-round boy, and he told me that he got 1/3d a week and a Christmas box every year from his customers. He also told me that he got a ticket once a year for the Paper-Boys' Tea, which I had already heard was a real bean-feast. To me, having a paper-round seemed just as good as being an errand boy, so I asked 'Mr. Harold' if he would give me a job in his shop. He put me off for quite a time saying that I was too young, but when I was ten he would think about it. He eventually gave me a small round for which the wages were ninepence a week. Ninepence a week was a good start I thought, and as I knew the boys with bigger rounds got as much as 1/6d the prospects in the newspaper business seemed good. I was at Stott's shop bright and early on my first day at work: 6.45 a.m. to collect the papers which had arrived on the early morning train from London. With Mr. Harold's help I arranged my little batch in order and tucked them in the *Daily Mail* bag provided. One newspaper was given to me carefully wrapped in brown paper with instructions to deliver it secretively. It was the newly-published *Daily Herald*. Another call I clearly recollect was one to a house where I delivered a weekly journal (*Pearson's Weekly*). This magazine had to be delivered via the back gate as the front letterbox was sealed, even to the postman. The *Pearson's Weekly* was also wrapped up in brown paper as it had to be placed behind a box of plants on a window sill where my customers (two maiden ladies whom I never did see) always left a ha'penny and invariably two lemon curd tarts. On the whole paper boys did quite well. One boy who de-livered to the big houses in the posh part of Peterborough had a marvellous customer in an old lady who gave him a penny every morning for going into her bedroom and scratching her back with a back-scratcher. I did not do quite as well as this, but an occasional extra copper came my way.

Mr. Harold kept his promise about giving me a bigger round when I was older. Before my eleventh birthday I was taking home 1/3d a week from Stott's and feeling as fit as a fiddle in the bargain: the weather needed to be more than foul to warrant such luxuries as wearing a cap or coat. The little overcoat that my father made for me was so seldom worn that it was passed on in turn to my three brothers (there was now baby brother Cecil). As for gloves, when I was a boy we had something much more exciting: a winter warmer, which consisted of a perforated tin filled with old rag. The idea was to set the rag alight with red-hot cinders, then run along with the perforated lid facing the wind to keep the rag aglow. A winter warmer was a marvellous thing on a cold and frosty morning.

Being a paper-boy, I was in touch with much of the commercial life of Peterborough, other errand boys in particular. Jobs were discussed, such as who was doing what and where a boy was wanted, and it came to my knowledge that an errand boy was wanted Friday nights and Saturdays at Blackman's tobacco shop in Narrow Street – wages a shilling a week. I lost no time in getting on my Sunday collar and making myself known to Mr. Will Blackman who, eyeing me up and down (more down than up) said I was on the small side, but as the parcels were also on the small side, I could make a start. So I trotted round Peterborough every Friday evening with my little barrow used for horse-mucking delivering parcels of tobacco and running errands and helping in the shop from 9 a.m. to 8 p.m. on Saturday, for which I received the brightest new shilling in the till.

Working all day on Saturday at Blackman's, as well as my paper round, meant a great change for me, as until then the day had been pretty well filled with spending the Saturday ha'penny, a trip to see Perce Poole, who had got a job in a barber's shop as a lather-boy, and, if funds permitted, a ha'porth at the Hippodrome in the afternoon to see the moving pictures. Now I could manage only the first of these pleasures but to get to Blackman's in good time I was obliged to buy my usual aniseed balls straight away (they lasted longest and were good for swapping) and could no longer spend time gazing into Box's shop window at the 'What-ho's – my they're ripping' liquorice comfits, everlasting sticks (which belied their name), gob-stoppers, Spanish liquorice, un-claimed (jelly) babies, lucky bags, pop corns and sherbet powder for making lemonade. Being unable to see Perce Poole was a great loss, for Bob Barber (the barber for whom Percy worked) had let me see the comics such as *Chips* and *Comic Cuts* without having a haircut. Mr. Barber knew that my Uncle Dick cut the four Blades brothers' hair at one sitting. He must have known that Uncle Dick used a basin on our heads and that we were 'cropped' as a job lot four for a penny (if Mam had one!); but this made no difference because Bob was a jolly chap, and not only let me see the comic papers and sometimes *The Police News* (if the artist's impression of a man cutting his wife's throat

23

with a razor, or chopping off her head with a hatchet was not more gruesome than usual), he also told everybody in the shop what was on at the Hippodrome because he got a free seat there every Friday night in return for showing a bill in his shop.

Just as bad as missing the comic papers was missing the moving pictures, for there never was a better ha'porth than the Saturday matinee. First came the lady who played the piano (and was often booed), then the newsreel, followed by the Paris fashions – the latter greeted by tremendous whoops and jeers from the entire audience. Then came a comedy film. This was always received with great applause, for everyone on the screen got into the most hopeless tangles, and there was always someone getting a knock on the head with a rolling pin or a slap on the face with a lump of dough. After the comedy picture came the serial, which never failed to finish with the heroine hanging over a cliff or roped to a railway line with a Canadian Pacific or American Railroad express just about to run her down, when on flashed the caption, 'Will she escape? See next week,' at which groans came from the audience almost as loud as the shouts the villain had received as he roped the girl to the railway track. The final item was the 'big' picture. This was always about cowboys and Indians, and as there was generally plenty of scalping of the 'whites' and shooting of the Red Indians in return, followed by the pipe of peace, you certainly got your money's worth. The only drawback was that it always seemed to be raining or snowing on the screen, and the cinematograph machine made a terrible noise, very much like the rain on the zinc roof if there was a storm outside.

Life at Blackman's tobacconist's shop was just as exciting in its way as the pictures, perhaps most of all when Mr. Blackman was at his meal in the house at the back of the shop, for then Len the assistant let me help serve behind the counter. Admittedly I served only such things as matches or cigarette papers, but nevertheless 'behind counter'. Len Ward was a marvellous chap and quickly became one of my heroes. He was up to all sorts of tricks and possessed sundry accomplishments, not the least the feat of whistling and step dancing at the same time, and being able to slice an ounce of thick twist, or accurately gauge the weight of loose tobacco at the first go. One of Len's pranks was to give Mrs. Blackman's tabby cat an occasional pinch of snuff. Most of the Blackman parcels were for country customers who called with their orders during the morning. My first job after dinner was to take the parcels to the various hotel yards and place them in the customers' traps which were awaiting the ostler and the pony, and which by the afternoon were fairly well packed with purchases. Though the yards were open to the public, there was little worry about things being stolen – an interesting reflection bearing in mind the burglar-proof locks and other security methods so necessary in this age of enlightenment. My favourite delivery was to get a parcel aboard the 3.5 p.m. train at the North Station which, in spite of what the porter's fen brogue intimated, went – as far as I can recollect – to: Eye Green–Thorney–Wryde–Murrow–Wisbech–Sutton Bridge–Lynn–Yarmouth–Wroxham and Cromer. As well as the parcel I was responsible for seeing its owner (a Mr. Cave from Thorney) aboard the train. The parcel was quite an expensive one, and Mr. Cave like a number of other people who came to town to do business on Saturday was, by 3 p.m., a bit the worse for wear. My routine was the same every Saturday. Having located Mr. Cave at the station entrance I piloted him over the footbridge, dumped him on a seat on the train and placing the parcel firmly on his lap, said, 'There you are Mr. Cave, you're on the 3.5 train, Thorney's the second stop and you've got your bacca'. I never heard of Mr. Cave missing the stop at Thorney, nor for that matter him missing thanking me warmly, and after fumbling in his trousers pocket giving me the whole of tuppence. This princely sum I spent on my way home at night on something for us all for Sunday breakfast, the best investment being, when in season, two penny-worth of 'tacked' tomatoes.

After Sunday breakfast we boys were not allowed to do anything before going to church other than read, or go for a short walk. Sunday was a quiet and somewhat austere day. No games and no mouth-organ playing except for hymns, but with the compensation, as far as I was concerned, of going to Auntie Liddy's for dinner, drumming to Uncle George's gramophone and listening to Mr. Pack playing his big drum in the Salvation Army band in the evening. On Sunday afternoon my brothers and I were permitted the luxury of the front room. Luxury as far as seating accommodation was concerned – the chairs were softer – but by no means the most exciting experience for four growing boys who had strict orders to be quiet and to sit down and read. And what literature! Not *Treasure Island*, *The Boy Slave in Bokhara*, *Twenty Thousand Leagues Under The Sea* or *The Dog Crusoe* and such like, but *The Church Family Newspaper* (passed on to Dad by the vicar), or our one Sunday book: *Christie's Old Organ*: a heart-rending story about a poor old man named Treffy who was dying in a garret and whose only comfort was a little and rather wheezy barrel organ which he taught a poor ragged orphan to play. This book was shared by two of us, or at least until a tug-of-war developed. In the meantime, the other two amused themselves with a summary of a sermon reported in the aforementioned *Church Family Newspaper*, or a light work from Dad's bookshelf, such as Darwin's *Origin of Species*, the *Oxford House Papers* (a form of Hansard) which, though not specifically for the convenience of the Blades brothers, was in two volumes. Not that it was always as heavy going as studying the past curriculum at the various Oxford colleges or the sad death of Treffy, for in the summer months after evensong there was, for me at least, an occasional visit to the grounds of Westwood House to hear such famous bands as Besses o' the Barn, and have the music explained to me by my father, who was quite a musician in his own way and knew a lot about a great composer named Handel.

Telling Arthur Gooding (the assistant head teacher) all about the band was of course quite an unnecessary procedure, for he was a keen musician and never missed a concert. As well as being able to play the harmonium, Arthur Gooding could also play a cornet. The instrument may have been known to St. John's boys as a trumpet or a bugle, but whatever it was called he could play it remarkably well. On special days such as the King's birthday, Empire Day or Trafalgar Day, Teacher Gooding brought his instrument to school and played marching tunes and patriotic melodies whilst the whole school marched in class order round the playground, waving small Union Jacks and saluting the big one held by the Boss. If it was a fine day the Head addressed the whole school in the open, using as his theme the grandeur of Britain and its Empire, the sterling qualities of those who governed us, and the value of obedience to the powers-that-be and our parents; all extremely interesting to schoolboys, especially to those who had been bundled off to school with an empty tummy or a smack on the ear. Not that Mr. Adams was unaware of there being a few tummies not as replenished as his own – which seemed to be constantly expanding and had earned for him the nickname of 'Plunky'. His manner of dealing with hungry boys was typical of his compassionate nature. Each day after dinner he addressed the school with the words, 'Stand out any boy who has not had a dinner'. Rarely a day passed without one or two boys lining up in front of the Head's desk.[3] The Head then gave as many ha'pennies as there were hungry boys to the head boy (myself in my last year at St. John's), who marched the file of boys to Pyle's shop at the corner of School Place. Here, each

[3] An impostor was rare.

boy would be given a hefty cheese roll which was consumed under my supervision at the pavement edge outside Pyle's shop. There was a great deal of poverty among the boys at St. John's and Boss Adams and the teachers did all in their power to help genuine cases of hardship. In some instances boys whose parents were in no way short of money would fare badly at home. Far too often a good deal of the father's wages went into the publican's pocket and the harassed mother would struggle to make ends meet.

A cheese roll was not the only thing Boss Adams gave away.[4] He gave prizes in addition to the yearly books allowed by the education authorities. One of Boss Adams' most popular prizes was for swimming: he gave sixpence for swimming across the river and back. The prizes were presented with the yearly reports at prizegiving day before breaking for the August holidays.

Summer Holidays

In our household and a good many others, the preparations for summer holidays did not entail a visit to a tourist office or preparing a wardrobe to suit a Mediterranean climate. Few people got further than the nearest seaside resort, and most of them who saw the sea did so on a day excursion on August Bank Holiday to a place like Great Yarmouth – all the 104 miles and return for 1/3d., children under 14 half fare. Very reasonable if you had the price of the trip, but the Blades family's chances of going en bloc to Great Yarmouth, or for that matter to places nearer, such as Skegness or Hunstanton, were about as remote as a trip to the Himalayas. A trip to the North Bank on Shanks's pony, or a halfpenny tram ride to the suburb of Walton to see the fireworks was the extent of our 'travel arrangements'. There was an economical alternative: a walk to see the fireworks display on the football ground, or to be precise to see the display from the outside of the ground. Here we could at least count the rockets that went up and try to guess what was happening on the other side of the fence. When the firework display was over Dad partook of one of his rare extravagances: 'a penny plate' of cockles, whelks, winkles and mussels. The cockles and whelks looked like snails to me and I was never certain of the winkles and mussels, but no doubt they were very tasty.

A day such as August Monday invariably finished with a romp

---

[4] At Christmas he never failed to start my collection for The Waifs and Strays with two bright new pennies. Subsequent contributions were more often halfpennies.

at bedtime. There were the usual pillow fights, throwing Cecil – the youngest – from one end of the bed to the other, and jumping up and down on the bed (as on a trampoline), the winner being the one who touched the ceiling first. These games were soon put a stop to – if Mam or Dad could make themselves heard from the foot of the stairs or Dad's footsteps were heard on his way up. Quieter games followed. These included being millionaires and mad singing. As millionaires we pressed or rang imaginary bells and ordered the most fantastic dishes imaginable. Mad singing not only amused us but increased our vocal range for we stretched our voices to the limit using intervals and progressions that would do justice to any avant-garde masterpiece. Our 'mad music' of nearly sixty years ago may not have been as mad as we thought, or do some composers write mad music today? Our boyish mad music was never encored, in fact it was invariably cut short by Grandad who, though getting a bit on the deaf side, would open his bedroom door and tell us to 'Shut that blasted row' and to get off to sleep before we got a flea in our ears – an admonition which, coming from Grandad and his sepulchral bedroom, caused immediate silence. By the time Mam and Dad came to bed the Blades Brothers were all asleep, or feigning sleep, as I was on the occasion I heard Dad say to Mam, 'What a pity we can't take them on a real seaside holiday'. But why bother about the seaside and places like Yarmouth when there was the North Bank and the fun of fishing in the River Nene?

Underneath the bridge was where the fish were supposed to bite best, but it was also a good place to make for if a storm brewed, and fierce as a fen storm could be there was a remarkable feeling of safety under this old wooden bridge where, incidentally, there was a realistic effect of thunder if a farm cart rumbled over the slatted surface of the arch – a veritable theatre bronteron, an effect machine with which I was due to make acquaintance.[5] Sitting on the river bank it seemed out of the question that in a few months' time the whole landscape would be in the grip of winter and the flowing water a huge skating rink, with contests taking place on a stretch of 20 miles of frozen water and the degrees of frost so low (and constant) that there might be a repetition of a winter a little before my birth when a carriage and pair was driven on the ice and chestnuts and potatoes were roasted under the water bridge for days on end. Have the seasons changed? I remember a great deal of frost

[5] Bronteron: in some cases a slatted ramp down which heavy stones or balls of lead were rolled. (The slats in the water bridge provided a grip for the horses' hooves.)

and snow in the winters of my boyhood and almost constant sunshine in the summer. If there were wet days during summer holidays then I have forgotten them. My memories are of the sunshine and rolling fields of wheat and barley shimmering in the heat, and the sound of a reaper which meant that gleaning time was at hand, and that meant an extra copper to be earned because Mr. Tebbs the farmer or anybody who kept chickens would give a penny for a sack of ears of wheat or barley.

A wonderful surprise came one August morning: a letter from my father's Auntie Polly at Belton (near Uppingham) to say that the two elder boys could have a few days' holiday with her, and what is more she sent the railway fare. And what a holiday we had! It is as clear in my memory as if it were yesterday. Auntie fed us like turkey cocks, never allowing us to go out on a ramble without a large slice of cake, to keep our stomachs 'comfortable'. I have vivid memories of clambering up the ladder each night to our little bed in the loft above Uncle's bakery, and the sweet sound of the small organ in the village church and standing at the side of Dad's cousin Alice as she practised on it. One day Tom and I were taken to Uppingham by way of the notorious Wardley Hill which seemed like a mountain to us. At Uppingham we were shown the famous school, neither of us dreaming that in years to come I would take part in symphony concerts held there, or address a large audience from the platform in the main hall.

With my summer holiday, my paper round, Blackman's on Saturdays, and the annual Sunday School outing and choir trip, the August holidays went by all too quickly, and before I knew where I was it was time to go back to school, and to take my place in a new class, one standard nearer to Standard 7, reaching the age of fourteen and really going out to work.

☙ 3 ❧

Growing Up

A new class at St. John's did not mean that I was separated from my Star Road companions. There was a new teacher, but class mates remained much the same, as with the exception of a few real dunces all boys moved up automatically each September. The Boss told the school – as usual – about his holiday at Brighton and how he swam every day in the English Channel, and floated (as no doubt his fat tummy allowed him) from Brighton to Hove on several oc- casions before 'lunch'. Luncheon he explained was the real name for midday dinner. Meanwhile all was going well with my paper round and at Mr. Blackman's. The tobacco business – like Peter- borough – was expanding, and soon after getting back to school and my eleventh birthday I was given a rise of sixpence a week, for which I took over Len Ward's delivery of parcels on Thursday dinner time and Friday evenings. Though my week was beginning to fill up, the extra work did not interfere with my being a choir- boy, as choir practice was on Thursday evening. I was becoming quite familiar with Tallis, Stainer and Maunder, and so was Tom who had become a probationer at St. Mary's. Anthems such as 'What are these, what are these, that are arrayed in white robes?' and 'I know that my Redeemer liveth' as an encore had become addi- tional items in our bedtime repertoire; though I must confess we changed – as have many thousands of choristers – 'What are these, what are these?' to 'What are these, bags of peas?'

It was at this time, the late summer of 1912, that we nearly lost Dad. He was taken seriously ill with pleurisy and lay for several weeks in Peterborough Infirmary, and prayers were said for him in church. Whilst Dad was ill I got into, or to be nearer the truth got out of, Peterborough Cathedral choir. As was customary, when a vacancy occurred for a Minster chorister, a notice was placed in the vestry of every church. With my various activities the notice in St. Mary's vestry meant little to me, but it interested Tom, whose voice was in any case superior to mine. Tom, however, was a very nervous boy, and it fell to me to take him along to be tested by Dr. Haydn Keeton, the organist and choirmaster at the Minster. (Dr.

Keeton had at that time two articled pupils who were destined 'to go places'. Their names were Thomas Armstrong and Malcolm Sargent. Both Tom and I were to meet these young musicians a great many times in years to come.) Dr. Keeton proved to be all that had been said about him by generations of choristers – a real old sergeant-major, and as nimble with a penny cane as he was at the keyboard. Tom wilted at the sight of the Doctor who, having just finished 5.15 Evensong, was wearing his full though somewhat untidy ecclesiastical paraphernalia. Keeton – as he was known for short – first told Tom to open his mouth, into which he popped a tuning fork to widen the gap and rattled it up and down between Tom's teeth. Then after striking the fork, he said, 'Sing that note, boy'. Not a sound came from Tom who seemed to be bordering on collapse so, thinking to encourage him, I said, 'Come on Tom, you can do that,' and sang the note for him. 'Sing that again,' Keeton rasped at me, and being too frightened to disobey him, I piped up with an A or something sufficiently near to it, for he immediately got to work testing *my* voice instead of Tom's. 'You'll do,' he said, 'and your brother can try another time.' By this time Tom was blubbering and I was far too scared to tender my immediate resignation as a cathedral chorister on the grounds of pressing public engagements. This I did the following evening explaining to Dr. Keeton that I could not become a chorister because of my work. At first I thought he was going to eat me, but instead he said that it was a pity and added kindly that my brother must try again. So ended my term as a cathedral chorister: possibly the shortest on record. Tom certainly did try again and became solo boy. Chris, the third of the Blades Brothers, also became a cathedral chorister, as did my son Douglas; in fact they all left their mark. They are there to this day: small blobs of tar on the stone gateway leading to the precincts.

Soon after this incident, I joined the Scouts as a tenderfoot. I soon qualified as a scout, and then was able to have one ambition realised – to play a kettledrum, for that is what most people called a side drum when I was a boy. It was some time before I was allowed to play my drum on the march, but this I did in due course, though I fear without the panache of my hero Mr. Jim Pack on his big drum. Scout night was one of the highlights of the week. It was hungry work too and if funds permitted I bought a ha'porth of hot peas on the way home.

Another of my heroes was Mr. Ingamells, who lived next door to a house that took lodgers, with a card in the window reading:

YOUNG MEN TAKEN IN AND DONE FOR. Mr. Ingamells had – in my opinion – one of the most marvellous jobs in the world, for he was in charge of a big stationary steam engine at a factory. His job, as well as being a responsible one, was without doubt a thirsty one as he seemed obliged to drink a great deal of ale, either at the Durham Ox – the nearest of the numerous 'locals' – or from Mr. Box's off-licence, to which Mr. Ingamells made regular evening trips with a white jug into which Mr. Box put half a pint of the best, drawn from the wood. This Mr. Ingamells took outside to drink. When the jug was quite empty, he went back into the shop for a re-fill which he took home to share with his wife over supper. One hot summer night an accident happened to Mr. Ingamells: he was drinking his beer outside the shop when a wasp flew into the jug and he swallowed it and had to be taken to the Infirmary. This I felt was a terrible thing to happen to a man who knew all about steam engines, but Grandad only said, 'That'll larn him'.

Incidents such as the wasp swallowing; a horse falling down and breaking a leg and having to be shot; someone's dog going mad; Mrs. Kendrick throwing a bucket of cold water thickened with coal-dust over Old Frosty for clipping Charlie's ear; or Mr. Kendrick getting his motor bike to go first time – although never reported in the national press – set many tongues wagging in the vicinity of Star Road.[1] In the main, however, things went along in a fairly steady routine, with the exception of high spots such as the Sunday School treat, the choir trip, Bridge Fair, the visit of Sanger's circus in the summer and a travelling show in the winter. One show that came to Peterborough included the Fat Boy of Peckham, and a very thin man whose place of birth was not advertised, but who was on a thirty-days complete fast. I never saw inside the show, but was told that the boy, though not as young as people expected, was very fat indeed, and that the man was as thin as a rake and, because of his sorry condition, did better with his enamel collection plate than the fat boy. Mam said they put sugar in the thin man's drinking water to keep him going, but Grandad was of the opinion that he probably got more grub down him than the fat boy, and that like a lot of other things the whole affair was a bit of a 'catch-penny'. Whether or not, it was all very exciting to me, but not as exciting as the thought of carol singing on Christmas Eve and Christmas Day and especially Christmas breakfast, dinner and tea, and the

[1] As did the bloomers worn by a niece of my Grandad who, according to most of the women in our road, was a brazen hussy for daring to ride a bicycle like a man.

fun of Boxing Day when we were allowed to pull crackers (an annual present from Mr. Manley the grocer), and to play real games at Auntie Liddy's and see Uncle George's magic lantern show. The screen was a white tablecloth and what fun it was when Uncle played his prize joke and put on a slide upside down!

As for our festive board I can say immediately that we were not great poultry eaters in our house. Occasionally on such days as August Monday we had chicken and ham paste instead of bloater paste, but even then Grandad said it was new-fangled stuff and hadn't the flavour of fish paste. Turkey and such like did not make regular appearances at our table though I must admit they looked very nice in the shops and I always said that when I grew up I would buy Mam a goose for Christmas – and actually did from my first Christmas bonus as an engineer's apprentice. Grandad said that he had tasted a pheasant now and again, and also eaten fowl when he used to keep hens and Mam said they had once had turkey at a Christmas party at Thorpe Hall when she was in service. Dad had actually tasted venison at the Bishop's Palace in the precincts when he went to a conference to do with the Church of England Men's Society. But we were not concerned about such things. There was surely nothing like the roast beef of England, particularly if it was a beautiful piece of sirloin like the joint we had on Christmas Day. As for game pie, what about cold rabbit pie with a good solid crust and jelly gravy after a run home from early morning choral communion? What a feast! I have taken breakfast in one of London's finest hotels with Robert Zildjian, the world famous cymbal manufacturer; partaken of an immense Australian snapper in Adelaide; struggled through a yard-long menu in a Perth hydro; regularly consumed a large North Sea sole with innumerable trimmings (a speciality of my hostess Mrs. Kirby) during the Aldeburgh Festival; done considerable justice to ham and eggs and a series of desserts in Montreal; feasted on jam omelettes and caviare in Moscow; taken refreshment in Windsor Castle and Buckingham Palace; and whilst on a Continental tour with Daniel Barenboim and the English Chamber Orchestra spent an hour or so coping with the delightful fare offered on the Rhinegold Express ending with coffee laced with schnapps: an inspiration I seem to remember of the flautist Norman Knight and bassist Adrian Beers who, though never playing in the same clef 'on the stand' were (until both 'signed the pledge') always in complete unison in the bar. But for sheer gastronomic delight give me Mam's cold rabbit pie on a frosty Christmas morning, and for a close second, Christmas dinner of Yorkshire pudding followed by sirloin of beef with plenty of gravy on the potatoes and Brussels sprouts, and for 'afters' a real Christmas pudding crowned with a sprig of holly, and a piece set aside for Grandad aglow with flaming brandy. And if there was room for it, one of Auntie Liddy's mince pies. Over such a meal even Dad and Grandad forgot to argue about the relative merits of church and chapel and the long note in the Old Hundredth, and for once Grandad was too involved to tell Tom and me to 'git ye furrader throm him', or if we asked for another helping to say, 'You've had anew for the likes o' you'.

❧ 4 ❧

Dark Days

The early days of 1914 were dark days for the Blades family. Two branches of the family suffered bereavement. We also lost one of the Star Roadites: Harry Cottom. No more wheeling Harry to school and settling him down by the 'Slow but Sure' combustion stove, or in a sunny place near the window. The farewell was made as his former entourage walked tearfully round his coffin, and I was not the only one who was startled by Harry's appearance, for the poor hunchback boy whom we had so often trundled along to school in his modest push-chair was, with his frail limbs straightened in their final resting place, every bit of six feet tall. Grandad, who continued to be at variance with my father on matters of politics, religion, and the singing of the Old Hundredth, had grown a trifle more 'rheumaticky' and was fast losing the sight in his remaining eye. He and his crony Matty Goodley remained of the opinion that the Government was responsible for the state of things, the weather in particular. Both were convinced that the goings on of the younger generation were a disgrace, and that things were different in their day. Dad was well, though hiding a terrible depression due to the insecurity of his employment. Mam's main problem was to make ends meet, and with her four boys growing out of their clothes, getting heavier and heavier on boot leather and all with healthy appetites, her days were long and anxious ones. How could they be otherwise with the weekly income averaging something less than a sovereign to pay the rent and feed and clothe seven people? Not surprisingly, money, or the lack of it, was a constant topic in our house. Is there any wonder that I became money conscious, and that I have since been considered financially minded? If I *am* financially minded, then the chief reason is that as a boy I saw so many people suffering the want of money, and that goes for my own folk.

Not that we were unhappy in our house: quite the reverse. We had much for which to be thankful. What mattered that we only saw an egg for breakfast once a week – on Sunday – at the time of the year when pullets' eggs were twenty-four a shilling, for then there was the fun of sharing this luxury: my turn one week for the

35

eggcup and to spoon Tom's portion onto his bread, and Tom's turn to act as chef the following Sunday. And what friends we had! For example Auntie Fanny and Uncle Harry who paid for me to spend a few days with them during the Easter holidays. I was taken to see ocean liners on Manchester Ship Canal and where one canal crossed another over the Barton Aqueduct. All the more wonderful because I had a picture of it in my school prize: *Conquest of Engineering*. Another adventure was being taken to see the black stone that had been put in a wall to mark the spot where Charlie Peace shot and killed a policeman – miles better than reading about it in Bob the Barber's *Police News*. There was also a trip to the Zoo at Belle Vue, followed by a visit to a music hall, where a comedian (Jack Rickaby, I think) made a joke about his bow-legs of which he said, 'anything is good enough to go to work in!' His songs included one about tripe which went 'Tripe, tripe, tripe, that's the stuff for me. I like it for my dinner and I like it for my tea.' Another song was about seaside bathing beauties whose virtues he extolled but (according to the song) his wife did not share his opinion for she said 'the beauty of form I fail to see, if you want to see better come home with me', which brought the reply 'Oh yes my dear with you I agree, but you're not as young as you used to be.' Most people in the audience laughed a great deal at this song, but my cousins and I agreed that the bit about the bow-legs and the tripe song were the best jokes by a long way, and that the man who played the drums in the band was jolly clever as he seemed to be playing two or three instruments at the same time.[1]

Soon after this memorable Easter holiday I heard that Roger's the hardware shop in Cowgate, required an errand boy – dinner time, nights and Saturdays. I quickly went to Cowgate, and in view of my experience to date the manager of Roger's gave me the job. Roger's was certainly hard work and I am sure that I earned every penny of my half-a-crown; but the extra money was worth the extra work and made my addition to the family income quite size-able for a boy, as with my wages from Stott's which were now one-and-sixpence, I was taking home the whole of four shillings weekly (not far short of the rent). At Roger's I came under the wing of a quiet little man named Fred. He was a kindly man, though not as jolly as Len Ward, and I must admit I really missed Len and his – and my own – pranks. But again I had a slice of luck (in fact I have often been called Lucky Jim). One night Len Ward came round to our house to tell me that Mr. Blackman wanted to see me.

[1] He would have been known as a 'trap-drummer'.

He hinted that the boy who had taken my place had lost some parcels and that Mr. Blackman wanted me back. The upshot was that I returned to the tobacco trade, dinner times, nights and Saturdays for what I had been getting at Roger's.

With my morning paper round and extra work during the dinner hour and evenings, I was obliged to forgo the Boy Scouts, but I was able to keep my place in the choir, admittedly with an occasional 'deputy' or absence on practice nights – a procedure I developed rather successfully as a professional. It might be said that for a boy of thirteen I was robbed of a great deal of fun; but there was still plenty for me to enjoy, one really special treat being the Saturday night 'Penny Pop'. The 'Penny Pop' was a popular concert held weekly in St. Mary's Church Hall. It was organised by the congregation of St. Mary's Church, my father included. Dad, who was marvellous as a light entertainer, being able to sing a comic song, recite, or deliver a 'stump speech' as well as the next, did a 'turn' each week.

The winter evenings slipped by, and in no time came the Sunday School treat and the choir trip, and of the latter, by far the most memorable the choir trip to Great Yarmouth on Tuesday, 4th August 1914. At school, the Head had spoken of the assassination of the Archduke Ferdinand, and the Kaiser's threat to the peace of the world, much of which I did not fully comprehend as to me Germany was a place where cheap toys came from, and jolly good toys they were with their trademark D.R.G.M. Tuesday, 4th August, the day of the choir trip, dawned clear and bright. To the younger members of the choir the long train journey and the sight of such places as Ely Cathedral was a major event. In contrast, the grown-ups took on an air of indifference as to the length of the journey and talked of much longer rides. During the afternoon I saw something I shall ever remember: a news-vendor with a placard which read: WAR DECLARED. BATTLESHIPS IN YARMOUTH ROADS. There was rush to the beach to see the ships and a brave sight it was indeed with the smoke pouring out of the funnels, and the splash of the waves and white foam in contrast. Momentous as the occasion was it registered little with the younger members of the group, and we spent the rest of the afternoon as boys would, searching the shore for souvenir shells and so forth. After tea the journey back to Peterborough. Here crowds were assembled everywhere, waving Union Jacks and doing all the things people do on exciting occasions. Some of the more high-spirited had already wrecked the shops of the two German pork butchers. Remains of pork pies such as had often made my mouth water (and I had promised myself to sample when I grew up) were strewn about the pavement, and strings of sausages were hanging on the overhead tramway lines. We were told that the mayor had been obliged to read the Riot Act and that the two pork butchers had already been arrested as German spies.

War and My Last Year at School

The whole of the month of August seethed with excitement and a hubbub similar to that on an election day. The streets were alive with Union Jacks and wherever you went there was a large picture of Lord Kitchener with his finger pointing straight at you. Regimental bands marched round the town and men and youths by the dozen followed them to the recruiting office. I followed the bands for another reason: there were some marvellous drum beaters among them, though not as good I felt as Jim Pack. Dad, Uncle George, Uncle Dick, Uncle David, and Mr. Playford and Len Ward were among the early volunteers. Dad was passed medically fit by the same doctor who had as good as 'given him up' two years previously, and was immediately enrolled in the garrison battalion of the Third Essex Regiment. By the time I returned to school things were settling down to grim reality. Mr. Adams had prepared a map of the battlefront and one of my first duties in the morning, as I was now a monitor and head boy, was to help him pin the little flags in position. Mr. Hankins and pupil teacher Jim Gooding had volunteered and we at St. John's School were horrified by being given a lady teacher who, to our surprise, turned out a real trump. Despite my new duties as a monitor, I managed to listen to Teacher Arthur's harmonium just before school started. If we were alone he played such tunes as *Alexander's Ragtime Band*, to which I tapped an accompaniment on the lid of the harmonium, at the same time keeping an ear open for the Boss's tread on the stone steps so as to warn Mr. Gooding, who then quickly modulated into a hymn or something similar. As far as lessons were concerned I was doing well, and soon after my thirteenth birthday had made the jump to the top class (Standard X7). I had received my usual birthday card from Cousin Lil, and had replied to the effect that by this time next year I would have left school and would be out at work. Maybe not the regular job at the Post Office that Dad had envisaged, as many boys on leaving school were now going into munition factories and from what I had been told were earning good money as well as learning a trade. So the thought of becoming an engineer passed through my mind, and as my last year at school flowed along I visualised being concerned with the building of torpedo boats and huge cannons or, alternatively, joining up as a drummer or a bugle boy. There were many things to be thankful for, not the least that the Blades family were all as fit as fiddles, due I am certain to our mode of life: a not too-rich or heavy diet, and Mam's iron powder for strength, and liquorice powder for 'inner cleanliness'. We missed Dad, who on enlisting was posted to Weymouth, and though supposedly for home service was eventually sent with the first draft to the Dardanelles. Before the end of the year Uncle George and Playford were in the trenches in France, and Auntie Liddy and Mrs. Playford had joined the ranks of the thousands of British housewives who lived for the morning post and dreaded a War Office envelope containing 'reported killed, wounded, or missing'. One bright spot for many at home was the now regular weekly income. My mother's army allowance was 25 shillings weekly; in addition, there was the billeting money as we had two soldiers from the Norfolk Regiment sleeping in the front room. So as far as the things of the flesh were concerned, we had never been better off in our lives; a factor (according to some) not altogether unconnected with the early enlistment of many a married man. Like most boys at St. John's I found the war exciting. The Head gave vivid accounts of the action on land and sea – often in the place of a lesson – and the whole town was full of the throb of war and, to my delight, the throb of the Drum Corps and the bugles of the Norfolk Regiment which was being trained in Peterborough. (I suppose the Northants Regiment was being trained in Norwich!)

Christmas 1914, my last as a schoolboy and an errand boy, was a sad one for many, myself included. Len Ward's and Mr. Playford's names had been among the names of the killed on the lists hung daily outside the General Post Office. Playford, so Uncle George told me on his first leave, had been blown to smithereens at his side, the first time they went 'over the top'. I got to know those dreadful lists fairly well, as among my several domestic duties I helped a bit with Grandad, who was now almost bed-ridden and totally blind. It fell to me to keep Grandad informed of the progress of the war and what was on the 'lisses' – the 'lisses' being Grandad's plural of lists! Every night I reported what he called the 'state of things'. As soon as he heard me enter his bedroom he would rasp out, 'What's going on along at the front with them Proosians?' The information on the 'lisses' and the state of the war generally I rarely disclosed, deducting from the losses of the Allies and adding considerably to those of Kaiser 'Bill'. I constantly assured Grandad that the Huns were as good as beaten and Matty Goodley was a long way out in saying that the war could last up to a twelvemonth. I never (thank God) had to report a single loss in our own family. (Uncle David, Uncle Dick, Dad and Uncle George returned from active service with but slight injuries – trench feet or a touch of gas – a remarkable family record in view of the losses of the Allies being over a million men.) But though the war showed no sign of a close, Grandad's life certainly did. In his last month or so I was reminded from his ramblings of incidents in his early manhood. He constantly told me that he was 'over a hundred' but this is not the figure on his gravestone. He died (in the Workhouse Infirmary) at the age of 81 and lies 'along of Grandmam' in the old cemetery at Peterborough. We missed him of course, and I for one have never forgotten his strong facial features, his resonant bass voice, and his extemporisation on the melodion.

Whatever Matty Goodley had wrongly forecast in his time he was certainly nearer the mark than Grandad in his prediction as to the length of the war. The effort of all was being sought and given, and there seemed no doubt that I was for the munitions factory, and during my last few months at school I assessed as far as I was able the various merits of the several engineering firms in my home town. Messrs. Peter Brotherhood's took my fancy, for in addition to making ship's turbines, centrifugal pumps and even torpedo engines, a boy told me that his big brother, who was a Brotherhood's apprentice, had actually been to sea in a warship that was out on test. Uncle George knew all about Brotherhood's, and on his first leave from France he told me that it was a famous firm and that it had an orchestra; so there was no question as to which establishment it was to be for J.B. At last the month of July came round, and on my last day at school with a letter and character from the Head plus my school books, I presented myself to Mr. Johnson, the manager of Messrs. Peter Brotherhood's: an appointment arranged by Mr. Adams who, like other school masters in those days, did all he could to see his boys well launched in life. Brotherhood's was a large firm and I was bewildered by the mass and the whirr of machinery as I was escorted to the manager's office. Mr Johnson, a benign and to me quite elderly man, after perusing my report and school books, said 'So you want to be an engineer my boy?' On my replying in the affirmative he said 'And what sort of an engineer son – a fitter or a turner, or maybe a coppersmith?' 'Oh no sir,' I replied, 'I don't want to be anything like that. I want to be a *real* engineer and build ship's engines and bridges and go abroad or out to sea.' 'Well,' said Mr. Johnson (whether laughingly or not I cannot remember), 'you're very good at algebra so I'm sure we can do something about that when you're old enough.'

The month of August 1915 seemed to creep by. There was no choir trip and such like, but I was happy. Who would not be at the thought of starting at Brotherhood's in early September? But it was not to be. Whilst I was washing down in the scullery one evening towards the end of August, Auntie Liddy who had popped in to see Mam, happened to glance my way and caught sight of me scratching my back with my school ruler: something I had been doing for a week or so. 'Kitty – quick,' Auntie shouted to my mother, 'the boy's a'peelin' '. Now Auntie was an authority on the matter of young people's ailments. She had been in service in a large family and her own three children had survived every known complaint from nappy rash to diphtheria, so if Auntie said I was 'a'peelin' ' there was no possible doubt about my condition. Doctor Latham was sent for and it transpired that I had been knocking about during the previous week or so with a mild bout of scarlet fever. I was quickly isolated in the back bedroom with a heavily-disinfected blanket over the doorway, awaiting admittance to the fever hospital. Soon after I had 'done a'peelin' ' I returned home, and following a period of convalescence in the fresh air of Star Road, the Common, and the Park Meadows, I made my way to Brotherhood's to report fit. Here, I was told to start the following Monday in the drawings stores under Mr. George Snow. Not quite what I had anticipated, especially in view of my record in algebra. Nothing now but to wait until Monday; so good-bye to St. John's and taking boys for cheese rolls, good-bye paper round and the jam or lemon curd tarts from the ladies who had the *Pearson's Weekly*, good-bye Mr. Blackman and getting twopence from dear old Mr. Cave after settling him down in the train for Thorney and telling him that his was the second stop, and good-bye to some extent to Jim Pack's bass drum for I was now fourteen and growing up, though still singing treble even if a trifle husky. What lay ahead? The bench? A machine? The engine room of a battleship? The Zambesi? Or a concert hall? My immediate care, however, was trying on my overalls and getting all prepared for 9 a.m. Monday morning.[2]

[2] My overalls were my first pair of long trousers (long-uns) as no working class boy wore anything but 'britches' until leaving school.

41

5

A British Workman

There were three ways of getting to Brotherhood's: walking the whole three miles, walking ¾ mile to the Market Place and getting a penny ticket on the tram, or walking 1¼ miles to the tram depot and joining the tram for half the cost. Need I say that the best way to me seemed the ½d ride? On this, my second trip to Brotherhood's, I had no letter of introduction or school books – nothing more than my dinner basket to qualify me – so on enquiry at the main gate I was told to wait until I was vouched for: a necessary procedure I soon realised as all the workmen showed a pass as they went through the gate. In due course I was collected by George Snow, who informed me that my hours from tomorrow would be 6 a.m. to 5.30 p.m. with overtime if I wanted. Mr. Snow, who said I could call him George, took me to the time office where I was given a number (722), my time card, and a pass which not only allowed me to enter and leave the works, but testified to my doing my bit for my 'King and Country'. George then piloted me through a maze of whirring machinery to a time-clock where he showed me how to punch my card, at the same time giving me information that after three minutes past the hour, a quarter-of-an-hour was lost – and so on up to one hour. No one was allowed to clock in between 7 a.m. and 8.15 a.m. breakfast time, meaning that a 'quarter' (of a day) was lost if one had not clocked in by 7 a.m. Anyone losing a 'quarter' by starting at 9 a.m. came in for a good deal of banter, such as 'who were you with last night?' Newly-married men were mildly ridiculed with such questions as: 'Has she been sleeping on your shirt?' and so forth. Having clocked in George Snow took me along to the drawings store, pointing out the various 'shops' en route. At first sight the 'office', as George called it, disappointed me. It was a small room containing a largish desk at which sat two elderly clerks who, like the desk, were engulfed by rows of shelves packed with blueprints pasted onto boards. These blueprints were known as 'job numbers' and it was explained to me that my job was to hand out a particular drawing on request. If it was 'out' my duty was to collect it and deliver it to wherever it was required. George

42

Snow, who was said to know nearly every job number by heart, and pretty well where every drawing was (or should be) at any time, proved a splendid teacher, and I quickly got the hang of the position of the drawings on the shelves, and even emulated him as a detective in tracking down a lost blueprint: a mighty interesting job as it often entailed following the course of a particular component through the whole factory, and meeting at close quarters such finished products as torpedo engines and massive centrifugal pumps – all most exciting, particularly if they were 'on test'. In the office I had a place next to 'Charlie', the younger of the two elderly clerks. Both were over seventy, in fact Sam the elder brother was reported to be approaching his eightieth birthday. These brothers Tavener were both bachelors and lived with their mother who was heading for the world's record in longevity. The whole family had solved the problem of ration cards and were a splendid recommendation for the brewery trade, as their staple diet, combined with huge quantities of snuff, was a local brew of stout, which Charlie assured me he used in place of tea in the morning and also went to bed on it. He was known to be keeping company with a widow who had a similar palate to his own, but had promised his mother that he would not marry whilst she was alive. Sam and Charlie spent their working hours in entering orders and deliveries into huge ledgers: books which were graced with their fine handwriting (I have never seen better) and such famous names in the engineering world as Harland and Wolfe, Dormond Long, coupled with such exciting references as a 'turbine for H.M.S. . . . .'

As the end of my first week at Brotherhood's approached I speculated on the contents of my first pay packet. An apprentice's wages were 5 shillings for the normal 54 hour week, this being 6 a.m. to 5.30 p.m. Monday to Friday, and 6 a.m. to noon on Saturday. The allotted mealtimes were ¾ hour for breakfast, 1 hour for dinner. Added to my normal money would be overtime, as after my first day I worked almost the same hours as George Snow and others where there was no night shift. The double-shift hours were 6 a.m. to 6 p.m. and 6 p.m. to 6 a.m. six nights a week, Saturday night off and one free Sunday each month. The day workers (one shift) worked 6 a.m. to 8.30 p.m. Monday, Tuesday and Thursday; 6 a.m. to 5.30 p.m. on Wednesday; 6 a.m. on Friday to 12 noon on Saturday (known as 'working through'); and 9 a.m. to 5.30 p.m. three Sundays in each month. My wages that week came to over seven shillings.

Work at Brotherhood's did not mean that I lost touch with my school pals. Saturday afternoon and evening was spent with Charlie

Kendrick and Den Leach. On most Sunday evenings I was just able to take my place in the choir for evensong; but not for long, as my voice was getting decidedly hoarse. I enjoyed the relief of the evening service after the constant roar of machinery. I enjoyed those Sunday evenings for another reason: I had been smitten by a girl named Emma Beecroft who, with her mother, was a regular member of the congregation at St. Mary's. Seeing her in church was as far as I got, making my romance an extremely tame one. To say that life at Brotherhood's was pleasant is much of an understatement. George Snow and the Brothers Tavener proved veritable mines of information on all manner of subjects, and I made hosts of acquaintances among the men in the various shops, some of whom had wonderful tales to tell about going to sea in battleships to test out firms' engines. In the shops there were numerous diversions. One prank was for one person to engage another in conversation whilst dripping oil onto his shoe, or a third party painted white the heels of the unsuspecting one. A new boy was usually sent to the stores for a handful of half-inch holes, or given a lengthy steel rod in each hand – just about as much as he could carry – which he was told to take up to so-and-so in a department on the far side of the works. So-and-so would ponder for a moment, and then tell the boy that the rods were really meant for a department near to where the lad had come from. This department of course directed the boy elsewhere, and so the game went on. Parodies of well-known songs were used as occasion demanded, as for example, if a man was showing an apprentice how to do something or other some wag would be bound to strike up with 'tell me the old, old story', or 'he knows all about it'. One of the best-known songs at Brotherhood's was the song the apprentices sang (at a discreet distance) to one of the firm's greatest characters, a man by the name of Dan. My recollection of it is as follows:

> 'Dan, Dan, the lavatory man
> Sitting in his box all day,
> Playing ha'penny nap
> In among the crap
> Never was a man like Dan, Dan, Dan.'

Such was the song dedicated to Dan – custodian of the main conveniences or toilets if you wish. Having been shown the rather grim-looking edifice and learned the shortest cut to it – preferably by a route that avoided the foreman's box – the next thing was to make the acquaintance of Dan; a necessary procedure as this somewhat benign looking old gentleman (on sight) was due to play no small part in one's daily routine and general welfare. It can be said immediately that Dan's job was no bed of roses and was by no means the most coveted position in the works. In addition to keeping his 'house' clean and orderly, he functioned as a guardian of the firm's interest in the capacity of time keeper, as all employees were allowed ten minutes and 'ten minutes only' in the abode which Dan so effectively controlled. In the matter of cleanliness Dan was exemplary. How on earth he managed to keep those twenty or more cubicles and other necessary arrangements in good trim is a mystery. But he did it; though admittedly not without a good deal of carbolic and 'elbow grease' – the latter to erase the occasional poetic efforts of certain shallow-minded individuals. To pay a visit to one of these cubicles was no light matter, for to do so one had first to face up to interrogation from Dan who presided in a small hut which he termed his office. 'Number and department?' he would say in a stern dark voice, particularly stern with nervous apprentices. Having given the number Dan would glance at a large watch on his desk, make a mental or a written note of the time and take a further look at the enquirer for admission. Dan had a remarkable knack of knowing if an applicant was really in a state of distress or was 'miking' (malingering). If Dan felt your case proved, in you went with a sharp reminder that it was for ten minutes and ten minutes only. If for any reason you over-ran your time in the cubicle in would come Dan. 'Number so-and-so – out.' And out you got nearly as quickly as you went in. Martinet as Dan was, he was a kindly man at heart and would always oblige if within his power. His 'house' in some respects was something of a retreat and the place, if one had time in hand, for a smoke and a chat away from the noise of the shops. In addition to his powers of observation Dan was no mean craftsman. He could cut squares of newspaper as true as a die. These served a most useful purpose, their only disadvantage as far as I can remember was their distinct failure as reading matter for it was only on isolated occasions that one reached the end of any particular subject.

Friendly as Dan could be, out of his 'house' he was somewhat lonely, particularly in the mess room, for here he took his meals at a private table. Some said he wished to be alone at such times. It could have been that his close contact with his not altogether salubrious territory rendered him a trifle unpopular. It is not improbable that he had a different opinion regarding certain atmospheric conditions; which is a reminder of the story of the London equivalent of Dan who, on a dreadfully sultry summer day was taking a breather and having a chat with his female counterpart at the top of the steps of their respective underground conveniences, and after sundry friendly exchanges as to the state of business etc. closed the conversation by remarking to the lady that he was going down for a breath of fresh air !

Remembering Uncle George's advice I kept my eye on Harry Flint who played the drums in the works band (the Belvedere Orchestra). Harry was (or seemed to me) a wizard, for he played drums and cymbals and instruments like the triangle and tambourine at the same time. I took every opportunity of listening to Harry and got as near to him as I could at the Saturday night concerts, but try as I would I could not get him to talk about drumming. He certainly practised the 'closed shop' that was prevalent in those days.[1]

A week or so before Christmas, George Snow told me that I was to leave him and go on the con-rod bench to start my apprenticeship as a fitter (the formality of a boy and his parents or guardians putting the seal to indentures which bound him to his master were waived at this period). On the con-rod bench, I came under the wing (no exaggeration) of the charge-hand Bill Churchyard who was so tall (6 feet 4 inches) that his vice was raised on blocks. Next to him worked Billy Conyers, a very small man of over seventy who was obliged to stand on a block of wood in order to reach his vice. These men were known as Big Bill and Little Bill, and a jolly pair they were, as indeed were the rest of the con-rod crew: ten in all, among them a very stout gentleman by the name of Charlie Tumbelty ('Tump') a Manchester man to whom I took immediately and he to me. I became in every way Tump's slave, removing burrs from newly-machined pieces he was working on, doing his rough scraping prior to bedding parts together, running errands, cleaning his bike and eventually spending an hour or so of my free time in his private workshop where he did a bit of contract work. 'So you want to be a turner as well as a fitter?' he said to me one day. 'I'll teach you turning,' he said, and he did: on a small lathe he owned that was not power driven; or at least not until I turned the handle whilst Tump made the cuts on the job in the chuck. Mr. Tumbelty was the finest engineer I have ever met. He knew all about stresses in bridge building, cantilever systems, how to cast metal, and he could tell the thickness of every one of a set of feeler gauges (one

[1] A completely different picture today with the mass of printed material and expert tuition in the various academic institutions.

thousandth of an inch to twenty-thou.) by placing the thin strip of steel between his teeth. And what a musician he was! He had a glorious baritone voice and could play a mandolin, and many a pleasant hour was spent in playing mandolin and mouth-organ duets.[2]

I should explain that the con-rod bench at Brotherhood's was where heavy connecting rods were assembled before they were positioned in the various engines. After a trial of a day or so, Big Bill consulted Little Bill and then said I was suitable to him and the rest of the bench, and that I must be initiated according to ancient custom. I had heard of this thing being done to young seamen as the ship 'crossed the line' and steeled myself for the ceremony, whatever it might be. My charge-hand informed me that the ritual was of long standing in the engineering world. The ceremony was a simple one but an impressive one. First the working tools were explained to me; then I was questioned as to my desire to learn and become a good workman; I was then 'tarred and feathered' (a private part being smeared with oil and ornamented with a piece of cotton waste). During this interesting procedure (interesting, of course, to all but the participant) Little Bill, as senior member of the team, delivered the charge, consisting of advice on moral conduct and that I was to grow up a credit to my parents and all who were about to take me in hand. I suffered no ill effects from my initiation, and on reflection am convinced of certain parallels and the value of these time-honoured customs.

On rare occasions the management allowed minor diversions in the workers' time. One event receiving their full approbation was the Bun and Lemon Competition. This was an annual affair at Peter Brotherhood's. The contestants were boys chosen from each department, myself representing the con-rod bench. The competition took place after the dinner break on Christmas Eve. It consisted of eating a lemon and then a bun, the first to finish received the prize of a shilling. I had a small dinner that day and lined up for the event, the whole 4 feet 11 inches of me – the smallest boy in the competition. We all stood on a long bench, with a man standing beneath each of us with a newspaper to catch any pieces of the lemon or crumbs of the bun that were dropped; these were handed back to be disposed of. The advice given me by the men on our bench – most of whom claiming to be Bun and Lemon Competition veterans – was to *eat slowly and swallow every morsel before taking another bite.*

[2] 'Tump' became chief engineer at the famous Farrow's factory in Peterborough and an international authority on bee-keeping.

I attacked the lemon (we were allowed to leave the peel), and after a good deal of squirming finished off the whole of the inside. I then made a start on the bun. I seemed to be behind most of the other boys, who were already well on with their buns. My mouth felt parched and the process of swallowing pieces of dry bun was a great effort. By this time there was a good deal of spluttering and coughing up and down the line, and many boys who had taken large mouthfuls were being made to eat the pieces they had dropped onto the newspaper. I plodded on, small bites, chewing assiduously and swallowing slowly as per my instructions. By the time I was halfway through my bun, several of the contestants had paused for breath – and saliva. The act of swallowing was, for the time at least, completely beyond them. On the other hand, I had got my second wind. Slowly the bun disappeared, helped probably by the moisture from an odd currant (it was more bun than currant at that time), and it soon became clear that I was taking the lead. Encouraged by the cheers of the audience (a vast one, including the management) and particularly by the shouts of 'hurrah' from the men of the con-rod bench – and of course the thought of the shilling – I pegged away. The tail end of the bun seemed like sawdust, but I got it down eventually and beat a boy from the light turnery by a short head. But the contest was not quite over; the winner had to sing a song of his own choice. I piped up with 'For the moon shines bright on Charlie Chaplin'.[3] What with my voice being in the breaking stage and the effect of the bun and lemon, my vocal effort was decidedly croaky and halting. But the men cheered, and two of the chaps from our bench carried me shoulder high round the shop. I was presented with the shilling and a draught of cold tea by our foreman Andy Burnett: a grand Scot and a fine engineer. He added sixpence from his own pocket to the shilling, and I remember that he took off his bowler hat which all foremen wore in those days and placed it as a crown on my head. Most of the men gave me a small Christmas box, and I collected a fair sum which Mam let me keep towards paying off my bike. But when giving her a full account of the competition I remember that she suddenly looked hard at me and said, 'I hope you haven't been wasting your master's time!'

So the days and weeks and the following year sped on. Dad was posted to the Dardanelles, and following the evacuation, to Egypt. His letters gave us such details of his duties as censorship would allow. One thing which gave us a feeling of pride was that he had preached to the greater part of his regiment (the Third Battalion

[3] A personality I was to meet and work with later.

Essex) on the steps of Khartoum Cathedral. There is no doubt that
he was built for, and should have been, a parson. We sent him all
(or nearly all) the news from home. I told him of my work and he
seemed delighted that I was to be an engineer. I kept mum about
my desire to be a musician; I was meeting with opposition in that
direction nearer home. Mr. Tumbelty, who was now very much of
a second father to me, saw little future in music and was constantly
advising me regarding my trade. After several months on the con-rod
bench he insisted that I should ask for a move to the machine shop.
'Get on the lathe,' he said, 'be an all-round man.' So I moved to the
light turnery and became immersed in facing, boring, setting up for
thread cutting and the like. In the machine shop I worked a month
on days and a month on nights, and before you could say Jack
Robinson it was my fifteenth birthday.

I Join Up

Fifteen! I was really growing up, nearly old enough to join the
army I thought. Why not go as a drummer or a bugle boy? Every
time I heard the drums of the 'Norfolks' or listened to Harry Flint
my wrists tingled to play a real drum. So, in spite of 'Tump's' advice
I made a bold decision: I would go for a soldier. A visit to a local
recruiting office on a certain Friday morning in October 1916 got
rid of the preliminaries – officialdom was not all that particular about
age details at that time. I passed for just over sixteen and was given
a railway warrant for Northampton. On the following Monday
morning (I was on nights) I left the house saying to Mam that I
was having a day on my new bike and would be home in good time
for a sleep before going to work. I duly presented myself at
Northampton Barracks and was directed to a hut where a line of
chaps were being marshalled along a long table, signing a paper or
two and receiving the King's shilling. I signed on, received the
bright new shilling, and was given instructions to report in seven
days' time with as little 'clobber' as possible. On leaving the hut my
exit coincided with the entry of a solid-looking sergeant-major. I
side-stepped to give him way and he did the same for me. We each
repeated the process a couple of times after which he picked me up
and dumped me – rather ungraciously I thought – on the duck
boards outside the hut. 'So this is the army,' I thought, but I celebrated the occasion by spending sixpence of the King's shilling on a
beef dinner. The best part of my return journey to Peterborough
was absorbed in planning my method of approach to Mam. The

immediate truth seemed the safest, so on my return home I burst into the house, saying, 'Mam, I'm in the army.' My mood of exaltation (if there was one – I felt scared really) was short-lived. A smack on the ear with the whole 'four-feet-ten' of her behind it brought me to earth. She rushed me round to Reverend Law, who more than rushed me back to the recruiting office, and after parley with the recruiting officer to whom he revealed my age and the fact that my father was a service soldier, I was summarily discharged without honourable mention. So terminated what could well be one of the shortest military careers on record.

I go to Jail and then to London

Life went on, and another Christmas passed and 1917 slipped along with still no sign of Dad who, from his letters, seemed likely to remain in Egypt until the war was over. Uncle George came home from time to time and on each occasion renewed his promise about making a drummer of me. In contrast, Mr. Tumbelty became more vigilant than ever respecting my prospects in the world of engineering. On his advice I left Brotherhood's to gain experience in other firms, and by the middle of 1918 was doing what he called a 'man's job' on the maintenance lathe in one of the largest shell shops in Peterborough. Shell making however came to an abrupt end in November 1918. November 11th saw the Armistice, and like the whole of Great Britain, Peterborough 'went mad'. I joined the throngs that paraded the main streets of the town singing patriotic songs and doing all the things, wise and otherwise, that people do on such occasions. One escapade was walking in the tramway track and holding up a Corporation tram. This led to Den Leach, Curly Kendrick and myself being bundled off to Thorpe Road jail. Here our names and addresses were taken, but after being duly admonished we returned (much subdued) to our Star Road homes.[4]

There was no work on the following day, and with Mam's approval I made my first trip to London to see Auntie Lizzie and Cousin Lil and the sights I had heard so much about. London! I could hardly contain myself on the journey from Peterborough North to King's Cross. By way of the Metropolitan Line to Bow Road, and an 'open decker' 25 bus to Manor Park, I reached Auntie's home. Nothing would do but to make our way 'up west' to meet Lil who worked in a Lyons teashop, and have tea at Lyons Strand

[4] I have been in a few prisons since but on a different errand: helping to entertain those who were doing a stretch there.

Corner House and 'do a theatre' – and this we did. Though London was not yet fully lit up it was the most brilliant place I had ever seen. Lyons Corner House proved to be everything Lil said it was, and what is more there was a band which we looked down on from our balcony seats.[5] The man who played the drums seemed to do the impossible, even eclipsing Harry Flint. Surely, I thought, here's the life for me. But I changed my mind in the gallery seat in the Alhambra Theatre as I watched the drummer in the pit, who to my mind was Harry Flint and the man in the Corner House rolled into one. It must be a London theatre for me.

Peace

Back home after my first trip to the great city I settled down (rather badly I fear) to my work on the maintenance lathe. Interesting as my work was I hankered after what I had seen in London, and with Uncle George's promise always in mind I eagerly awaited his coming home. This soon happened and he returned from France with a drum, a German bugle he said he had captured, and above all a catalogue from Hawkes full of illustrations of wonderful instruments such as kettledrums, side drums, bass drums, glockenspiels, xylophones, tubular bells and drummers' 'traps' such as bird whistles and cuckoo effects. What a feast! And how we pored over the pages night after night deciding what Uncle would buy when he won the football competition in *Answers*,[6] and what I would have when I played (in evening dress) in a London 'theayter'. The first thing for me to buy was a pair of real orchestral drumsticks and a printed drum tutor. Uncle made me a practice pad and gave me my first real lesson: how to hold the sticks; play a five-stroke roll and practise two strokes on each hand alternately (Daddy-Mammy) to make the long roll. Here was enough to keep me busy in my spare time, and also to make me unpopular at home (and with the neighbours) to the extent of being given the pigsty at the far end of the garden as a practice den.

The pigsty was not the most salubrious of quarters, but it was at least private, the pig having been disposed of during the short ration period during the war. I cleaned up the place and managed to remove all traces of the pig with the exception of its effluvium. With my practice pad and Langey Drum Tutor I got to work most

[5] I think the conductor called himself 'Loony' and that he had done yeoman service in entertaining the boys on leave.
[6] He had a win on one occasion: a postal order for ninepence.

evenings and over the weekends, reporting progress as often as possible to Uncle who, the moment Auntie Liddy's back was turned would say 'Git 'em out', which meant my getting his drumsticks out of the cupboard drawer. Uncle (who incidentally was a small sprightly man) had resumed his trade as a joiner and was augmenting his wages by doing an odd drumming job with a pianist or a small band, playing at dances and so on, including an occasional Saturday night dance at the parish church hall – a venture on his part. His kit, like his list of engagements, was unprepossessing: a rope bass drum; a side drum with a brass shell; one brass cymbal; a pair of home-made foot cymbals; and a few 'traps' such as triangle, castanets, wood block, a siren whistle, and row of pots and pans for 'jazzing on'. The bulk of what drumming work there was in Peterborough at this time was done by a Harry Sculthorpe, a fine player recently home from the war, his younger brother Eric, and Harry Flint, leaving only an occasional date for people like Uncle George. I had not as yet got a look in and was in no way considered seriously.

One Saturday afternoon just after dinner Uncle George's son, George – a hardy youth a bit younger than myself – called round at our house with the information that Dad had got a new instrument, and I lost no time in getting round to Charles Street. Here Uncle told me that he had acquired a new instrument: a Chinese gong. He said that he had found it near Peterborough North Station, and then took me into his workshed and showed me his find. It was a curious type of gong as it was not circular. It was in fact a rectangular metal plate about 2 feet by 18 inches and $\frac{1}{8}$ inch or $\frac{3}{16}$ inch in thickness. One side of the plate was finished in a sort of grey enamel, and the other bore some strange characters which may or may not have been Eastern in origin. Uncle George had suspended the instrument vertically, but on close inspection I found that when I screwed myself in a position to see the gong horizontally, the characters – in spite of some obliteration – read: VAN HOUTEN'S COCOA. There was a further adornment, Eastern or otherwise, in the form of a cup-shaped vessel resting in a concave receptacle in which was placed a spoon-shaped implement. The cup-shaped vessel had a handle and fumes could be seen issuing from the vessel. It is possible of course that the vessel signified some form of incense burner, though it looked very much like a breakfast cup and saucer. Uncle George, who was making a beater for his treasure from an old bass drum stick covered with a red sock, seemed in no way disturbed by the fact that the Chinese temple gong bore a strange resemblance to the advertisement plates on hoardings such as those at Peterborough North Station. I was certain that I had seen a similar plate in between an advertisement for Mazawattee Tea, and a form of style-fountain pen which, in addition to the pen and a goose with a feather quill in its mouth, bore the following inscription: 'Oh no! Mrs. Goose your quills are no use. Go back to your fens – we use Suavita pens.' I did not mention this to Uncle George on a point of discretion, and who was I to doubt the word of a man I loved and admired and who was so good to me? Uncle said he had 'found' the gong, and though on investigation I found a suspicious gap between the advertisements already mentioned, I left it at that. In addition, let it be remembered that Uncle had recently returned from four years in France, and what British Tommy would lay his hands on something that did not belong to him – unless of course it could be said that he felt he had more right to it than the legal owner.

Uncle George finished making the beater and quickly rigged up a wooden stand for the gong. Now came the great moment. He struck the plate, and I must confess that it certainly sounded Eastern in character. He said he had already worked out a place for it in his programme, and explained that he intended to play a solo on it to open a popular foxtrot: *Indianola*. His solo consisted of two bars of foxtrot tempo, the gong beat being followed by a few taps on the wooden frame to represent a wood drum and ran so:

Uncle let me try his instrument and his composition which I did by counting four beats in a bar to myself, and whilst playing it I got a sudden brainwave. 'Let's jazz it up Uncle,' I said, and I played

Uncle somewhat reluctantly agreed to my suggestion, and he tried this new introduction a few times with me following up with the tune on my mouth-organ – an instrument I was never without. The overall effect was marvellous (to me), though I have since had misgivings regarding the use of a gong and wood drum in Indian music.

We were preparing to get the gong indoors ready for taking with the rest of the gear to St. Mary's Church Hall in time for a 7.30 p.m. start, when a knock came on the shed door – Uncle's sanctuary – and a voice shouted, 'Are you there George Cox? It's Bert Brandon.' Uncle lost no time in letting Bert Brandon know that he *was* there for a very simple reason: Bert Brandon, who owned a small garage, was a fair violin player and did a few jobs with a small band he had formed. Bert had no small opinion of his violin playing, particularly when he was 'in the mood' as he called it. One of his favourite sayings was, 'Give me a couple of pints and I'll fiddle "Wraggy" any day.' ('Wraggy' was Urban Wragg who ran a rival dance band.) Uncle, who owed no allegiance to the said 'Wraggy', lost no time in opening the shed door to Bert Brandon, though not before he had put his finger to his closed lips to me as a warning. 'Bert', he said, 'half a minute, I'm getting my kit ready for tonight.' We then left the shed and Uncle invited Bert into the living room and I sensed a distinct air of business. 'George,' said Bert when they got inside, 'are you working next Friday night?' Uncle, a superb strategist, never batted an eyelid. Of course he was not working on Friday night. Apart from an occasional Saturday night venture at the Church Hall, you could count his 'dates' on the fingers of one hand. Uncle, putting his hand to his stubbly chin (the shave came later in the day) and looking thoughtful said, 'You *did* say Friday of next week Bert?', to which Bert suitably replied. 'Eva,' shouted Uncle to his youngest daughter who was helping Auntie Liddy in the kitchen with the scones and suchlike for the night's refreshments,[7] 'get me my date book.' Eva made her way through the living room to the front room and returned with a book about the size of a Victorian family album which Uncle, after having put on his spectacles, inspected privately. After due consideration he turned to Mr. Brandon and said, 'Bert, you're lucky, I'm free.' 'Good.' said Bert, 'pick you up at half-past six in my old bus, the job is at Thorney (seven miles away); seven-and-six, and as much as you can eat at refreshment time!' They settled the deal with a hand-shake, and Bert made his exit by way of the back door and the passage; but not quite alone. I nipped out with him, and when we got clear of the house I said, 'Mr. Brandon, will there be room for me on the bus as I always help Uncle to fix up?' 'If you promise to behave yourself and not hang about on the stand too much you can come,' he said. I did not mention this arrangement to Uncle on my

[7] The sale of these scones and tea often made those Saturday night dances just pay their way.

54

return to the house: it needed a more opportune moment, perhaps when he had found the introductory music successful.

We got the kit to the church hall in good time to experiment with the Chinese temple gong. Uncle fixed it up with the plain side facing the audience: possibly having in mind the musical illiteracy of the majority of the dancers. He covered the back with a screen, and I must say that what with his drum, and pots and pans, the stage looked quite impressive. The 'orchestra' was not large – piano and drums. The pianist (an acquaintance) got five shillings a night and refreshments, and Uncle George took a trifle for his pocket if there was a profit, and on good nights gave me a few coppers. *Indianola* was a riot and got several encores, and Uncle gave the gong a slight tap in the other items of a lugubrious nature, such as *Delilah Waltz*: again not strictly Chinese – but what mattered? I longed for the interval when Uncle allowed me to take over with a relief pianist who played a waltz to which I discreetly played

all through. The Chinese temple gong however was taboo as far as I was concerned, for, apart from taking the beater away, Uncle, by now informed of my accompanying him on the Friday, said that if I touched the gong he would tell Bert Brandon to leave me out. Uncle got to work on the gong on the Monday night of the following week as he had decided to give Bert Brandon's combination and the people of Thorney the benefit of his discovery. He completely covered the puzzling hieroglyphics with black paint, and substituted an ornate Chinese temple, surmounted by his name. The gong was a huge success at Thorney and subsequently. With his customary re-

Uncle George's 'Chinese' gong

sourcefulness Uncle George continued to find a place for it in his programmes long after *Indianola* had died out, especially in tunes like *The Sheik of Araby*.

Uncle did everything possible to help me with my drumming but, as he put it, 'he'd had no proper tuition and couldn't read from the music'. Nothing less would do but for me to learn to 'read from the music' as he had always promised, and accordingly he arranged for me to have a weekly lesson at half-a-crown a time from Harry Sculthorpe: a marvellous arrangement, but one that did not last for long as Harry became a real 'pro', by getting a summer job on the Britannia Pier, Great Yarmouth. Nevertheless I pegged away in the pigsty and so did my brother Tom (now an apprentice moulder) who had been smitten by the urge to drum, and between us we rigged up our den with such things as foot cymbals made from saucepan lids, a bass drum from an old trunk, and a gong of similar material and ancestry as the one belonging to Uncle George.

Dad's Return

Life was great and there was another pleasure to come: Dad was on his way home from Egypt. He duly arrived, still in khaki but except for the uniform, very little changed. And how delighted he was with us all. On a couple of points, however, Dad was not at all happy about me: my flitting about as he called it from job to job, and the drumming business. This led to Dad reminding us of the insecurity of his *own* occupation and of his lifelong desire to see his boys enjoying security. As far as music was concerned, Dad contended that this was laudable enough in its way, but not as a mode of livelihood. As it happened a small engineering firm in Peterborough required apprentice labour, and Dad lost no time in getting me along to Messrs. Harry F. Atkins to get me settled (as he termed it) – and settled I soon was. With a little more than three years to go before I was twenty-one, Mr. Atkins agreed to accept me as an indentured apprentice. My previous experience he said would be noted. A visit to a solicitor's office resulted in my becoming bound to serve my master faithfully and well until I became of age. On becoming of age, I was certainly serving a master faithfully and well, I trust, but not quite as Dad had visualised – as we shall see. Work at Atkins proved pleasant and interesting. I was given the maintenance lathe which meant a constant variety of jobs as opposed to repetition work, and my foreman – Willoughby Upex, an ardent chapel man and a bass singer – was always ready for a chat on music and would get me to show him a stroke or so in the way of a paradiddle (L.R.L.L. R.L.R.R.), which he called 'para-fara-diddle'.

However opposed Dad might have been to my becoming a professional, he made no attempt to stifle my musical interest, nor curtail my time spent in the pigsty. And was the practice den cold in the winter! So cold that I am reminded of Christmas Eve 1919. A bitter evening, but one that found me doing my 'nightly dozen' in the pigsty. Whilst pausing to warm up the thought struck me, why not take my instruments into the house? Dad and Mam were out doing a bit of Christmas shopping, to be followed by a chat of undetermined length at Auntie Liddy's. My kit to date consisted of a small side drum, purchased secondhand from Harry Sculthorpe, my homemade foot cymbals and bass drum, and a triangle made from a length of silver steel which I felt was of no further value to Messrs. Harry Atkins Ltd. Into the house this went, and above all – into the front room – the 'holy of holies' – which in my opinion deserved something better than homemade stuff, so why not a real bass drum? And I knew where there was one: at the Britannia Inn, made famous as far as I was concerned by the choirmaster's regular trips during the Sunday evening service at the Mission Church opposite, and by the fact that a local band rehearsed there on Sunday mornings. I had a nodding acquaintance with the proprietor of the Britannia, having delivered his morning paper as a boy, and on request – he being in a particularly benign Christmas mood – saw no reason why I should not borrow the band's big drum for an hour or so. What a marvellous sound it made in our front room! I tried to emulate Jim Pack 'on the march' and imitate the soft rumbling sounds like distant thunder that he made in the hymns; and then combining the big drum with my side drum and cymbals in the piece I was currently practising: the drum part to a popular waltz called 'I'm forever blowing bubbles'.

This Harry Sculthorpe had taught me to play from the music, though on this occasion I was performing in the dark, because if I had used the gas and the penny had run out Mam would have had something to say about my equipment in the front room. After several runs through the

in 'I'm forever blowing bubbles' I turned my hand to a slog at the Mam-my, Dad-dy practice for the long roll on the side drum and then paused for a breather. To my surprise I heard music, and sweet music too, which on investigation proved to be a small brass band clustered round the street lamp a short distance up the road. In due course the band moved along, collecting a copper or two en route. I was about to close our front door and return to my drumming when I perceived our opposite neighbours Mr. and Mrs. Duffield talking at *their* open door. Mr. Duffield was as usual wearing his frock coat. This frock coat had puzzled my three brothers and me for some years as we could never connect the garment with his occupation at the sewage farm. He may of course have considered that the coat gave his job some sort of a flavour; but no matter, there he was in his regalia, and to my chagrin I heard him say to his wife, 'Well, it wasn't much of a band, but at least it stopped that young b—— from drumming!' Not a nice thing to say about a boy whose aim was to be a professional. I decided to retaliate with a further spell of practice before getting clear of the front room for my parents' return.

Though Mr. Duffield's remark about my drumming grieved me, it did not spoil my appetite for Mam's cold rabbit pie on the following morning. Christmas 1919 was a much happier occasion than those of the war years. With Dad back in 'civvy street' and Brother Tom and myself at work, Mam's budget was now less drastic. Not that we were millionaires: Dad's work was still very much of a seasonal trade, and on reflection I realise how grossly underpaid he was, having in mind his skill as a craftsman tailor, and it was a lucky thing for me that he had no desire for me to be a 'snip' as a tailor was known. Mr. Atkins and my father were fully satisfied with my progress as an engineer. On my part, I made certain that my drumming also progressed, but not at the expense of my trade – in fact during my first year as a bound apprentice I tied with a youth for the annual apprentice's prize, consisting of the return fare to London and a ticket to the Engineering Exhibition held each January. I saved the rail fare by cycling in company with Curly Kendrick to Auntie Lizzie's place at Manor Park, the eighty-mile journey being no problem to us as we were strong cyclists and not unaccustomed to night riding in any weather. An early breakfast and a bus ride to Olympia refreshed us. We whipped round the exhibition, each making sufficient notes to give a satisfactory report back home. The exhibition was followed by a scramble to Piccadilly Circus, allowing me a look round Hawkes & Sons' music shop in Denman Street before an afternoon roaming round the West End. In the Strand we had a London haircut and had our photographs taken. The evening was spent with my cousins at East Ham Palais, a well-known dance hall where one of the most famous jazz bands in history, the Southern Syncopaters, was playing.

I doubt whether Curly Kendrick enjoyed that evening at East Ham as much as I did. Unfortunately, he and my other friend, Den Leach, were not at all musical. Curly Kendrick's chief hobby was messing about with petrol engines. His musical pitch was on a par with Den's. In a singsong both brayed like asses in keys of their own which, unless by accident, were certainly foreign to the correct one. For some unaccountable reason Den frequently expressed a desire to play a trombone, inspired I'm sure by watching the efforts of a huge man known as 'Tiny Tim' who played the tenor trombone in the Peterborough Military Band, and who was of such proportions that he completely dwarfed his instrument, which in his hands had the appearance of an alto trombone. Den, in spite of his failings musically, was a splendid fellow and quite an athlete, being a strong wrestler and a top-hole tree climber – favourite pastimes with us all (the tree climbing being particularly useful when taking turns to raid Old Frosty's orchard). We were, in our opinion, quite 'he-men'. We were known as 'erbs' and prided ourselves among other things on our disdain for the fair sex. Apart from the mildest of 'clickings' as light flirtations were known, we were – or felt we were – impervious to the wiles of the girls from the corset factory, and the 'behind-the-counter beauties' in Woolworths, whose ambition was to be 'taken out regular', which invariably led to strict courting and admittance to the girl's home (from which there was rarely an escape). Not that we did not join the lads about Town now and again. We had learned to dance and were not above disporting ourselves at the Co-op Hall on a Saturday night to take a hand in the Lancers, or a partner in a foxtrot or quick step. Waltzes were a bit dangerous, being very much on the romantic side, and danced in the twilight (hall lights dimmed) – as was the last waltz at a Cinderella dance – could lead to the Waterloo of an unsuspecting young man. Listening to the music was a much safer proposition, and to me decidedly more profitable if Harry Sculthorpe was 'on the drums' as he so often was, accompanying a lady pianist named Dorothy Holbrooke who played the 'raggy' music of the 1918–19 era as well as any man. Saturday night in spite of its dangers was something to look forward to, either at the Co-op Hall or St. Mary's Church Hall with Uncle George. It meant a real spruce up, including a shave with what Grandad would have called 'one of them new-fangled safety razors'. Den sported a double-breasted jacket which he always wore open to show a gold watch chain with a medal (won at a tug-of-war), the whole, including the watch (not gold), being borrowed from his father. He was certainly one of the boys, but to Curly Kendrick's and my own dismay he began to grow secretive and we feared the worst: a sweetheart. Our fears were not unfounded. Den was the first of the trio to fall, and we lost him to a girl named 'Glad'.

I missed Den; but there was still Curly Kendrick, and also I had made the acquaintance of a keen cyclist some years my senior, by the name of Charlie Cooper, with whom I did a good deal of cycling. In addition to being a good man on the track, Charlie was a first-class 'road man'. He was a member of the Century Road Club (a famous London club) of which I eventually became a member. Our jaunts included an occasional weekend trip to London, and of these the one I remember well was the return journey following our Easter visit to Herne Hill. The Saturday morning was spent 'up West', where I purchased a few small effects, including a cuckoo whistle. We left Auntie's place at Manor Park in the early evening of Easter Sunday. It was a beastly night during late March, raining and blowing hard, with a cutting cross wind from the east. We slogged away, club fashion (wheel to wheel), changing the lead at each milestone, exchanging only an occasional word as the miles slipped away. At Eaton Socon we sheltered in the porch of a cottage and munched our sandwiches. Our snack finished, Charlie rolled a cigarette and enjoyed a quiet smoke during which time my mind turned to my cuckoo whistle, and to what exciting uses I would eventually put it. For the moment I became unaware of it being midnight and my immediate surroundings, imagining myself in an orchestra. I gave one or two toots on the whistle, but was immediately brought back to earth by a sharp jab from Charlie who put his finger to his lips. Above the sound of the storm we heard an upper window being opened, and after a pause a husky voice said, 'I heard it, I heard it, but I 'aint never heard a cuckoo at this time of the year afore'. We waited quietly until all seemed clear and then got under way again, probably cogitating en route on the type of reception the news of the early arrival of the cuckoo would receive in Eaton Socon on the following day, and as far as I was concerned musing on how long it might be before I played in a real band. It happened I had not all that long to wait. It was quite a modest affair but not without incident, for there cannot be many people who have called on the arm of the law to help them fulfil their first public engagement.

I Play in a Real Band

My début was not recorded in the local press, in fact it passed unnoticed other than with those directly concerned. The occasion was
one sunny Thursday afternoon in early June 1920 at a garden fête
at which I was due to deputise (for the first hour) for my teacher
Harry. The band was the Peterborough City Military Band, and
the occasion sufficiently important – or made to appear so – for my
being given an afternoon off from work. The gear would be there,
Harry said – all there was to take was my drumsticks. After a rush
home to change and an even more rushed dinner, I tore off to the
fête and found all there as Harry had said but, in my excitement, I
had forgotten my drumsticks. By breaking all cycling records I
might just get home and back in time for the opening march, so off
I went; but not for the whole distance, for I met a policeman who
was one of our neighbours. He was on his bike and I excitedly explained the position to him. He became almost as animated as I was
and agreed to go to get the drumsticks, allowing me to return to
the bandstand, where at a pinch I could at least play the cymbals
in the opening march. The sticks however arrived in time, and I made
a bold effort at the march during which, with the help of Mr. Page the
conductor, I at least kept in time with the rest of the band. With
more eye on Mr. Page than on my music, I managed to 'oom-pa-pa'
through the waltz which followed. This I coloured with an occasional
discreet ting on the triangle,[8] discreet being the correct expression,
for to be truthful I was feeling extremely nervous, and looking
forward to Harry Sculthorpe making an early appearance, as
indeed was Mr. Page, and for a very good reason: it was getting
dangerously near to the time for the *pièce de résistance*, the *Chu
Chin Chow* overture: a drum part quite beyond my reading powers
and my ability to improvise. Mr. Page, anticipating the worst, spent
the whole of a 'break' in the programme in teaching me the opening
bars and the pattern on the woodblock for the stitching in the
cobbler's song, which he said would be very nice if I could manage
it. Due to Harry's absence I was obliged to play in the overture, and
did tolerably well with the 'Ching' (cymbal) 2 3 4   1 2 Boom (bass
drum):

[8] The triangle is a seemingly simple instrument to play, but not according to the player who proudly held one aloft whilst counting 69 bars
rest and then struck his thumb.

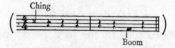

following the opening theme 'I am Chu Chin Chow from China', and the sewing business on the woodblock. Fortunately Harry crept in to add lustre to the finale. I was allowed to sit in for the rest of the afternoon, and join in the free tea and the evening dancing on the lantern-lit lawn. I told the prettiest of my partners that I had played in the band during the afternoon, but I must confess she seemed in no way impressed by the fact, or by me.

Such is the unfathomable nature of women; and of men come to that, for I was due for another shock. Curly Kendrick of all people fell heavily for a girl who lived some distance from Peterborough. This, together with the fact that my cycling friend's wife was having her second baby, left me chumless – but not for long. A girl with a pretty face backed by a plait of golden hair with whom I danced at the Co-op Hall knocked me for six and I started a-sweethearting with Vera Vere. For several months Ve-Ve gladdened my heart, and then saddened it for as many more, for she dropped me for a young Welsh farmer, which I'm sure turned out a good thing for her, and incidentally proved no ill to me, as among other things it had a good deal to do with my obtaining my first paid engagement. It was not necessary for me to open a banking account for the investment of my first fee as, including what is known today as hire and porterage, the sum amounted to half-a-crown. I was contracted for this auspicious engagement by a young man named Frank Hitchborn whose acquaintance I made whilst listening to the music at a Saturday evening dance. Frank, who looked and seemed as disconsolate as me, confessed that the girl who was playing the piano had recently 'packed him up', and that he felt like chucking himself over the Water Bridge. It was obvious that Frank and I had a good deal in common regarding the fair sex, and in other directions too, for it transpired that Frank could play the piano – so why not form an orchestra? we thought. This we did, not quite as originally planned, as no one seemed anxious to join us. So we decided on a duo, and a small advertisement appeared in the local press to the effect that the Blades-Hitchborn Duo was open for engagements at dances, weddings, garden fêtes, and other festive occasions with all communications to Frank Hitchborn. The fact that Frank was not immediately overwhelmed with correspondence did not damp our enthusiasm, and we rehearsed on every favourable occasion in his front room. Here we were joined from time to time by Frank's two elder brothers, who were talented entertainers, and with whom we occasionally played (unpaid) at a nearby public house, The Peacock, giving rise to the 'Peacock Feathers Concert Party' with which Frank and I performed at various houses of refreshment in and around Peterborough for drinks all round. Modest and remunerative engagements admittedly, but to use a professional term, they (or the advertisement) led to something, and for that something Frank booked me by word of mouth, saying, 'Jim, we've got a date. Stanground Football Club dance, Thursday fortnight, Stanground Church Hall 7.30–11; bring all you've got.'

The 'all I had' did not require a pantechnicon, though for this important event, which we felt might turn out to be something of a shop window, I managed to borrow a small bass drum from a local dancing teacher who used it to accentuate the beat at his classes. I polished my cymbal and the brass shell of my side drum, and with a bit of titivating and the help of the bass drum my kit looked quite gay. Getting it to Stanground and back (seven miles in all) was no easy matter as the gear was too bulky to be strapped to my bike. I solved the problem by cleaning up the wheelbarrow which for years we had used for collecting horse muck and the like, and got my instruments to Stanground in fine style and in plenty of time to warm up by running over a number or two with Frank who, like me, had purchased a black bow tie as the first instalment on eventual evening dress. The caretaker of the hall who was busy waxing the floor with candle scrapings said we both looked 'real dandy' and that it would be a good do – if anyone came! Fortunately some did come, it turned out to be a good do and Frank really went to town. He was one of the finest buskers I have ever met; he had only to hear a tune once and he could play it in any key. His sense of rhythm was infectious and he was adept with the 'marmalade' – a term used for frittering around the melody. On my part I was quite at home with Frank and put in some good work on my drums, the triangle in particular in 'The Bells are Ringing for me and my Girl', and joined with Frank in singing such numbers as 'Last Night on the Back Porch' and 'Back Home in Tennessee'. For the Eastern numbers I would have liked Uncle George's temple gong, but he was using it – or said he was. Towards the end of the first half the floor was in prime condition, the result of the candle scrapings having been worked in. In the interval Frank and I were given refreshments: tea and some fairly hefty sandwiches. We were bucked by the fact that a chap from Manea (a nearby village of about 250 inhabitants) said he would have us in mind if his football club ever had a dance, and the Blades-Hitchborn Duo returned to the stand considerably strengthened physically and morally. Apart from a few minor skirmishes in the hall, the second half went even better than before the interval. At 11 p.m. the 'do' packed up and so did we. We were paid on the nail, in sixpenny pieces – sixpence being the price of admission including tea and a bun. We were both ninepence down on the black bow, but having in mind the success of our début and the fellow from Manea, we made our way home in excellent spirits. Frank, who lived on the Stanground side of the town, trudged as far as the Water Bridge with me, taking turns with the barrow. We parted as St. John's Church struck midnight, both full of hope as to the future of the Blades-Hitchborn Duo.

With the exception of the jobs with the Peacock Feathers Concert Party and the promised football dance at Manea, we had what could be termed a quiet winter, and an even quieter spring. Not that we were idle: we rehearsed regularly, and in our own words 'felt ready for anything'. What lay ahead? For the Blades family a terrible sadness: the death of Mam. Such disasters are all too frequent in family life for me to dwell on the immediate condition of the occupants of 171, Star Road. Suffice to say that after dispensing with the services of two consecutive housekeepers – both with reputations for looking after people, but who like 'Mrs. Gamp', were also extremely capable of looking after themselves to the extent of augmenting their chattels with some of our spare bed linen, we were eventually blessed with 'our Lizzie', a model housekeeper who eventually became Mrs. Thomas Weston Blades, though she remained Lizzie to us for the rest of her long and active life. Lizzie's cooking, particularly her pastry making, was unsurpassed; in fact there was only one dish to vie with anything that Lizzie made: Mam's cold rabbit pie. And so our house got under way again. It was not always the quietest of establishments. My brother Tom was doing quite well with the drumsticks, and Chris and Cecil were already showing signs of hankering after a tap on my kit, which often led to a rumpus. Due (again) to Uncle George's interest I had a few lessons with the drummer in our local Theatre Royal who let me sit in the pit and watch him tune his 'timps', and I have to thank Freddy Walton for having introduced me to the use and sound of tonics and dominants, and the fact that drums could be made to play in tune as well as in time.

Certain of this information I imparted to my partner Frank, though our expanding knowledge did not seem to expand the activities of the Blades-Hitchborn Duo, but we were nearing an annual event which we figured could be used to our advantage: the Prince of Wales was to open the Peterborough Agricultural Show. Here was an opportunity not to be missed. The great day arrived, and the whole city was alive with the streets from the North Station to the showground being lined with people. Frank, with a melodion borrowed from his uncle, and I with my side drum, obtained a strategic position near the entrance to the main gate where we awaited the arrival of the Prince. Along came the procession headed by the town band who had (fortunately from our point of view) blown themselves out. Following the band came the Fire Brigade, the Independent Order of Oddfellows, representatives of the Masonic Order – complete with aprons and headed by my old schoolmaster – and various other denominations all with their respective banners, followed by the Mayor and Corporation with the Prince. As His Royal Highness passed us we struck up with *God Bless the Prince of Wales* – or the nearest we could get to it. We were immediately grabbed by a policeman who told us in no uncertain terms to 'hop it' and that if he hadn't known our fathers he would have run us in. We hopped it all right and at a good pace: straight to Stott's the stationers where we ordered cards to be printed: *Played before Royalty*. The Duo did a bit better after this, but I seemed a long way from becoming a professional, and truth to tell I had much to learn. To gain experience in my young days was no easy matter. There was no opportunity (at least for the likes of me) to take a three-year course at the Royal Academy of Music, or the Royal College of Music, or to go from a school orchestra into a youth or training orchestra. People like Harry Sculthorpe and Freddy Walton had gained experience in army bands, but helpful as they were to me it was clear that it was practical experience I needed.

With Harry leaving Peterborough there came a vacant seat in the small orchestra at the 'Kinema'[9] and I was given a fortnight's trial. How I tried, but as Wylie Price the conductor said on the final evening, I wasn't fully experienced. Uncle George said, 'Never mind, you'll get into a London Theayter in time', and Dad, who was grieved at my disappointment, did his best to console me by saying that 'a prophet is not without honour save in his own city'. Not that

[9] The picture house where I first experienced the artistry of the Charlie Chaplin comedies. Incidentally, on the erection of a new electrical sign at this theatre the red lights halted the 8.20 p.m. King's Cross to Edinburgh, the system giving the impression of a signal of danger.

Dad was anxious for me to leave home I am sure, but my apprenticeship was not quite working out to plan. The firm of Messrs. H. F. Atkins was in the throes of a slump, and though as a bound apprentice I worked a full week, my time in the factory was spent in performing such miserable tasks as cleaning and greasing the machines that would not sell. On enquiry I was told that there would be no difficulty in getting released from my apprenticeship so, taking all into account, there seemed no reason why I should not try for a job away from home. According to Freddy Walton, jobs in the musical profession were occasionally advertised in a London paper called *The Era*, published each Wednesday. This I ordered, and after several abortive applications by letter I decided on a new tack. In answer to an advertisement for a drummer in a circus band I sent the following telegram: 'Experienced drummer unexpectedly disengaged. Blades. . . .' I received a reply (written on a piece of fish and chip paper). It read: 'Start Monday. Ginnett's Circus, Henley-on-Thames. £3 5s. od. a week, uniform and tent.' I started. I got the uniform and the tent, but *never* the £3 5s. od.

✤ 6 ✤

I Become a Professional

A 'pro.' at last – if I could qualify the claim made in my telegram. With less than four days to go before making my way to Henley-on-Thames (as an 'experienced drummer') there was little time to waste. Every moment was spent in building up my kit. Uncle George made me a marvellous foot cymbal pedal, to which he added, on loan until the winter season, a couple of brass cymbals. He also unearthed, from a source he never disclosed, an old bass drum. It had one burst skin, but this Uncle skilfully covered with a circle of canvas, and my pianist friend Frank who, like me, laughed and cried in turn over my forthcoming departure, painted the canvas drumhead all colours of the rainbow, and in his true artistic style emblazoned the shell of the drum with my initials. Sunday was spent in taking stock of my equipment which, together with a spare shirt, socks, and a change of underwear, was dumped by means of the barrow in Peterborough North left luggage office awaiting my taking the 8.40 (the business man's train) for King's Cross the following morning. Most goodbyes were said on the Sunday evening, and on the fine Monday morning in June 1921 I left home with the blessings of my family, and a sigh of relief from the neighbours. My only escort was Frank, with whom I parted as we felt men of the world should. Aboard the 8.40 I made several journeys to the guard's van to check on my precious equipment – the bass drum in its cover of ticking made in record time by Auntie Liddy, and a smallish tin trunk containing my wardrobe and small gear, which consisted of my drumsticks, a side drum, a pair of foot cymbals, a 'loose' Chinese crash cymbal, a triangle, tambourine, castanets, sleigh bells, woodblock, and the inevitable syren whistle. I carried just enough ready cash for my immediate needs. It constituted (with my kit and my bicycle) the whole of my worldly wealth; but why worry with a job worth £3 5s. od. plus uniform and tent?

Crossing from King's Cross to Paddington and getting to Henley-on-Thames was an adventure in itself. The walk from King's Cross main line station to the Metropolitan Line platform for Paddington with the bass drum under one arm and the tin trunk grasped in the opposite hand, seemed – as far as stairs were concerned – like climbing the Monument. A friendly guard allowed me to stow my gear on the Underground train before giving the away signal by making contact with his metal-covered staff on the overhead wires, and Paddington was reached without mishap. The trip to the main line platform was, to the best of my memory, on a par with my experience at King's Cross. What I more clearly remember is my first sight of what was to be my home for the next few months: Ginnett's Circus. The circus tent, a 'single-poler', was in the middle of a small field. Dotted around were one or two small tents, a couple of caravans, and such equipment as goes to make up a circus. I found the band tent and met Sam of the fish and chip paper contractual letter. It is possible that he was as taken aback with me as I was with him, and the appearance of the circus in general. Sam was a small stout man, quite old, and shabbily dressed. He eyed me up and down (every bit of my 5 feet three inches), and so did a shaggy lion in a nearby cage. Then, with more eye on my big drum than me, Sam said, 'So you'll be the new drummer, my boy'. To which I replied appropriately, for Sam's voice belied his appearance: it was husky, but so friendly that the circus tent seemed to grow larger and the shaggy lion in his cage quite noble.

Sam took me to the big tent and showed me my perch, and then back to the band tent to give me my uniform. My predecessor must have been a Life Guard but Sam said 'not to worry'. He also told me that the circus was doing so badly that the company had agreed for the time being to take pot luck on what came in in the way of wages which meant feeding 'catch as catch can'. To this shattering information he hurriedly added that he was sure things would buck up and that it was dinner time. By this time I was hungry enough for anything and fed 'catch as catch can' on a couple of slices of bread and marg, and sausages fried in an empty salmon tin. The chef was a lean-looking young man by the name of Slim. Slim, a Welshman, was the trombone player, and we were joined at 'table' by the rest of the band: Alf, the second cornet – a man in middle age – and Len, a cheery-looking man of uncertain age who was introduced as the finest euphonium player the Luton Red Cross Band had ever had. Nice as were the sausages (and only those who have eaten sausages fried in a salmon tin over a wood fire by a trombone player with a bare torso and three days' growth of beard, know how tasty such a dish can be), my immediate concern was to know what was expected of me in the main tent. 'When do we rehearse?' I asked Sam. Sam replied that I was to rig up my kit and not bother about rehearsal, as in any case there would most likely be no audience to speak of for the afternoon show. One of my jobs, he said, was to keep an eye open for whatever act seemed to be making an entry as 'things had got muddled'. Sometimes, he said, the elephant came on first, for which we played slow music, and if Robin Redbreast, the red-coated ringmaster, gave the signal that the horses were coming on we played a galop – and so forth. Sam also gave me a few scraps of music which I must confess looked a bit Greek to me, particularly the opening march. After perusing this I made certain of one thing: at the start I must play for two bars, then count two bars' rest, and then start the drumming again. At three o'clock Sam started off the band by a movement of his elbow (he played a cornet as well as conducted). I went, 'Pom-tiddy-pom-tiddy-pom-pom-pom', and counted softly 'one-two-two-two'. 'Stop,' yelled Sam, and turning to me, shouted, 'What the so-and-so do you think you're doing?' I replied rather quakingly, 'Two bars rest sir'. He said, 'Now look here my boy, circus drummers never ruddy well rest, from the time we start to the time we finish you flog them drums as hard as you can go'. That single experience was worth a fortune; it taught me my greatest lesson: the conductor is always right! Acting on Sam's advice about circus drummers never resting, I did tolerably well with the second run of the march, the galop for the prancing horses, and the plodding music for Jumbo the elephant. Jumbo was a grand old fellow and never above helping out with a piece of bread and margarine. The same could be said of the horses, who on occasions in the small hours would break halter, and it was not at all unusual to be awakened at 2 a.m. by a warm nose which had made its way under the tent flap in search of the bread box.

Sam was right about the size of the audience on my first afternoon. The residents of Henley-on-Thames no doubt found regattas more interesting, but as yet I was not concerned about the number of people in the tent; that came later when I learned that a fair house meant a fish and chip supper, and a poor one an empty tummy to go to bed on. I survived that first afternoon thanks to the tolerance of Sam and the rest of the band. My two most important moments were playing a long roll on the side drum for the act called 'sawing through a woman' and nipping under the flap of the tent a quarter-of-an-hour before the finish of the show to light a small primus stove and put on the kettle for tea. Sawing through a woman was a current novelty. A coffin-shaped box was placed in the centre of the ring. Then on came a lady dressed in the customary circus tights, followed by her male partner carrying a carpenter's saw. The lady was then laid fully stretched in the box and the lid battened down. These proceedings were accompanied by appropriate music until at a signal from Robin Redbreast the band 'dried up'. This was my cue to start a loud roll on the side drum. When this had made certain of the required hush, the male artist started to saw through the centre of the box (the sound of my drum and his sawing covering the rustle of the curling up of the lady contortionist inside the box). At the conclusion of the sawing I continued with the drum roll until the lid of the box was removed, finishing with a terrific stroke on my suspended cymbal as the lady jumped to the ground completely unscathed – a grand act and as good practice for me as the tight rope act which demanded numerous rolls and crashes.

The evening performance was a repeat of the matinee with one addition: a display of the noble art by George Beckett – supposedly deputising for his heavy-weight champion brother Joe. George took on all comers in a round of three minutes' duration – arousing great excitement, as on occasions he met a really stiff opponent and was only saved by the bell. This he accepted philosophically. And could he fry eggs! His source of supply may have been questionable, as one or two hen houses were certainly raided in the still of the dawn (we broke camp and were on the road each day by 5 a.m.). On one occasion with the help of the band, me included, George 'found' a stray sheep on Dunstable Downs and put an end to its loneliness by preparing it as humanely as possible for the common pot.

Henley-on-Thames was followed by Beaconsfield and such places as High Wycombe, Aylesbury and Leighton Buzzard, the routine being the same every day. We in the band were responsible for pitching and striking our own tent. We were awakened between 4 and 5 a.m. according to the distance to travel, and after a cup of tea from the main pot (a huge iron saucepan), we struck our tent and piled this together with our belongings into the pole waggon (an old army lorry) on which we travelled to the next pitch. Going to sleep on wooden poles is not the easiest thing to do, but I usually dozed off during the journey. On arrival at the next port of call the tents were pitched and by 8 a.m. breakfast was taken. This was followed by the 'ghost walking'[1] if there was any ghost to walk. We were paid out daily as the management had reached the low ebb of paying the company with what came in, resulting in an occasional half-a-crown or more as the case might be. Sam was given the band's

[1] Being paid.

70

share and this was paid out to us according to tradition 'down on the drum' – a form of indisputable receipt.

In due course I wrote home giving such news as I felt would please them. In telling them that I was happy this was no untruth for the circus, rough as it was on occasions, was a tremendous experience, and playing my drums afternoon and evening six days a week was worth a measure of inconvenience. No need to reveal that my bedding consisted of the red felt that covered the forms constituting the best seats, and that if it was a wet night and the best seats were occupied, we in the band slept on what we could find; though of course with a bit in the 'kitty' a 'sub' meant a fish and chip supper. The circus was full of kind hearts. Sam, whose hair grew whiter as the season proceeded (for the simple reason that he ran out of hair dye) was kindness itself and forgave my inexperience, helping me – as did the other men – with my music. On occasions, however, I found it best to sleep outside the tent, for if we played in a place where there was a brass band, Sam and the 'boys' were treated to a good deal of beer by the local players, which led to a bit of rowdyism in the tent on their return. To say that I was constantly hungry is putting it mildly; but it was a hot summer and a slim diet did me no harm I am sure. I practised whenever conditions made it possible. On one occasion Sam found me alone in the band tent practising Mam-my-Dad-dy on the heel on my shoe. 'You'll get on drummer,' he said (and what a thrill it was to be called 'drummer' !). Sam told me a good deal about his hard life playing in circuses, exhibitions, and so forth. He also told me about my predecessor who was a fine drummer, but a bit of a rascal and that he had scarpered.[2]

The Ninepenny Dinner

Sam's prophecy regarding things bucking up was never fulfilled. This was in no way due to the quality of the circus, as it was a top-hole little company; but we were faced with an industrial depression and a terribly hot summer. On odd occasions we had a sizeable audience and once or twice I came near to receiving my £3 5s. od. and this meant a pound or two put aside for the future. In general however we were hard pressed, prompting Slim on the day we were in Irthlingborough to persuade me to join him on a busking expedition in the main street where our trombone and drum

[2] I am reminded of the story of the conductor of a travelling show (a gentleman of foreign origin) who, on finding a player short at rehearsal exclaimed, 'He is a washdown, he have escaped'.

duets from the circus repertoire enriched us by ninepence before a policeman told us to quit. I cannot believe that the serenading of Slim and myself was responsible for the good house that night, resulting in the company receiving five shillings when we reached Rushden on the following morning. This 'manna from heaven' as Slim called it, was all the more acceptable; it being Saturday. Whilst stocking up for the weekend I came across a dining room with a tempting array of viands in the window. The sight of the luscious food and the tempting smell emerging from the spick-and-span interior convinced me that I deserved the luxury of a sit-down meal, so after smoothing myself down a bit I took my place on a dark brown high-backed wooden form and ordered beef, potatoes and carrots, with roly-poly pudding to follow; the whole of ninepenny-worth, and the first good sit-down meal I had had since leaving home. On my way back to camp I met Sam to whom I related the qualities of the ninepenny meal, and advised him to 'stoke-up' as I had done. 'Son,' he said, 'I ain't got ninepence'. 'But Sam,' I said, 'we all had five shillings this morning'. 'Yes,' he replied, 'I know we did, but I've just been to the Post Office and sent mine to my old woman in Camden Town'. The only thing to do of course was to take him along to the source of the boiled beef dinner and set him up with one – and how he enjoyed it, though more than once I (near to blubbering) had to tell him to stop crying or he would spoil his dinner.

Those ninepenny dinners in Rushden remain treasured memories, though Rushden itself caused me, indirectly, some concern, for Ginnett's Circus was getting dangerously near to Peterborough, and what is more we were to play there. This called for a bit of sprucing up, for though I had kept as clean as my surroundings would permit (we were rarely far from a river and carbolic soap was cheap enough), my ten weeks of living rough in the sun had left its mark. As I anticipated, Dad and Uncle George came to see how I was getting on, and though both agreed that my playing was growing confident, they tried to persuade me to pack up the job; in fact Uncle made a start on removing my gear from the field.[3] Sam and Robin Redbreast entreated Dad and Uncle to let me see the season out, particularly as there was only a week or so to go, and to get another drummer under the circumstances would be difficult they said. So it was agreed that I would finish the run, and with a change of underclothing, a few of Lizzie's lemon curd tarts and my bike, we started our final run: a short tour of the Fen

[3] The fairground where I had spent many pleasant moments as a boy.

country with Wisbech the first objective, and unbeknown to me at that time a place that was to be a milestone in my career. Wisbech, like one or two other places Ginnett's Circus had visited, was sufficiently large to boast of a picture house, and according to Sam all these places would soon follow the trend in London and employ sizeable orchestras to accompany the silent films. In each place of consequence I left my name and details of my experience (with those who would take them) in case a drummer was needed. At Wisbech I went further and begged an interview with the manager of the picture house (the Hippodrome), where I was told a small orchestra was employed. In answer to my enquiry as to whether an experienced drummer was required the manager, a small and extremely kind-looking man of obvious Jewish persuasion, said: 'How experienced are you my boy?' Something of a flattener in its way, but I stated my case as well as I could, for after all, was I not playing professionally, and had I not deputised in the Peterborough City Military Band? The manager promised me that he would think it over. I had already been told on a number of occasions that things would be thought over, but there was something about Mr. Harry Bancroft that gave me a feeling of encouragement, and I speculated hopefully.

Soon after the tour Ginnett's Circus came to an end – or to be precise it collapsed on a certain Saturday in Downham Market in the county of Norfolk. By this time the outfit was certainly in low water. Numerous debts had accumulated en route, and more than one tradesman was looking for his money. Robin Redbreast, who had obviously encountered similar situations in his long career as a Ringmaster, advised me to get my belongings clear of the field the moment the evening show was over: advice I promptly heeded by seeking the help of a Downham Market railway porter who agreed to help me to get my instruments into the nearby station left luggage office, and to store them until I could get them back to Peterborough. By good fortune all went according to plan that evening – but only just, for on my return to the field to say goodbye to Sam I found the police in charge and Robin Redbreast doing his best to recompense the various claimants with what seemed negotiable. After a few hurried goodbyes I got under way on my thirty-four-mile cycle ride home to Peterborough. A lonely enough journey with scarcely a soul with whom to pass the time of night, but I had plenty to think about. Perhaps my thoughts went back to my one-time sweetheart and I may have saluted her old home in Eye village fifteen minutes ride from Star Road where, with very little seat left in

my trousers, I dismounted about 2 a.m. completely unheralded and
by no means the local boy made good, but richer in experience and
a pound or two better off in pocket, and with Mr. Bancroft's promise
that he would get in touch with me if ever he needed a drummer.
No great achievement, but nevertheless I had reached the first rung of
the ladder in my climb to the concert hall.

The Second Rung

My first job on the Monday morning following the abrupt termina-
tion of my circus engagement was to sign on at the Labour Exchange.
The clerk nearly had a fit when I registered as a professional musician. I was informed that there was nothing in my line – and little
in any other come to that – so I joined the ranks of the unemployed
in receipt of the dole; but not for long. My period of 'resting', as
being out of work is more politely known professionally, was a short
one: [4] two weeks exactly, for on the following Sunday, on my return
home from an evening of listening to the City Military Band, I found
a note to the effect that the manager of the Wisbech Hippodrome
wished to see me at my earliest convenience. My earliest convenience
was to be first in the signing on queue at the Labour Exchange on
the following morning, and then do the 21-mile cycle ride to Wisbech in record time. I reached the Hippodrome by noon, and after
taking a few minutes to cool down, I tapped (once again) on the
door marked MANAGER. I found Mr. Bancroft in an excellent mood,
having just returned from the bank. He told me he had decided to
add a drummer to his small orchestra and that he would give me
a week's trial to start the following Monday as the big picture
needed plenty of sound effects. 'Two-pounds-ten a week if you can
do the job,' he said, and added 'and you can get good digs in
Wisbech for a pound a week'. On my ride home I worked it all out:
two-pounds-ten a week; not more than a pound for lodgings as I
would cycle home each weekend: I would give Lizzie five shillings
for meals on Sunday and for doing my laundry; have five shillings
pocket money, and put a pound a week aside for buying equipment –
and all for playing the drums six nights a week two shows a night !
Admittedly no uniform and tent, but the cash as regular as clockwork if I knew Mr. Bancroft; and of course if I could keep the
job.

Uncle George and Frank Hitchborn were kept busy during the
rest of the week helping me to give my equipment something of an

[4] My only period of strict unemployment in the whole of my career.

orchestral appearance. The canvas head came off the bass drum and was replaced by a brand-new vellum from London, and between us we made a small glockenspiel and a more faithful reproduction of Uncle's famous gong. The barrow was again called into service to get the instruments to the station, and at Wisbech with the help of an ancient-looking taxi driver and an even more ancient vehicle, the whole arrived intact at The Hippodrome, where I awaited Mr. Bancroft, and his instructions. These, like Mr. Bancroft, were precise. 'Your conductor is Mr. Rainbow. Rehearsal for the variety act is at two o'clock. Here's an address for lodgings, and whatever you do don't take too much notice of your music when the films are showing – keep an eye on the screen for the effects.'

Don't take too much notice of your music! If ever a young man on the threshold of his career was handed out a present I was. Music for the drums was still much of a puzzle to me (some of it remains so), and to be given the opportunity of skipping a difficult part in favour of inventing an alternative in the way of sound effects was to prove a veritable godsend.[5] I was duly introduced to Mr. Rainbow and the members of the orchestra: a second violin (Mr. Rainbow played first), a pianist, a trumpeter (yes, a trumpet, not the more usual cornet), a 'cellist, and a double bass player – a gentleman more than past his prime who I was to learn had perfected the knack of watching the film and his music simultaneously, particularly during the newsreel with its customary bevy of bathing beauties. Mr. Rainbow belied his name for he was somewhat austere. He accepted me, I felt, as a necessary evil, and straightaway told me to 'keep it down' – instructions I obeyed implicitly, or at least until I became reasonably conversant with his repertoire. The variety act proved to be a comedian whose music was in the usual state of dilapidation, and at first sight was as decipherable to me as if it had been written in Chinese. By playing to a great extent by ear ('lugging') I floundered through the act's two songs and such of the music for the films that Mr. Rainbow felt inclined to rehearse. There were the usual love themes (*Hearts and Flowers* among them, of course), a 'Hurry' or two, and a tragic motif. 'Close-fitting' by means of the conductor operating coloured cue lights for the various themes and main changes had not reached Wisbech, and in any case Mr. Rainbow favoured the playing of the standard repertoire with as few cuts as possible. A march or standard overture did well for the newsreel,

[5] My powers of invention have saved my bacon on a few occasions since; in fact Benjamin Britten once said that he knew no percussionist in the world who could alter composers' works as successfully as me.

and current popular tunes or a light selection for the comedy. The 'big' picture usually required heavier, or more romantic material, and for this Mr. Rainbow – like all conductors in the days of the silent films – drew where suitable from Beethoven and such masters who, it seems fair to say, had they lived in the present century would doubtless have written superb film music and earned the fortunes denied to them in their lifetime. Apart from the music for the act, my greatest test at this first rehearsal was coping with Auber's *Masaniello* overture which opens tutti with a series of rapid quaver beats finishing with a 'poom-poom' followed by a brief silence. That 'poom-poom' and the silence to follow so scared me that I enlisted the help of the player sitting directly in front of me – the trumpeter. He whispered that he would drop his elbow to his side as a cue for the 'poom-poom'. I 'dried up' as directed and we decided to extend the semaphore tactics as and when required. With the help of this friendly and experienced musician I survived the rehearsal, and with my music for further study, set out for my digs well pleased with my good fortune to date. The digs certainly justified Mr. Brancroft's recommendation. The landlady, a Mrs. Stimson, combined the business of 'doing' for people with assisting her husband in a small dairy business. The latter occupation I became painfully aware of as this industrious woman was for ever emptying, filling, or washing out two rather hefty milk churns. She was equally industrious in her 'doing' for people, and I sat down to a feast of a high tea with the act's music propped up in front of me. And here my good luck continued, for who should join me at tea but the comedian himself. He was – as many comedians are in private life – a quiet, unassuming man. He immediately agreed to go through his book with me, and from the horse's mouth so to speak, I learned the full meaning of ad-lib; 'vamp till ready'; 1-1, 2-2-; 'cue for tabs' and similar enigmatic signs known only to the initiated.

I spent the whole of my week's trial in what is known profession-ally as 'playing safe', as for example, the 'poom-pooms' in *Masaniello* which were approached judiciously. These and similar risky situa-tions were helped along by the aforementioned semaphore system. My chief concern I felt was to satisfy the manager, which justified my paying the bulk of my attention to the screen. Had not Mr. Bancroft told me not to bother too much about my music? For-tunately, the programme required plenty of action on my part, the big picture in particular – it being a Western with plenty of gallop-ing horses, whip cracking, and revolver shots. When Mr. Rainbow could catch my eye he pointed angrily to his music, but I fenced by pointing to the screen and to the manager's office. If I felt reasonably sure of my drum part I obliged Mr. Rainbow, then down would come the manager and point to the screen to which I replied by pointing to the conductor. By keeping these two gentlemen at bay, and with the help of the semaphore system, I reached the end of my week's trial and was duly appointed the drummer at The Hippodrome, Wisbech, where I was to spend two and a half rewarding years.

It was during my time at Wisbech that many of the problems and mysteries connected with music and professional life were unfolded for me, and all in a kind and friendly manner. For a few weeks I found the clatter of the milk churns around 5.30 a.m. a trifle disturbing, but was soon able to sleep through the noise – like the Londoner living near Paddington station who was obliged to return from a country holiday to get a good night's rest! I soon became aware that the 'lady-next-door' gave lessons on the piano, and registered with her for a weekly 'drill' of five finger exercises at a 'bob' a visit. At the theatre, in addition to playing such standard overtures as Zampa, Light Cavalry, Pique Dame, Raymond, Poet and Peasant, Lustspiel, The Caliph of Baghdad and The Bronze Horse, I became acquainted with works by the classical and operatic composers, in general in such splendid reduced arrangements as those by Tavan and Mouton. It was good for me that Mr. Rainbow, a fine musician, had an extensive library, and that he became interested in my progress to the extent of condoning my constant efforts to keep on the right side of Mr. Bancroft.

As time went on I developed the knack of watching the screen, the music, the conductor, the trumpet player's arm, and the manager's door simultaneously, and got as far as 'jumping in' with a roll on a cymbal or a drum to make a change from the frequent piano modulations forming 'links' between numbers. For epic films such as The Four Horsemen of the Apocalypse (in which Rudolph Valentino made his name) and Orphans of the Storm (Lillian Gish), special scores in book form were included with the film, or alternatively the conductor was provided with a cue sheet and occasionally the drummer with an effect sheet.[6] These effect sheets kept me in touch with what was expected of a cinema drummer, and to keep up to date, I was frequently obliged to purchase further instruments and construct gadgets. The most used 'traps' were a slapstick, syren, and a tray of broken glass for the comedies; coconut shells, a rail-

[6] In some large cinemas a back stage effects man was employed.

road bell, train whistle, and large slapstick for revolver shots for the Westerns; and such all-round effects as a thunder sheet (a metal sheet), surf on the shore (lead shot on drumhead or beads on a tin tray), klaxon or bulb motor horns, ship's bell, hooter and foghorn, and others too numerous to mention. Manipulating these effects kept both hands and feet well employed, demanding an independent technique such as pressing a bulb horn with one foot and a klaxon with the other whilst playing the written drum part, or substituting an effective improvisation, as for example rolling on a suspended cymbal or bass drum with one hand whilst playing a rhythm on the side drum or some other instrument with the other hand.

The cleaners at the theatre certainly got to know the sound of my drums as I spent most mornings practising the rudiments: the orchestral repertoire as included in my printed tutors, and the music for the coming week from Mr. Rainbow's library. If the variety act was a musical one I took note of their mode of daily rehearsal. Among other things I learned from those dedicated performers was to leave nothing to chance. One act was an American xylophonist who assiduously rehearsed his evening programme every morning. He not only allowed me on the stage whilst he practised, but also let me examine his instrument, the bars of which were not arranged in the then more usual pattern of four rows (known as Continental style), but were set out as the piano keyboard – a style which he assured me would one day be generally accepted. He also drew my attention to another possibility. Tapping me on the shoulder with a xylophone mallet he pointed dramatically to the screen and said: 'Boy, one day that screen is gonna talk.' A prophet indeed and one who fired my enthusiasm to own and play a xylophone. But the first main addition to my steadily expanding equipment was to be a pair of timpani. 'Real drums,' said Mr. Rainbow; so acting on Freddy Walton's advice I paid five pounds deposit on a pair of Parsons' 'Super Ideal' timpani, the balance to be worked off at the rate of five shillings weekly. The drums duly arrived by rail, and proved to be everything that was said about them by the makers: Messrs. E. A. Parsons of Birmingham. The gleaming copper bowls were a joy to my eye. I tensioned the skins with a beating heart. Would they sound as well as Freddy Walton's? Yes, indeed they did, and I spent some time accustoming my ear to their pitch and tuning them in fourths and fifths (the common intervals).[7] By evening I felt

---

[7] Immediate recognition of the true pitch of orchestral timpani is no easy matter: even to excellent musicians certain of the numerous upper harmonics tend to register more strongly than the principal note.

sufficiently confident to ask Mr. Rainbow's permission to try them out, and was greatly bucked by his telling me at the end of the night that 'I had a good ear'. My new drums must have pleased Mr. Bancroft also as I was promised a rise of five shillings a week when I was twenty-one which was in a few weeks' time.

I attained my majority and the five shillings rise on Friday, 9th September 1922. I was not given indentures proving me a 'journeyman' as my father had visualised would be the case on this important day of my life, but both he and I had the satisfaction of feeling that I was serving my present master 'faithfully and well'.[8] Apart from a drink all round for the band, the day of my coming-of-age was uneventful. A modest tea-party at home on the following Sunday celebrated my receiving the key of the door and the family's 21st birthday present: a leather suitcase (which is still being put to good use housing my collection of printed tutors). My friends Frank Hitchborn, Freddy Walton and Charlie Cooper swelled the family gathering, which included Uncle George who was in excellent form and prophesied my securing a job in a London 'theayter' in next to no time. Not surprisingly, drumming, drummers, and my new drums were among the topics of conversation. Another topic was an event which had puzzled the whole household: the arrival of a large tin of a famous brand of toffees-de-luxe, addressed to my youngest brother. The puzzle was solved by my explaining that I had entered (in Cecil's name) a caption in a competition advertised by Andrew's Liver Salts. The subject to be captioned was an illustration of a policeman drinking a glass of sparkling liquid obviously given to him by a servant girl who was holding a tin of the famous liver salt whilst admiring the arm of the law. My entry, which was awarded a consolation prize was 'The Master's Health'. The winning caption, far better than mine, was 'On duty, health and pleasure bent'. Family news was of course a major topic. Dad had now set up business on his own by converting the front room into a workshop; a venture which did not prove a success and he eventually decided against the tailoring trade and became an employee of the London Brick Company, a position he held until his retirement. My three brothers were all working: Tom as an apprentice moulder, Chris as an apprentice joiner, and Cecil in the office of the Peterborough Coal Company. They were all keeping the pigsty warm practising the drums, Tom and Chris being as keen to become professionals as

[8] The engineering indentures, which were cancelled by agreement some sixteen months earlier, were delivered to me a few days after my birthday.

I had been.[9] Such was the position at my home on that pleasant September Sunday in 1922, a house that had rung with small voices, and in little more than twelve months' time was to ring with another, for Lizzie duly presented my father with a daughter and his four sons with their much-loved 'tomboy' sister Margaret.

Building Castles

Those weekend trips kept me in touch with my friends and haunts. I never tired of the Peterborough Market Place on a Sunday evening and studying Jim Pack's technique on his bass drum, or having dinner at Auntie Liddy's and listening once again to Uncle George's gramophone. Uncle was as keen as ever on my progress, and between us we built many castles in the air. 'I'm going to see you wearing evening dress playing in a London theayter' he would often say and in my own mind I pictured myself in Lyons Corner House band, or the pit of the Alhambra. I saw quite a lot of my old teacher, Freddy Walton, with whom I occasionally spent a Sunday in London. Sometimes we stayed overnight, enabling us to browse round Hawkes & Sons on Monday mornings. Once I persuaded Freddy to join me in a look down 'the street' (Archer Street, Piccadilly) which from an early hour, particularly on Monday, was crowded with musicians fixing engagements. I am sure that had it not been for Freddy's intervention I would have been late for rehearsal at Wisbech. (I visit Archer Street regularly these days as the London Orchestral Association Club is situated there, and on all occasions I am reminded of Freddy Walton's advice. It was: 'Come away my boy. You've got a regular job worth looking after, and in any case the business is finished'.) Despite my teacher's warning I continued to build castles, many of them on those lonely weekend cycle rides to and from Wisbech, though to be fair to Wisbech it was a pleasant place in which to live. As well as the excitement of my work there was plenty of fun at the Hippodrome. One prank I remember being concerned with was putting a kipper through the sound holes of the double bass. Marmaduke, as our bassist was known, was a bit of a joke among the band. He had grown quite deaf and drew some atrocious sounds from his instrument – a three-string bass which he 'played' with a 'Dragonetti' bow in the original style. He had, unbeknown to us, lost his sense of smell as well as his hearing, and after a lapse of time I was obliged to retrieve what was left of the kipper. We were not without our sad moments. The

[9] Both had their ambitions realised.

1 My mother

2 My father

3 Myself on my second birthday

4 Grandad Close, *c.* 1907, in his Sunday
suit that always smelt of moth-balls

5 St John's – Class 3, 1911. The author is fourth from the left, bottom row

6 Uncle George, c. 1914

7 My three brothers. Left to right: Cecil, Tom and Chris, c. 1914

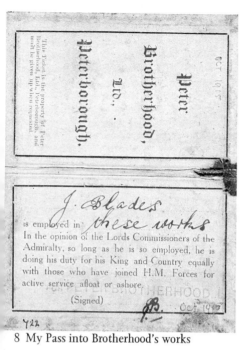

Peter Brotherhood, Ltd. Peterborough.

OCT 1915

J. Blades is employed in *these works*

In the opinion of the Lords Commissioners of the Admiralty, so long as he is so employed, he is doing his duty for his King and Country equally with those who have joined H.M. Forces for active service afloat or ashore.

(Signed)

Oct 1915

8 My Pass into Brotherhood's works

9 Myself and (left) chum 'Curly Kendrick'. The lads of the village in London, 1919.

10 Wisbech Hippodrome

11 Jarrow Empire

12 The Oxford Picture House,
Workington 1924

13 The Loonies, Workington 1925

14 Olive, my first wife

15 At the Villa Marina, Douglas I.O.M., 1929

16 With Jerry Hoey at the Piccadilly Hotel, *c.* 1935

17 The Rank gong. By courtesy of the Rank Organisation
18 The Chinese tam-tam (gong) used for recording the
original Rank gong strokes. *Photo: Godfrey New*

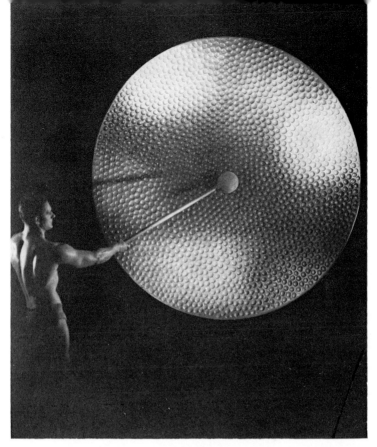

17

18

19 Drum-head autographed at conclusion of the first E.N.S.A. concert
given to the British Expeditionary Force somewhere in France,
5th November 1939

20 Autographed drum-head. 1930 onwards

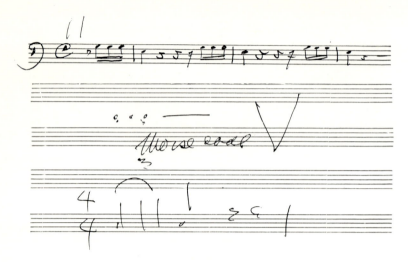

21, 22 The B.B.C. V for victory signal: manuscript scribbled in Bush House, 1940, and the African drum used for the recording

23 My wife Joan on our Swiss honeymoon, 1948
24 My son and his bride Doreen, 1954

25 Auntie Lizzie complete with her little black bag

26 Benjamin Britten and J.B. at the recording of Britten's opera *Albert Herring*, Jubilee Hall, Aldeburgh, 1963. *Photo:* Decca Record Company

27 A still from *We Make Music* World Mirror Productions. *Photo* by courtesy of World Mirror Productions

28 J.B. at a Royal Albert Hall Promenade Concert rehearsal with Sir Malcolm Sargent, 1962. *Photo:* Eric Sargon

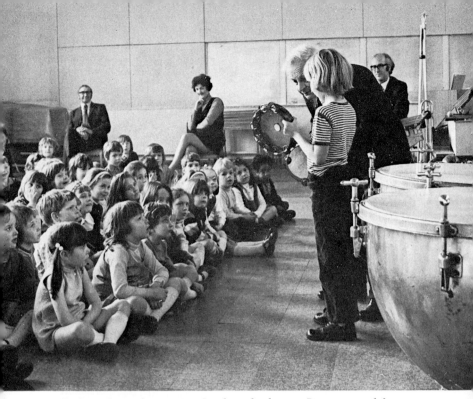

29 The lure of a tambourine in a London school, 1973. By courtesy of the
London Borough of Waltham Forest. *Photo*: Paul Hancock

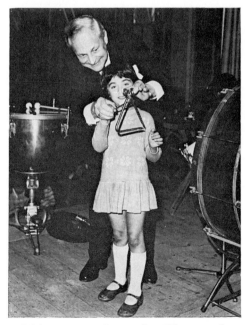

30 Making music : Bermondsey Library, 1969.
Photo: A. I. Wood

Anvil effect

Babylonian bass drum

Four-toned whip

Tuned wood blocks

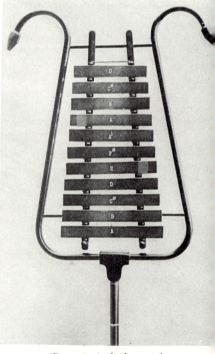

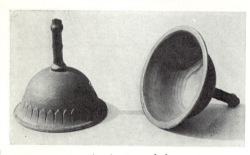

Ancient cymbals

'Portative' glockenspiel

31 The percussion used in Benjamin Britten's church parable opera
The Burning Fiery Furnace. Photographs by G. Durham

32 J.B. with Daniel Barenboim (conductor and soloist) and the English Chamber Orchestra. Royal Festival Hall 1969. Photo: Jack Wilson

33 Being introduced by Imogen Holst to an Aldeburgh Festival audience. Jubilee Hall, 1973. By courtesy of 'The Aldeburgh Festival'. *Photo:* Anthony Askew

34 *A World of Percussion.* Saying goodbye on our BBC 2 Television programme. ('Music on Two' series, producer Denis Moriarty, 1975)

trumpeter, a sufferer from chronic arthritis, had reached the stage of being wheeled to the theatre in a bathchair, and during my second year at Wisbech he gave up playing. One man's ill luck however is often another man's good fortune, and I was able to introduce to Mr. Bancroft a Peterborough cornetist who was in need of work. I wish I could have done the same for 'Tiny Tim', the City Military Band trombone player (in private life a painter and decorator), who frequently asked me if there was any chance of a job at Wisbech as he was 'getting too heavy for the ladder'. Such incidents were a constant reminder of my own good fortune. At the Hippodrome my new pair of timpani had more than proved their worth, leading me to my next investment: a xylophone. I was attracted by advertisements in the current catalogues featuring four-row models as 'invaluable solo instruments', and as xylophone solos were current novelties, I committed myself to a further hire purchase agreement – this time with Hawkes & Son. My knowledge of such instruments as the xylophone was scant, so for the time being my latest acquisition found a place with my practice drums in the corner of my bedroom. But here came a problem. For some time I had felt the lack of practice facilities at Mrs. Stimson's. A 'business house' was definitely not the best place to add the practising of a further instrument, so it was decided with goodwill on both sides that I make a change.

I had no difficulty in finding fresh digs. My new landlady was a Mrs. Johnson, a lady with a keen interest in music and whose home was in every way a hive of musical industry.[10] Mrs. Johnson, herself a fair pianist, had two daughters, both talented musicians: Kath playing the violin and Rita the piano. In contrast, Mr. Johnson, a market gardener (who gossips said was having an affair with a lady connected with the same obscure religious organisation as himself), was completely unmusical and had no time for such nonsense as musical evenings. The remaining member of the Johnson household, if I exclude the two young men, both musical, to whom the charming daughters were (to my intense disappointment) engaged, was an old lurcher dog named Rex who became a constant companion of mine. Rex was really the head of the house, and I did not become a full member of the establishment until he had accepted me by allowing me to collect the door key last thing at night from a hook inside his kennel.

In my new home (and it certainly was a home) I had every facility for practice. My xylophone was given a corner in the pleasant

[10] It also had a bathroom – a new experience for me.

room used for musical evenings. These kept me in Wisbech on many a winter weekend, and also kept me busy preparing simple xylophone solos for these occasions. There were diversions from music of course, one being to take tea once a week with two spinster sisters who lived opposite – both a trifle beyond the bloom of youth. Their curiosity regarding their friend Mrs. Johnson, and a few others, was only equalled by Mrs. Johnson's desire to hear about the sisters, who were reputed to be heiresses to a small fortune and a good catch for anyone looking out for a bank balance. Whether one or both had designs on me I was never sure, but I certainly had no designs on them or their fortune, and merely continued as a (discreet) source of information on the outside world for which I received, in Victorian style, several cups of delicious tea served in elegant china cups, together with brown bread and butter, milk scones and plum cake.

Another cup of tea I took – in quite different surroundings – was at the home of a blind boy to whom I was introduced by Mrs. Johnson. This boy, Tommy Nurse by name, was one of the many who came under the influence of Mrs. Johnson's benevolence. Tommy was a lonely boy, and I would like to believe that I brightened up an occasional hour for him by teaching him to play the mouth-organ and letting him hear me practise on my xylophone.[11]

Life was certainly pleasant at Mrs. Johnson's and in Wisbech generally. Perhaps a bit too pleasant – in fact getting dangerously comfortable for a young man who was supposed to be ambitious. What of the future? The only way to get into that London theatre was to forge ahead, and that meant taking heed of most of my friends whose advice was to get moving and gain experience up and down the country. So 'an experienced drummer, xylophone soloist, etc.' – not unexpectedly disengaged this time – answered any advertisements in The Era that seemed attractive, including posts in London. But for a provincial to break into London was no easy matter, and my first reasonable offer came from The Empire, Jarrow-on-Tyne, salary to be £3 10s. od. a week, for which I was to provide a 'full kit', wear a dinner jacket, and play a xylophone solo as and when required. It was not easy informing Mr. Bancroft of my decision to leave the Hippodrome, but he accepted my fortnight's notice with good grace. He kindly agreed to my timorous suggestion that my brother Tom who had recently done a Christmas pantomime for him be given a trial in my job; so all that was left was to do as

[11] We remain friends.

Tim Reed the cornet player had advised: join the Musicians' Union in case my card was wanted up North;[12] say goodbye to all at home and in Wisbech, and prepare for making my way 200 miles north to Jarrow-on-Tyne and meet what was coming – and how little I knew what was coming!

[12] The Birmingham branch: the nearest provincial centre of Union activity.

83

7

'Black Jarrow' – January 1924

A cold, blustery January morning saw my departure from Wisbech, or to be precise I saw the cold and blustery morning when I could give it attention, for the greater part of my time was spent in helping to transfer my precious equipment from a small furniture van to the guard's van on the train bound for Grantham where I was to join the main line express for Newcastle-upon-Tyne. Getting a third-class through ticket, and an excess baggage ticket, from Wisbech to Jarrow was no easy matter on that cold Sunday morning. It took me some time to convince the solitary railway official that as a 'theatrical' I was allowed 1½ cwt. of equipment before excess was charged. He finally told me to fix it up at the other end, adding that he hoped I got there as a strike was to start at midnight or possibly earlier. Cheering information for a chap who had spent a restless night pondering on whether it was wise to leave a safe job where there was little competition (the only drummer seen or heard near Wisbech was at a Hunt Ball), and plunge into the musical life of one of the best-known industrial centres in Great Britain. In addition, my worldly wealth was, with the exception of Grandad's silver watch and a few pounds in my pocket, invested in my instruments and two small life policies: one taken out to help my one-time cycling friend Charlie Cooper, and the other on the advice of my old Sunday School teacher (and what sound advice it proved). My ready cash had been depleted by the necessity of adding evening dress to my wardrobe. This at least made a small job for my father who put a velvet collar on a suit I purchased from the one and only second-hand clothes dealer in Wisbech. Dark clothing had been sufficient in Wisbech, as Mr. Bancroft believed in his orchestra being heard and not seen.

Eventually the Grantham-bound train steamed away and I ventured to pass the time of day with my one fellow passenger, none other than Bransby Williams, the celebrated character actor who had been the turn at the Hippodrome the previous week, and had sent down half-a-crown for the drummer for obliging with some background sounds during his portrayal of Scrooge (cymbal roll and

rattling of chains for Marley's ghost and so on). The famous actor
enquired of my immediate movements. I told him where I hoped to
be by late evening. He told me that I would find Jarrow a complete
change from Wisbech but that it could well lead to a job in Newcastle. We parted at Grantham where he wished me God-speed. The
railway porter gave me the cheering information that the north-
bound train was late and that he hoped it would arrive in time for
me to get to Newcastle before the strike started. He was most interested in my baggage, particularly the shining copper bowls of
the timpani. Like most of the general public at the time he was not
fully acquainted with their musical purpose, and asked me if the
parchment was 'to keep the rain out of the bowls'! At last the
main line train came in and my kit was hustled into the brake and
the express headed northwards, breaking all records, or so it seemed
to me, on the final hundred miles from Grantham to Newcastle, the
journey giving me my first sight of York Minster and Durham
Cathedral, in both of which (unbeknown to me on that journey) I
was later to play. Rumbling over the King Edward Bridge at Newcastle-upon-Tyne gave me a slight rumble in my tummy. One more
change and Jarrow Empire would be at hand. The confusion at
Newcastle Station was in my favour, as I was able to hustle my
equipment on to the local train for Jarrow without the formality of
being weighed for excess.

Jarrow Station was reached about 7 p.m. and I deposited my instruments in the small left luggage office. The ticket collector gave
me directions to the Empire and cheered me somewhat with a bit of
banter about my failing to understand his crisp Geordie accent and
my own Fenland drawl which, though decidedly 'Peterborough' was
not as authentic as the Fenland farmworker who, on being questioned
about his son who had moved to a nearby county, replied, 'My boy
Garge, he bin' a-gon' furrin this twelvemonth larst muck-knockin' '.[1]
I made my way (on foot) to the Empire to meet Mr. Connolly, the
manager. It was a cold wet night adding to the gloom and depression
of Jarrow, one of the most unfortunate of the unemployment-stricken
Tyneside towns. My first reaction to my new place of employment
was similar to my feeling of intense disappointment at the size of
the circus tent some few years earlier, for when compared with the
Hippodrome, Wisbech, the Jarrow theatre was indeed a poor-looking
place. I made my way into the dimly-lit entrance and was received
by the manager, a sad-looking man who, after enquiring as to my
journey and the safe deposit of my instruments, suggested that we

[1] Furrin : the next town; muck-knockin' : potato-picking.

should walk up the street to the lodgings he had booked for me – a humble place he said, but clean and homely. I had the feeling that all was not well in 'the state of Denmark' when Mr. Connolly asked if I were a Union man. On my replying in the affirmative he remarked that it was a pity in some ways as his orchestra had voted to strike late the previous evening, and that he would be obliged – for the time being at least – to carry on with a non-Union pianist. Here, to quote Dick Swiveller, was something of a 'flattener', and it was small comfort to me that Mr. Connolly apologised for having been unable to acquaint me of the situation, and that he intended to approach the Union officials at Newcastle early the following morning to ask permission for me to make a start on the job I had travelled so far to undertake. To this he could add nothing further and on reaching my lodgings we parted for the night.

The digs took the same dismal pattern as the picture to date: a poor-looking house and an even poorer-looking landlady who, however, made me most welcome by saying that supper was waiting – bread and butter (or could it have been margarine?), a piece of cheese, and an onion. The meal was taken in company with my fellow lodger, an older man who informed me that he worked at the waterworks and always rose at half-past five – a piece of information that did not disturb me unduly until I learned that he and I were to be bedfellows. After supper we drew up our chairs to a small fire; his chair incidentally had no back. I learned from my new acquaintance and the landlady – a war widow – more of the ghastly plight of Jarrow. This, coupled with the wet night, the shattering news from Mr. Connolly, and the poverty stricken appearance of my surroundings created an impression of unreality – almost a nightmare, and I retired to bed in a state of deep depression. I had barely sufficient money to return South; there was the rail strike; and in any case, I could not return home without my brother Tom feeling it necessary to relinquish his chance of a break by offering to give me back my job. The fact that I was to sleep in a red blanket on a hard bed with a waterworks man who was due to rise at 5.30 a.m. did little to cheer me up, and I said good-night to my room mate (by no means a bad fellow) with a sad heart, and being thoroughly exhausted by the events of the day soon fell asleep. I was awakened by the rising of the waterworks man who, whilst struggling out of his nightshirt, took a few draws from a clay pipe which he had lighted – rather dexterously I thought – with the aid of a candle. He coughed rather badly, and to this was added the asthmatic bark of the landlady who was cleaning out the downstairs fireplace prior to

86

preparing breakfast for herself and lodger No. 1 who, bidding me a gruff 'Good morning' put out the candle and left me to sleep until a more reasonable hour.

My feeling on awakening was that the events of the previous evening (and my present condition) was all a hideous dream; but the landlady's knock on the door with the information that my breakfast was ready, brought me to earth. I washed at the kitchen sink with a mental picture of Mrs. Johnson's comfortable bathroom, and then did what justice I could to the modest breakfast, after which my immediate care was my instruments. These I arranged to be moved from the almost deserted railway station to the theatre. Here, the manager gave me the information that the Union were prepared to allow me to work with the non-Union pianist on the understanding that if the strike continued I should make every effort to find another job, which prompted me to place an order for *The Era* at a nearby stationers before assembling my instruments prior to a run-through with the other half of the Jarrow Empire 'Symphony Orchestra'. Whatever my worries were at that moment I was to have none about reading my music, for the simple reason that there was no music to read! My 'partner in crime' was a relief pianist, a man several years my senior and one of those people who played by ear, and like my old partner Frank Hitchborn, could busk until the cows came home, as well as memorising after one hearing. Rehearsal consisted of running through a few items suitable for the news reel, the serial and the big picture – a film featuring the Ku Klux Klan. Much of what the pianist played was familiar to me, and for the remainder I used my powers of invention. The *Ku Klux Klan* theme used by my colleague gave me an idea: why not the popular *Ku Klux Klan* song as an intermission? The tune was a jaunty affair and suited florid extemporisation from us both, with plenty of tom-tom from me, plus a trifle of Oriental atmosphere from my near replica of Uncle George's famous gong. We decided to wear paper hats in the form of hoods on which we painted a skull and crossbones. It was arranged that I should sing the second chorus ('Ku Klux Klan was a Dark Old Man'),[2] and beat on a tom-tom whilst walking up and down the centre gangway. Whether or not a drum and a gong were important instruments in the ritual of the Ku Klux Klan I cannot say, but our intermission that evening proved a great success and was encored by the somewhat sparse audience. Mr. Connolly said he was completely satisfied with our interlude, adding that he was certain that Mr. George Black, who owned the

[2] Or something similar.

Empire and cinemas elsewhere, including Newcastle, would also be favourably impressed on his weekly visit to the Empire. In due course I met Mr. George Black, who expressed his regret for my being placed in an unfortunate situation. On congratulating me on my part in the intermission, he said that he would always bear me in mind.[3]

Settling down in Jarrow that first week helped to take my mind off my sudden change of circumstances. In any case I could not complain. I was surrounded by people in a much worse position than myself and who were bearing the brunt of mass unemployment with a good heart. Their fortitude and the way in which they accepted me gave me encouragement. My digs, in spite of a slender diet and sharing a red blanket with a waterworks man, were homely, and were (according to Mr. Connolly) a temporary lodging until I could get better suited. Much of my day was spent in the theatre, practising and preparing a stunt for my second week. My solo was to be *The Drummer's Birthday*, a jolly piece of 'trap' drumming and for those days quite spectacular. As a minor relaxation I took afternoon tea at the Co-op café where I was so extravagant as to have a pot of tea and a cream horn as a reminder of my somewhat more luxurious tea-taking at the Misses Messams. Mid-week was a period of excitement and speculation. What would be advertised in *The Era*? Would my next job take me further north, or would I return south? As it happened it took me to the North-West; but in the meantime there was work to be done in Jarrow; much to be learned from occasional afternoon visits to the large picture houses in Newcastle; and interesting people to meet – one in particular: 'Dear Sir and Brother Knight George A. Cliffe, K.O.M.' It was during my third week in Jarrow that I met the redoubtable 'G.A.C'. *The Drummer's Birthday* had gone down quite well during the previous week and I was brushing up the xylophone solo which, with a novelty piece for the pianist, was the present week's intermission. As I pegged away in the dim light of the pit, completely engrossed in my solo, I became conscious of an audience. Glancing upwards, I saw the round cheery-looking face of a man in his late prime peering over the curtain rail. 'Good morning young man', a friendly North Country voice said. 'I notice you are practising – that's the way to get on', to which I suitably replied. 'I'll introduce myself', said my new acquaintance. 'This is how my friends address me', and he handed me a letter which began: 'Dear Sir and Brother Knight Cliffe, K.O.M.' Having no idea what a K.O.M. or a Brother Knight

[3] This he certainly did as we will see later.

was, I ventured an enquiry as to whether my audience was in any way connected with the Musicians' Union, and was told that me was not a Union official; that his business in Jarrow was to do with his professional activities as an advertising agent; that he was an influential member of the Ancient Order of Buffaloes; and that he was a personal friend of my employer Mr. George Black, whom he assured me was a big man in the entertainment world – and was going to be a bigger one, and well worth keeping 'the right side of'. Brief as was our acquaintance to date, the 'K.O.M.' promised to put in a word for me with Mr. Black, and added if ever I was in need of accommodation at a reasonable price he could help me as he was directly concerned with a small boarding house in South Shields; a place no great distance from Jarrow and decidedly more healthy. I lost no time in making arrangements to become a member of his establishment, and within a few days took my abode at 47, Vespasian Avenue, South Shields: a large terraced house, no distance from the sea and not more than thirty minutes journey from the theatre. Mr. Cliffe was in every way the head of the house, which was domestically controlled by two maiden ladies, or to be more precise by a rather down-at-heel maid of all work who boasted a glass eye.

I have vivid recollections of that South Shields' boarding house and all of them pleasant: the substantial breakfasts brought to my room by the girl with the glass eye who kept me informed of events downstairs including the fact that the 'master' always took half-a-pound of jam with his morning toast; the pleasant lounge in which my supper was served, during which Mr. Cliffe entertained me with numerous anecdotes concerning his interesting life (he had made quite a 'bit of brass' as a waste paper merchant during the First World War); our joint perusal of *The Era*, and our united efforts at framing suitable replies to likely-looking advertisements. I learned much from 'Dear Sir, and Brother Knight Cliffe, K.O.M.' and I like to think that he found me not uninteresting; in fact on many an evening he used me as a foil – to keep him in practice, he explained, in his present occupation of selling advertisement space on theatre drop curtains. The part I played was that of a tough customer who considered advertising a waste of time and money. I found my opponent remarkably convincing, but it transpired that he was meeting his match in a Hebburn jeweller who refused point blank to renew his ad. on the local screen. But the 'K.O.M.' was undaunted; he had a plan, and one that was to involve me. My Midland accent would qualify me as a stranger to Hebburn, reasoned Mr. Cliffe, and it was arranged that I should pay a call on the Hebburn jeweller and purchase a shilling Albert watch chain. I was to make conversation with the jeweller who would no doubt ask the reason for my being in Hebburn, to which I was to reply as I felt best, making certain that I referred to a visit on the previous evening to the local cinema where his advertisement had reminded me that I was in need of a watch chain. Our plan worked, as did our reply to an advertisement in *The Era* for a drummer at the Oxford Picture Theatre, Workington, Cumberland (£3 15s. od. weekly). So my equipment spent another night in the small left luggage office in Jarrow (again active) awaiting an early morning 'local' to Newcastle and a trip to Workington via Carlisle.

'Black Jarrow' made a lasting impression on me. The daylight of my first Monday morning in that stricken town did little to dispel the gloom of the previous evening. A pall of smoke (domestic rather than industrial) darkened the already dull and biting morning. Large groups of men with seemingly little conversation were queueing to sign on for the dole, and harassed-looking housewives (equally silent) were scrubbing the front doorsteps as generations of housewives had done before them. There were few shoppers and fewer shopping baskets. Whether those with strange-looking bundles were making their way to establishments I knew as a boy as 'pop' shops, I cannot be certain, but I can with certainty speak on the sadness with which I watched numbers of small boys (many scantily clad and down-at-heel) feasting their eyes on the 'stills' advertising the films to be seen inside the Empire, and concluding that they – like me when I was their age – had little immediate chance of a glimpse of the real thing even from a seat in the 'fourpenny's'. 'Black Jarrow' taught me much; it certainly made me realise that though I had known what it was to have only bread and 'scrat' it was never less than that, and that I have good reason to be thankful to the Lord and 'especially unto them that brought me up by hand'.

8

Enter Percy Pegleg, John Henry Wright and the Barrow

The journey through Northumberland and Cumberland on that clear and frosty morning proved a pleasant ride. I felt reasonably confident about holding down my new job, and had no illusions as to what I might encounter: the circus and Jarrow had been a wonderful lesson for me, and I was ready for the best or the worst that Workington had to offer. The Cumbrian porter at 'Workington Main' seemed to be calling a different name from the one on the station board, and relying on my eyes and not on my ears I alighted. On looking round, whilst giving up my ticket, I observed two young men and a barrow. The young men were sharing a morning paper which, I learned later, had been borrowed from the ticket collector because they were both on the dole. I sensed that these young men were to escort me to the cinema. The elder introduced himself as Percy Pegleg, and said he was nicknamed so on account of his artificial limb: a replacement for the one he left in the mud of Flanders in 1917. He said, 'You must be Nathan's new drummer and John Henry Wright and I have come to take you to T'Oxford'. My equipment was loaded on the barrow and we made our way to T'Oxford – by which name the Oxford Picture House was known throughout Cumberland. The route was along one of the main streets of the town and my gleaming kettledrums caused a good deal of attention and comment from the groups of men standing or squatting miner fashion on their heels at street corners. Men grouped together at street corners during working hours was no new sight to me, and I realised that the busiest place in Workington was the Labour Exchange – not for reason of the dole being attractive (18s. per week).

In spite of his limp Percy Pegleg kept pace with the strong strides of John Henry Wright who pushed the barrow. We passed the 'Hip' which I was informed was the smallest of the three cinemas in 'Wukkinton'. I was also given the information that last week's picture at that establishment had been 'mustard' – the tone of my informant's voice leaving me in no doubt as to the meaning of 'mustard'. My new conductor Nathan Jones was, I was told, a cripple who played the piano as well as conducting the band. Percy told me that I would always know when to start playing the first tune because Nathan made a special point of getting the audience quiet by tapping loudly on the piano lid with his gold ring before beating out the time with his foot. Other useful information given to me on that walk was that t'band at T'Oxford was the best for miles around; that there were two performances nightly; and that Nathan (who always wore patent shoes and grey spats with pearl buttons), because he could not get out in the interval for a drink, always had a tot of whisky from a silver hip-pocket flask. When conversing privately my companions spoke in broad Cumberland dialect which was occasionally explained to me, and with this and other pleasantries in the way of salutations from numerous acquaintances of my porters, most of whom I was introduced to as 'T'Oxford drummer' – my *nom-de-plume* from now on – the Picture House was reached, and quite a smart-looking place T'Oxford turned out to be. (It was known locally as 'Brown's Palace' having been built by a famous 'brickie' of that name, 'Authy' Brown).

John Henry Wright, my 'batman' from henceforth, helped me to unload and fix up my equipment. He then took me to my lodgings (up t'hill). I felt that I knew my landlady Mrs. McNichol of 33, Guard Street, before I reached my digs as John Henry, who knew everyone and about everyone in the district, told me that she was 'Oirish'; a devout Catholic; 'a party who was always ready for a good crack' (gossip) and that she was recently widowed. I was also informed that her grown-up family lived with her. The family I was soon to learn consisted of two boys who worked on the 'line' (as had their respected father), and a daughter 'Kath', a charming though most outspoken young lady who was anyone's equal in a 'fratch' (argument), and was said to have recently told an official at the Town Hall that she wanted to speak to the butcher – not the block! I was given a warm welcome at 33, Guard Street, and after a good midday meal I returned to the theatre where the rehearsal proved to me that I was to play with some excellent musicians. The orchestra was small but up-to-date. In addition to the pianist/conductor there was a violinist doubling banjolin (an instrument with four strings which could for convenience be tuned as a violin); a 'cellist doubling tenor banjo (tuned as the 'cello); a clarinet player doubling E flat and tenor saxophones, and a flautist doubling piccolo on which instrument he was a brilliant soloist. The reason for my inclusion in this élite ensemble was due to my predecessor's failure to keep pace with the times. Not unnaturally I felt that a great deal was expected of me, and at the rehearsal and first performance I really 'played for my supper'. During the interval, Nathan, after taking his tot, expressed his approval of my playing and asked if after the second performance I would be interested in joining the flautist and play (for a friend of his) at a dance in Egremont, a smallish place on the fringe of the coal mining area some eight miles distant. This proposal I readily agreed to, and Mr. Ward and myself, with John Henry Wright in charge of my dance kit, were collected at 10.15 and driven in a small van of unknown age to the Parish Rooms in Egremont to take our place in Jack Dixon's 'Modern Dance Band'. The line-up of this group was: Jack (Johnnie) Dixon on violin, Mrs. Dixon on piano, a cornet player, plus Mr. Ward and myself. I found Jack and Millie Dixon two of the most genuine and lovable people it has ever been my pleasure to meet, and it was with difficulty that I wrestled myself from their friendly embraces to assist my 'batman' (who I noticed had already sized up the supper table and a few likely partners) to arrange my drums and other paraphernalia in a position near the rhythm section – a cottage piano !

The dance had barely got under way at the time of the arrival of the Workington contingent, the usual hours of such affairs in that part of the world at that time being 10 p.m. until 3 or 4 a.m., so that many a young miner went home after the last dance merely to have his breakfast, change into pit togs and collect his bait tin.[1] Through John Henry Wright I had been able to get word to my landlady that I would be rather late home. I did, in fact, arrive home in every respect with the milk: in the region of 5 a.m., not long before the break of dawn over the lakeland mountain range to the east. As I mounted the steep steps of my new abode – a series of three stone steps which, because they exposed the back of my neck to the almost-incessant chill wind from the Solway Firth, I eventually christened 'Pneumonia Steps' – I felt that I had made a doubtful start at 33, Guard Street. But Mrs. McNichol took it in good part and quickly became accustomed to my frequent similar perambulations, and was not disturbed by my nocturnal habits as was a certain landlady who catered for students of the Royal College of Music and who, when Hubert Dawkes – a quiet young man from Dorset – took a late bath on one occasion during his first year of studentship, demanded that Mr. Dawkes be found other accom-

[1] A bait tin (for meals throughout the shift) and a pit lamp signified a coal miner in those days.

modation, and that she be given a quieter young man in his place. She received one: a new boy – the ebullient Malcolm Arnold!

The whole of that first evening at Egremont was a riot. Jack Dixon, who was a fine folk fiddler, knew how to please the Cumbrians, who were as much at home dancing the foxtrot and one-step as they were the lancers and the quadrilles. Mr. Ward, an ex-Royal Marine whose proud boast was that he had studied with the illustrious Eli Hudson, did yeoman service in the lancers and the waltzes, and I 'jazzed up' such numbers as 'Felix keeps on walking' and 'Barney Google with his great big Googly eyes'. My efforts included a good deal of syncopation on the woodblock and tom-tom; a vocal chorus or two; and solos on the Swannee whistle and flexatone, the latter instrument evocative of a singing saw and, according to its decorated cardboard box, an instrument for making 'jazz jazzier'.[2] Over a huge supper (at 1 a.m.) of cold beef and pickles followed by drop scones and plum cake, Jack Dixon in booking me for the following evening at Biggrig told me that he had prearranged with Nathan Jones to book me if I was any good. Biggrig proved to be a smaller place than Egremont. Here we played in the hall of the Infants' School, and I remember a youth who sat listening to the band telling me during a quiet waltz to 'give it hell!' The supper at Biggrig was on the same grand scale as that as Egremont, in fact it was supplied by the same caterers. I was served by a daughter of the catering family, a rather nice-looking girl who it transpired had studied in Manchester and knew my cousin Sophie Howe. A mild friendship developed between us which led to all but three people deciding that the affair would end up at the altar. The three people were the two people most vitally concerned and the girl's mother who had a horror of musicians.

Those dances at Egremont and Biggrig, and such places as Aspatria ('Speatry'), and Cleator Moor, were typical of the many pleasant late night engagements with Jack Dixon's 'Modern Dance Band'. These engagements (at fifteen shillings a time less half-a-crown for John Henry Wright) took me to many places in West Cumberland and I learned a lot about those staunch folk, and saw the inside of many of their humble dwellings as quite often supper was served in a miner's home. In all, life was very exciting. Admittedly 'Wukkinton' was a little remote as far as the map was concerned – and T'Oxford not a London theatre – but I had reason to feel that I had made a move in the right direction.

[2] Swannee Whistle or Lotus Flute, known to one Workington youth as a 'Swansdown Whistle'.

Though I had to make up for a loss of sleep by frequently lying in, T'Oxford saw plenty of me during the day. Percy Pegleg became quite a fan of mine and rarely lost an opportunity of listening to my daily dozen in the theatre. John Henry Wright became my theatrical stooge, performing the most ludicrous antics and gymnastics which I endeavoured to catch with sound effects. Of these the most spectacular was his 'Blondin' act which he conceived for my practice of the long roll on the side drum. This daring stunt consisted of J.H.W. climbing a support from the centre gangway to the balcony seats and, whilst I rolled on my drum, walking with outstretched arms on the narrow cushioned arm rest of the long crescent-shaped parapet. These afternoon sprees were often followed by a game of snooker, and a cup of tea and a chat in the billiards saloon below the cinema. I soon got used to my companions' Cumbrian dialect, though they never quite mastered my Fenland drawl. Neither did the young lady in the paybox and the girl ushers who would engage me in conversation just to hear my quaint brogue. Despite an occasional mild passage at arms with Kath McNichol, I quickly became one of the family at 33, Guard Street, and was completely accepted as such by the head of the house, an old tabby cat named Darkie who always sat on my right shoulder at mealtimes. Darkie died during my stay at Mrs. McNichol's and was buried with full feline honours in a muck heap at the bottom of the back garden. The two McNichol boys who were choristers brought home their surplices for the occasion. I officiated as priest in a stiff white collar turned back to front, and wearing my dinner jacket with the velvet lapels.

Happy days and enlightening ones too. Nathan Jones introduced me to a great deal in music, including some tubaphone solos recorded on 78s which he helped me to transcribe for the xylophone (some of these solos I still play). To be in the fashion I changed my style of drumming from 'double drumming' (playing the side drum and bass drum simultaneously with side drum sticks) to the regular use of a foot pedal on the bass drum. This Nathan reluctantly accepted as the trend of the times and a necessity in the contemporary jazz. On his advice I forsook the four-row xylophone and re-built my instrument in the form of the piano keyboard, to resemble the instrument used by the American xylophone artist who had forcast that one day I would adopt this style and that the screen would talk. My domestic circumstances were ideally suited to my current mode of life: plenty to eat and drink and complete freedom to come and go as I pleased. My landlady, in addition to

looking after my physical needs extremely well, took a keen interest
in my spiritual welfare, doing her utmost to convert me to the 'true
faith'. But my memories of the Mission Church choir and the arguments between Grandad Close and my father as to the phrasing of
the Old Hundredth, and possibly Jim Pack's big bass drum, kept
me a 'heathen'; but not a bad one, Mrs. NcNichol admitted,
even if I did break the Sabbath by going on an occasional 'chara'
trip to see the Lakes, at half-a-crown a trip including high tea served
often in the converted stables of one of Buttermere's splendid
hotels.

I become a Loonie

After six months in Workington I took a holiday, the majority of
which was spent in London looking about me. Interesting of course,
but at heart I was anxious to get back to the fun of work and the
bustle of the coming season – and quite a bustling one it proved to
be. Soon after my return, a Workingtonian approached me with a
proposition to join a dance band he intended to form. 'Gale's Jazz
Band' he proposed to call it. I took an immediate liking to Herbert
Gale, a quietly spoken young man who had recently left the pits
due to silicosis. 'Gale's Jazz Band', Herbert said, was to consist of
himself on violin, a banjo player, a saxophonist, a pianist and, he
hoped, myself on drums.

I joined forces with Herbert and with his approval changed the
name of the band to 'Gale's Jazz Loonies', adopting for myself the
stage name of 'Hustlin' Jim'.[3] The Loonies became a sensation almost
overnight. People came from miles around, not only to dance, but
to hear the band play and watch their antics. As well as our particular brand of fun, which included a black-faced mascot, we
adopted a boisterous strict-tempo style of playing in one-steps and
fox-trots with a complete contrast by way of 'hush-hush' in waltzes,
with the added attraction of switching on a light inside my bass
drum in the 'twilights' to add lustre to the palm beach scene which
Herbert Gale (who was no mean artist) had painted on my drumskin. Every Loonie was a soloist and we all wore dinner jackets and
black bow ties. I included novelties on the xylophone and made
history – of a sort – by my use of my set of eight tubular bells in
'Three o'clock in the morning' and a special arrangement of that

[3] A crib: my Peterborough teacher Harry Sculthorpe called himself
'Hustlin' Harry'.

evergreen 'The Bells are ringing for me and my Gal'. My problem was how to cope with my gradually-expanding connection. In doing so (or nearly doing so) I gained an insight into the art of almost cutting myself in half which stood me in good stead at that time and has done so on numerous occasions since. The success of the Loonies fired the imagination of other local instrumentalists and the lack of drum players led to me being approached to join rival combinations. One quite tempting offer came from a Workington dentist whose chief hobby was playing the saxophone in his small dance band which he had dubbed 'Irwin's Rhythm Aces'. I must confess that I found Arnold Irwin a mighty persuasive gentleman. He became my dental surgeon; my host – his wife's brown bread-and-tomato sandwiches were fit for the gods; my medical adviser (he convinced me, and I remain convinced, of the value of vegetarianism and nature cure), and my financial adviser, to the extent of recommending me to buy Workington Brewery Shares, which advice I disregarded and have regretted ever since. I did not however become a 'Rhythm Ace', but acted in an advisory role at his rehearsals under a promise to find him an equivalent of 'Hustlin' Jim'.

News from home that winter and the months that followed was much as I had anticipated. My youngest brother (Cecil) had been smitten by the drumming bug and like Blades No. 3 (Chris) was making certain that the neighbours were suffering no loss as far as percussion recitals were concerned. These two boys were adding to their incomes by playing 'gigs'. Uncle George had severed his connection with free-lance drumming and, in addition to his work as a joiner, was playing six nights a week at a small cinema in a Peterborough suburb. Here he created some ingenious sound effects, which (as with me in my first few months at Wisbech) kept him far too busy to read from the music. My brother Tom, I heard, was hankering to make a move from Wisbech and it came my way to help him to do so, and at the same time to fall on much safer ground than I did when I made the move from Wisbech. This ground was the Empire, Maryport, the sister hall of the Oxford, Workington. Tom settled down immediately in Maryport, and in next to no time was helping me out with my work in Jack Dixon's band, the Jazz Loonies, and the newly-formed Nathan Jones' 'Radios' – a band that on a point of loyalty to my conductor I felt obliged to give precedence – even on occasions over the Loonies. With Tom in Cumberland I was able to keep my promise to my dentist friend, and among other things my brother became Hustlin' Tom of Irwin's Rhythm Aces,

97

and on necessary occasions Hustlin' Jim of the Loonies, whilst I in return became Hustlin' Tom.[4]

To say that the Loonies were a success is something of an understatement and in retrospect I have often thought that we made a mistake in not taking a chance in London. In many ways, however, it was just as well, for me at least, that we did not venture South, for it was at a Loonie dance towards the end of 1925 that I met and danced a waltz with a young lady who was to become my second sweetheart and eventually my partner for a good many years. This time it was not a pretty face with a plait of golden hair at the back that bowled me over, but a strong attractive face crowned with auburn hair. We danced, we talked, we agreed to meet again and so Olive Hewitt entered my life and I became acquainted with 19, Belle Isle Place, Workington, and the Hewitt family, headed by the redoubtable 'Charles E.', a signals electrician on the Cleator Moor Railway who, though deaf as a post, could detect a fault in a signalling system better than most – in fact he was often sent considerable distances to track down a fault. My future father-in-law was a staunch Conservative, which could have justified his spending most evenings in the Conservative Club, from which he invariably made his way home in a decidedly mellow condition. 'Pop' Hewitt had no time for Arnold Irwin's farinaceous-style diet and was no advertisement for it. He ate meat three times a day, rarely had a day's illness, and when in his eighties walked me off my feet on more than one of his tramps round London, during which he consumed at least four Walls' pork pies, several pots of Lyons' tea, and cleared his head in the evening with a bottle or two of beer or stout.

The prospect of setting-up home was an added spur to my almost constant round of activity in both the world of jazz and at the Oxford cinema, where, to accommodate the expansion in my equipment, I had been allowed a bulge in the curtain that surrounded the orchestra. My instruments now included a large set of tubular bells (thirteen), a new xylophone, and a genuine Chinese gong – obtained after much haggling from a Workington antique dealer. I purchased this gong (which I have since used in, for instance, a number of performances of the Sonata for Two Pianos and Percussion by Bartók

[4] This 'Jimmy/Tommy, Tommy/Jimmy business' as it later became known in London, was no great problem as at a glance Blades Nos 1 and 2 looked alike and also played similarly, so much so that on the occasion that Tommy could not perform on a particular session midway through a Charlie Kunz film, a sequence was shot with the drums in shadow (behind a gauze curtain) and Jimmy photographed very nicely as Charlie's drummer Tommy.

and certain of Benjamin Britten's chamber operas) specifically for the film *The Ten Commandments*. This epic masterpiece of Cecil B. de Mille's ran for two consecutive weeks, a record for Workington, after which it was presented – again for two weeks – at Tom's 'theatre' in Maryport. As I was familiar with the numerous effects (the parting of the Red Sea, etc.), Tom took my place at the Oxford, whilst I went to the Empire, Maryport. I may have made a slight impression on certain of the Empire's clientele, but not on the youth who, on walking past my corner on his way out said to his friend, 'He's all right, but you want to hear his young brother "larrup 'em"': evidence of Tom's popularity and that the current love of noise with young people is not novel.

A Mishap

Like a lot of other young chaps in the 1920s my brother Tom and I were bitten by the motor cycle bug and we purchased a second-hand B.S.A. machine. That B.S.A. motor bike gave us both a lot of pleasure; but it also led us into trouble, for as we were driving to see Wastwater on a sunny afternoon in midsummer 1926 we were pitched into the hedgerow by an idiot who was blinding on a Zenith. Tom, who was riding pillion, escaped injury, but I sustained a badly fractured tibia, and was in hospital for the best part of two months. What to me was a truly remarkable incident occurred shortly after midday on my second day in hospital. Though well before normal visiting hours, I was made sufficiently presentable to see my Uncle Harry and Auntie Fanny, who had made the journey from Manchester. Auntie Fanny, it may be remembered, was the ninth child of Grandad Close and was given to prophecy. My first question was to find out how they knew of my accident which had only happened the day before their visit. Uncle Harry gave me the answer. He said that on coming down to breakfast Auntie Fanny said, 'There's something wrong with one of Kitty's boys' (I suppose Uncle thought 'she's at it again'). He told me that on glancing through the short paragraphs that reported the weekend accidents in his morning paper he read of my mishap and the hospital to which I had been taken. There was no doubt that Auntie Fanny's sixth sense and psychic powers were as strong at this time as they had been twenty years earlier, when she had never failed to send a postcard to my mother whenever there was sickness in the family, asking 'who is ill this time?' An unusual incident perhaps, but many things that happened in that West Cumberland Hospital made me accept that there are powers which cannot be logically explained and not the least of these is the power of prayer.

After a few restless weeks it could not be concealed that my mutilated limb was giving the doctors considerable concern as gangrene was suspected. After a particularly bad day on which I had been frequently examined with screens around my bed, I spent much of the night that followed in prayer. The next morning I clearly remember the house surgeon saying as he inspected my leg, 'Good God, this is remarkable. This wound is almost ready for the nitrate stick.' The turn had come and from then on I made steady progress and was given as early a release from hospital as the circumstances permitted – the doctors agreeing that operating my bass drum pedal could act as a form of therapy, and with this and the fact of getting £500 insurance money, plus John Henry Wright taking me out a short distance in the Solway Firth in a rowboat and helping me to dangle my leg in the sea water I, to use a Lakeland expression, 'did champion'.

Despite the continued industrial depression and the havoc caused by the General Strike, the winter of 1926 proved as busy as previous seasons had done. I combined my work at the theatre with late night dances, with Nathan Jones' 'Radios', Jack Dixon's 'Modern Dance Band', and the now quite famous 'Gale's Jazz Loonies'. I was also busy in another way – preparing for my marriage. My bank account was sufficient to purchase outright a small house in Lakeland stone for £230. I was married on the morning of 27th January 1927. The ceremony was a simple one, but afterwards my wife and I were greeted with plenty of confetti and it was all white; for on leaving the church we encountered a severe snowstorm. We had a short honeymoon in London living in great style as we stayed with Auntie Lizzie at the sumptuous home of her employers (the Sainsburys). One morning whilst my new wife visited Harrods I went to the Premier Drum Co.'s shop in Berwick Street, for two reasons: to meet the eminent drummer Eric Little who had recently taken over the management of the Berwick Street establishment, and to see any new equipment. There were sufficient tempting innovations for me to put our house up for sale, but deciding that this would be unfair and possibly unwise, we returned to Workington and took up residence at 20 Brown Street, with brother Tom as a lodger. Life ran smoothly at No. 20 – a little too smoothly maybe. I was far too comfortable, and still a long way from that 'London theayter'. It was good that my wife, though by nature home-loving, saw eye to eye with my professional ambitions, and each Wednesday morning

The Era took precedence over our daily paper. However, no favourable replies came to my applications for the vacant positions in larger places. I even tried using Auntie Lizzie's London address for my postal address, but that may have done more harm than good by raising the question of the reason for a London player to play in Workington. Nevertheless I did get a reply to one advertisement in *The Era*. This concerned the sale of an orchestral glockenspiel 'in excellent condition, £3'. I sent a money order to the address given and waited! I waited so long for the instrument that I stopped payment on the post-dated money order – post-dated on the advice of a friendly clerk in the Workington Post Office. Later I had a visit from a local policeman who told me that I was required in two days time at Dale Street Police Station, Liverpool, regarding a falsified money order. Hurried arrangements were made to cover my professional duties, as it would be necessary for me to spend a night in Liverpool. I reported at Dale Street in the morning and was told that due to a gun-running case holding up proceedings, my evidence would not be taken until early the following day. The official also told me that I could have a look round Liverpool at the Court's expense. A lot could be done in an afternoon in Liverpool: a visit to the docks for example, and on a matter of business a visit to C. & F. N. Black's office to make myself known to the people who booked orchestras for the liners and local theatres. I was received by Mr. Charles Black who immediately whisked me round to a nearby cinema where I took the drummer's place for about a quarter-of-an-hour. After this brief audition Mr. Black said he would contact me as soon as something came along. Later I gave my evidence in court which merely amounted to verifying that it was my signature on the money order which the scoundrel who advertised the glockenspiel had persuaded an unsuspecting tradesman to cash.

I did quite well out of that trip to Liverpool. In addition to receiving my rail fare, a night's lodging, and the cost of my deputy, I also received a telegram from Charlie Black offering me a job on the luxury liner SS *Majestic*. I decided to stay at the Oxford for several reasons, not the least being an offer from the management of a pound a week increase in my salary. I did not receive that increase for long, for shortly after I was told that due to the steady worsening of the depression and the consequent decline in business at the Oxford, the management was obliged to lower costs, and rather than reduce the orchestra, the players would be obliged to 'take a cut'. Disturbing news indeed, but I was optimistic. My wife and I had just spent our first summer holiday together in London, and though

I had heard some good drummers there, I felt that I compared favourably with the majority, especially after my first 'date' in the big city during that holiday. This engagement I obtained through Eric Little, who asked me if I played the xylophone as a friend of his required 'a chap to play a bit of xylophone on some gramophone records'. I took a chance and borrowed a xylophone from Besson's in Euston Road (from whom I had recently purchased a xylophone) and spent the following day in the recording studio at the Chenil Galleries, Chelsea, playing a few glissandoes on my instrument in place of the then customary cymbal solos in popular numbers. These glissandoes were a novel idea of the leader Eric Siday, who said he was amazed at the way I read the 'parts' at sight and gave me £6 for the day's work, plus the cost of hiring the xylophone.[5] I must add that those sessions in Chelsea ran into the early evening and that I arrived rather late at Drury Lane Theatre where my wife had already seen part of the first half of Showboat. My excitement about the day's work excused me, and I was able to enjoy hearing Paul Robeson sing 'Ole Man River', little thinking that I would one day sit with him in a canoe, with me made up as his black servant and accompanying him on a mouth-organ (in the film Sanders of the River).

The cut in salary at 'T'Oxford', my experience with Eric Siday in London, and the difficulties of trying to serve so many masters, convinced me of the necessity of a move. In any case with all due respect to 'Wukkinton' I could see no possibility of improving my position in the small town and it was clear that the next step must be to a larger place. I had not long to wait for the next step – possibly because I quoted, somewhat enlarged, my recent 'London experience' in my reply to an advertisement for a 'Drummer with full effects' for the Kinnaird Picture House, Dundee. Nathan Jones was most understanding when I gave in my notice. He had often pointed out the possibilities open to me, stressing his own mistake in staying too long in his home town. I said goodbye to this fine musician with the utmost regret, for he had been a constant source of help and inspiration to me.[6] A similar sad farewell was said to our first little house – but our loss was another man's gain. A young husband-to-

---

[5] Eric Siday, among other qualifications, was a superb violinist. He shortly emigrated to America where he achieved considerable success as a composer – in particular as a 'Jingle King'.

[6] In the written recommendation he gave to me he referred to me as a percussionist – a term not generally accepted in Britain, at least until many years later.

be purchased 20, Brown Street and the bulk of its contents for £250, and I gave my one luxury, a black retriever dog, to the milk-man just before handing over the keys of the house to its new owner.

Exit John Henry Wright, Percy Pegleg and the Barrow

A crisp morning in March saw my arrival in Workington; and a fine Sunday morning in August with my faithful entourage, in their Sunday best, saw my departure from that friendly, if stricken town. I travelled alone to Dundee, it being agreed that my wife would join me after the settling down period. My journey was by way of Carlisle and Edinburgh, and as the train rumbled over the 2,364 yards of the famous Tay Bridge, I felt less of a rumble in my tummy than when crossing the Tyne on my journey to Jarrow some three years earlier. Accommodation had been arranged for me with a delightful Scottish family, from whom I learned the history of the Kinnaird. I quickly settled in at the Kinnaird Picture House which was a large hall, a little less elaborate than T'Oxford, Workington, as it had originally been the rather sombre City Hall. Much of the original interior remained, including a large pipe organ. This was used for the second of the three daily performances in place of a relief piano. Whilst the use of an organ in a picture house was not uncommon, the playing of it in the Kinnaird had its individuality, for it was played by an elderly blind organist who sat listening through the Monday afternoon performance, and for the next per-formance repeated almost note for note the repertoire played for the films by the orchestra. This feat of memory was the more remark-able for the particular reason that Frank Hubble, my new musical director (who conducted from the piano), had a decided flair for 'close fitting'. He used the coloured light system for the various themes: blue for 'love', red for 'hurry' and so forth. In the dim light of the cinema the small coloured cue lights were clearly visible in the orchestra pit which was screened by a heavy curtain. Each member of the orchestra had two music stands, one for the 'book' and the other for the separate themes, the pages of which were arranged as far as possible to avoid turnovers. In explaining his colour routine, Frank Hubble made certain that I was familiar with the fact that a constantly flashing red light meant an immediate performance of 'Three Blind Mice', the tune accepted throughout the entire entertainment industry as a staff alert signal in the case of

suspected fire and similar emergencies.[7] My conductor also informed
me that he felt an afternoon audience would include one or two
local drummers who were anxious to hear what the 'new man from
England' was like! I hope I did not disappoint them.

At the end of my first week in Dundee I met another new man
from England: Frank Anderson. Frank, with true Lancashire per-
ception, found me at my digs – at the tea-table. He had not had tea
and was delighted to join me whilst explaining that his mission was
to learn 'the weight' of the drummers in Dundee and what might
be expected of him. I subsequently saw a lot of Frank and his wife,
particularly about tea-time on Sunday afternoons when they 'happened to be taking a stroll' in the Logie district of Dundee: the
northern suburb of the city where my wife and I had found a
rather pleasant flat. Other frequent visitors to our Logie flat were a
Mr. and Mrs. Thomson. Bill Thomson, though not a professional,
was, in addition to being a fine pipe band drummer, no mean ex-
ponent at the current jazz. Like me he had a good collection of jazz
records, and whilst the ladies talked fashion, Bill and I spent a
pleasant and profitable hour or so listening to 'Red Nichols and the
Five Pennies', 'The Charleston Chasers', 'The Clevelanders', 'The
Rollini Brothers' and similar groups of those late 'twenties.

Bill Thomson was typical of the several Scottish drummers whose
acquaintance I made. They were grand fellows and fine players. I
learned much from them and from one in particular: a man some
years my senior, by the name of Kenny Gibson, who, some weeks
after my arrival in Dundee, asked if I would tutor him. I agreed
to meet him on the following Sunday. My first request was to hear
him play. He started by playing a Scottish pipe drum solo. After
eight bars I stopped him and said, 'I'll take the first six lessons from
you.' Drum-major Kenny Gibson of the 1st Battalion Black Watch
introduced me to the true skirl of the pipes by arranging that I
played the drum in a marching band – a privilege granted (then at
least) to few Sassenachs. Life in Dundee was so pleasant that I was
soon in a quandary over an offer of another post: I received a letter
from my Jarrow employer, Mr. George Black, offering me 'The Grey
Street Picture House', Newcastle-upon-Tyne. After much thought I
decided to decline Mr. Black's offer and to my great pleasure I
received a reply to the effect that if ever I needed a change I was to
contact him.

[7] The Kinnaird was almost entirely destroyed by fire in January 1968. It
was then (as many theatres that I have known) a Bingo hall.

I go on the Air

My début on the radio was as a xylophone soloist with my repertoire of one or two tunes for the young, the programme being the
tea-time broadcast 'Children's Corner'. I have played to, and addressed
many thousands of children since that broadcast, and I have lost
most of the dread I experienced whilst waiting for the red light to
appear in that small Dundee studio.[8] I made several appearances in
that Children's Corner programme, the inclusive fee for each performance being one guinea ! This emolument helped to pay for a set
of xylophone bars tuned to the New Philharmonic pitch (then
A439) of the BBC studio piano. Though there was an increasing
adoption of low pitch, the Kinnaird (like my previous theatres) used
the Old Philharmonic high pitch (A452). Fortunately the 'caps'
which closed the resonating tubes on my xylophone were adjustable,
enabling me before each broadcast to lower the pitch of each tube
by slightly lengthening the air column and then sharpen the pitch
before the evening performance. To do this I took occasional advantage of the high pitch of the conductor's practice piano, and the
fine ear of our cornet player, Albert White. Sound waves of another
kind were attracting me: the 'wireless' which was a source of inspiration to me. Every night I rushed home from the Kinnaird to
juggle with my 'cat's whisker' set to get 2LO and the late-night
dance music of The Savoy Orpheans (under Reginald Batten) and
Fred Elizalde and his Music. In addition to the music from the
Savoy Hotel there were frequent broadcasts from Kettner's Restaurant featuring (if my memory serves me well) the Kettner Five
with Rudy Starita and his xylophone. Listening to those broadcasts
was a constant reminder of the big city, and needless to say I applied
for every London post advertised in *The Era*, but in spite of mention-
ing my 'regular appearances' on the air, nothing came my way,
and I remember that I unburdened myself in a letter to George H.
Way: the famous American drummer and Editor of *Leedy Drum
Topics* whose kindly reply concluded, 'keep working, keep trying –
the break will come and be prepared for it when it comes.'

I become an Organ Stop

The break was possibly on its way, but in the meantime Dundee was
keeping me fully employed: on one or two occasions in a rather unusual way. The Kinnaird was facing a problem. A rival cinema had

[8] All broadcasts were live in those days.

come bang up-to-date by enlarging the orchestra and installing a mighty Wurlitzer organ. This instrument with its innumerable gadgets, including a variety of percussion instruments, was hydraulically raised for the purpose of an intermission featuring the organist, who made the most of his solo spot by employing every conceivable effect on his instrument. We at the Kinnaird were certainly faced with a difficulty – but not for long. My employer, Mr. Victor Hamilton of 'Hamilton's Diorama' fame, came from a family of travelling showmen and was, to say the least, resourceful. At the Kinnaird he had made use of a lady vocalist to sing appropriate items at sentimental points in an epic film. We had also employed the recently-introduced Panatrope to amplify the gramophone records used at times as an intermission. (The Panatrope I remember to my cost, for when playing a xylophone solo at a special performance of the film The Better 'Ole, I tripped over the wire cabling, which so accelerated my stage entry that the audience might have expected a comic. They were not entirely disappointed, for whilst acknowledging the applause at the conclusion of my performance, I leaned slightly on my instrument which, to my mortification, collapsed like a pack of cards.) Mr. Hamilton first tackled the matter of the opposition's larger orchestra. Assisted by his son, his son's friend, a young man by the name of Fred Hartley[*] and to some extent by myself, three dummy musicians were placed at strategic points in the orchestra pit. These 'extra' musicians were concocted by mounting three tailor's dummies on broom handles and equipping each figure with a white dickie, butterfly collar and a black bow tie. As only a glimpse of the orchestra could be seen, and the live musicians obeyed Mr. Hamilton's instructions to play louder, an impression was gained of an augmented orchestra. The question of the intermission on the rival Wurlitzer organ was speedily resolved by what must surely have been a unique intermission by our blind organist on the completely modernised Kinnaird organ. The method of modernising this rather ancient City Hall organ was also unique. As the interior of the organ was quite spacious it was decided that I should become a series of organ stops; so a glockenspiel, a xylophone, a set of tubular bells and a bass drum (the latter for the storm in our organist's pièce de résistance the William Tell overture) were hidden with me in the bowels of the organ, where a lighting system had been assembled to enable me to synchronise with the soloist. Our blind organist – a great favourite at any time – made a tremendous

[*] Young Fred subsequently joined the staff of the BBC in London and formed the well-known Fred Hartley sextet.

show as he manipulated the numerous stops, and aided by my quite realistic storm effects and the solos on my xylophone, glockenspiel and chimes, the Kinnaird patrons were given a novelty, to their delight and possibly to the chagrin of our competitors. I joined the organist on occasions other than those intermissions. For epic films such as *Ben Hur* I put in the effects during the tea-time perform-ance: to strengthen dramatic moments. For example, in the memor-able chariot race in *Ben Hur* I played a continuous gallop rhythm on my timpani whilst rattling chains which were wound round my ankles. For these extra performances I received a bonus of two pounds. The week's money for *Ben Hur* I spent on an easy chair which I christened by engraving with a red-hot poker the hero's name on the back of the headpiece.

Ominous Whispers

By this time our Logie home had become very much of a Blades' household. Scotland had already attracted my brother Tom, who had moved to a cinema in Perth and was able to spend each weekend with Olive and me. My brother Chris had also crossed the border, having like us forsaken his trade to become a professional. Blades No. 3 with a little help from Blades No. 1 had found employment in a small cinema in Dundee (Shand's Picture House), and he partook of all that our Logie establishment had to offer at something less than he would have paid elsewhere. Needless to say a good deal of drumming and drum talk went on at weekends. Much of our con-versation centred around our future. There was of course an oc-casional clash of opinions. On one thing however we were in com-plete agreement: it must be London for us, and if possible in the dance game or 'show biz' – and for a very good reason. Rumour had it that there would soon be no work for cinema musicians. The words of that vaudeville artist who had told me some five years earlier that the screen would talk were beginning to ring true. Already in the U.S.A. recorded sound tracks had been incorporated in silent films, so why not recorded speech? Talking screens or not, my concern was that London theatre and I came precious near to getting it whilst on our 1928 summer holiday. On one or two oc-casions as my wife was checking the value of some of London's fashionable establishments, I spent some time in Archer Street, where I chanced to hear that a drummer would soon be needed at the Palace Theatre. I was able to see Sims Waller (the musical director) who auditioned me in the pit of the theatre. The music I played was from the current production of *Hit the Deck*. Sims said that he would contact me in due course. This he certainly did for I received a telegram from him instructing me to hold on to my present job. A letter followed explaining that whilst on holiday his brother (his superior) had heard and engaged a drummer.[10] Disappointing of course, but as George Way advised, 'keep trying, the break will come.'

My next audition came by way of invitation – due entirely to my being heard on the air – for I was asked to do a solo spot with Leslie Jeffries at the Fountainbridge Palais, Edinburgh. The Fountainbridge Palais was a famous dance hall and featured Sunday evening concerts. At one of these I played my party pieces: 'The Doll Dance' and 'The Wedding of the Painted Doll'. At the end of the concert Leslie Jeffries asked me if I was interested in a London job: the Piccadilly Hotel. Was I interested? I did my best to conceal my enthusiasm; shades of Uncle George's 'Eva, fetch me my diary' when he knew he had not a date in the book! High hopes again for me, but another disappointment, for though Leslie Jeffries had fully expected a move South to the Piccadilly Hotel, he did not secure this London 'plum' – though I *did* a year or two later. (Leslie Jeffries became internationally known through his constant broadcasts from the Grand Hotel, Eastbourne.) It seemed obvious that London would not come to me. There was only one thing to do. I must go to London. We had some money in the bank (about £300) and I had a good kit. I took the plunge and handed in my notice to my conductor. I wrote to Mr. Black who, among other interests in the South, was in control at the London Palladium, and within a few days I received a reply, 'You can start at the Hippodrome, Crouch End, at your earliest convenience.' Once again our household furniture was sold and in due course my wife and I, with one or two black trunks, rumbled over the Tay Bridge in a southerly direction. Did I worry about what to expect at Crouch End? Not altogether, because I was wondering if the person who had acquired the 'Ben Hur' chair had discovered its christening mark, which my wife had cunningly concealed beneath a mock velvet cover.

A *Step Higher*

My entry into London, or to be nearer the truth a northern suburb, was not heralded by a fanfare of brass, the laying down of red

[10] Jack Collings who became the percussionist at H.M.V. studios, and a member of the BBC Unit which included his own Rendezvous Players.

carpets, or a blaze of lights. No, I arrived on a rather wet Monday morning in September at Crouch End Hippodrome on a coal cart, the only available conveyance I could find. Though unusual, it was, if compared with the circus pole waggon and the Workington barrow, a small step up the social ladder. It was a step for which I was thankful, as my search at Crouch Hill Station for a suitable conveyance for my equipment had been fruitless, and on observing an empty coal cart draw into the siding, I hailed the driver, who readily agreed to dump my gear and myself at the 'Hip' for five bob. He further agreed en route that for an extra 'tanner' for a nosegay for the horse, he would help to carry the equipment into the theatre. Whilst I prepared for the afternoon performance, my wife sought accommodation: ideally a furnished bed sitter with use of gas stove and bathroom, known professionally as a 'combined chat'. She secured one for fifteen shillings a week in Hornsey. At the Hippodrome my new conductor (Walter Spencer) wasted no time with preliminaries. After a glance at my instruments and then at me he told me not to expect too much from him during the first perform-ance as he was auditioning pianists. Pianists was certainly correct. Into the orchestra pit they came and went – some surviving for several minutes, others for only a matter of a few bars. Mr. Spencer was finally satisfied with a player called Vic Filmer. He also seemed satisfied with me, and I left the theatre that evening quite pleased with my first day in London. I was further gratified by being hailed in the dim light of the exit passage by a stranger who, tapping me on the shoulder whispered, 'Are you the drummer my friend?' When I replied that I was, he then asked, 'What are they paying you?' 'Five pounds eight a week,' I replied. 'Give yer six paand at Clapton Rink', came the reply. Not bad going, I thought, for my first day in town, although in view of the circumstances I declined the offer. (I learned from my conductor that this 'snooping' for players was quite common in London.)

I soon discovered that Walter Spencer (himself a fine musician) had made a wise choice in Vic Filmer, who was considerably more than a brilliant pianist. He had various compositions to his credit, was a first-class arranger, quite a wit and, in addition to his quaint stammer, delightfully eccentric. His idiosyncrasies included a rigid economy, such as wearing boots with tremendously thick soles, and being acquainted with eating houses where he got the biggest help-ings for the least money. He very soon introduced me to the last-named, for on learning that I went to Lyons for my tea he suggested that I join him at his hotel – a local coffee stall where a kipper, two thick slices of toast and a large cup of tea could be obtained for sixpence. I joined him at his kerbside rendezvous and over a (truly excellent) meal, he unfolded to me a plan he had in mind for an intermission. Vic's plan struck me as quite an interesting one. It was that I should accompany him on the drums during his piano solo 'Kitten on the Keys', and he accompany me whilst I played a xylophone solo. Nothing unusual about either it may be said, but mine was to be no ordinary solo. Vic's idea was for me to play 'Annie Laurie' in ballad form and at an arranged point he, armed with a revolver, was to point the weapon at me whilst shouting, 'Stop! We want jazz'. We rehearsed and it was agreed to present our double act at the Hippodrome on the following Friday – Novelty Night. All went well until my being held at pistol point and then . . . silence! We had completely overlooked Vic's stammer which, due to the addition of stage-fright, rendered him completely dumb. I feel I saved a complete collapse by shouting, 'You want jazz' and breaking into the arranged jazz solo. Whether we were encored or not I cannot recollect, but I do remember that we were never approached to make a subsequent appearance! The failure of Vic and myself as a double act did nothing to disturb our friendship and I have only the most pleasant memories of this quite remarkable musician.

A further recollection I have of my short stay at Crouch End is of the dreadful *faux pas* I made by not playing the solo drum roll to open the National Anthem at an operatic performance given in the Crouch End Hippodrome by a local operatic society. To date I had been accustomed to playing 'The King', or to be precise a hurried version of the first eight bars of it at the conclusion of a performance, so I took the visiting conductor's sign to me as a cue to start the overture. The tense silence that followed my muffing a rather splendid moment remains with me, though not as one of my most treasured memories! What gives me pleasure, however, is the recollection of being called to the front office to speak on the 'phone to George Black who merely said, 'I've found a place for you in the West End – Holborn Empire. Start as soon as convenient arrangements can be made at Crouch End.'

❧ 9 ❧

A London Theatre

A London 'theayter' at last! Not quite as I had visualised, for the acme in my opinion was a super-cinema like the Tivoli in the Strand or The New Gallery. Not that I was ungrateful to Mr. Black (soon to be one of the biggest men in the world of entertainment), for at that time the Holborn Empire brooked no rival, and was considered by most of the variety artists to be an even better shopwindow than the London Palladium. In addition, the movies had already started to talk. In *The Jazz Singer* featuring Al Jolson, a few patches of dialogue and one or two of the songs had been recorded and experiments were in progress with synchronised musical scores. There were however many cinema musicians who were convinced that recorded sound would never catch on, and quoted such cinemas as the Stoll Picture House, Kingsway, The Empire, Leicester Square, and The New Gallery in Regent Street, where people went irrespective of what film was being shown just to hear the orchestra.

Financially I had not improved myself by moving to the Holborn: £4 4s. 0d. a week against £5 8s. 0d. at Crouch End. For my four guineas I did two shows a night, six nights a week, with a three-hour rehearsal each Monday morning. And what a nightmare I found those Monday rehearsals! Ten or more acts, at least half of them with an effects cue sheet as long as your arm, and a 'book' that had been several times round the world with music so covered with additions, obliterations, and individual markings that a chart for de-coding secret ciphers should have been included. Furthermore, I had not made a good start with my new director – Sam Richardson – because he had not been fully responsible for my appointment. In making himself known to me, he merely said that the Holborn was 'lightning variety' and that he hoped I 'knew the game'. The 'game' was to know the routine of every act from memory, and the 'book' so well that every attention could be given to the stage and the conductor's beat (incidentally seen from the side). I must admit that I found that first rehearsal tough going, mainly due to the dilapidated state of the books, the (to me) scant amount of rehearsal time, and the jugglers and the comedy acts wanting everything on their

111

cue sheet, plus a few 'extras' to strengthen a joke. These extras included a motor horn together with a ratchet to give an impression of their trousers splitting if they bent down, to which at night some would add an occasional feint to catch out the drummer in the hope of getting a cheap laugh. The conductor quite naturally wanted *his* pound of flesh, particularly at a change of tempo during a dance, at which point there was invariably a high kick, or similar effect required by the dancers. Small wonder that being more used to the screen with its unchanging action I was caught out on a number of occasions, allowing Mr. Richardson to tell me in the interval between the two performances on my first night that at least my 'timps' were in tune in the intermission – *Pique Dame* overture I remember (and what a joy to play this fine overture with that 14-piece orchestra, my largest orchestra up to that time).

Sam Richardson was known to all (affectionately or otherwise) as 'The Guv'nor'. Guv'nor was an ideal name for him. He was a man in middle age, heavily built, six feet tall, and was considered something of a bully. I soon learned that the harsh side of his nature was much of a disguise, for deep down he was a kindly man, and not without a touch of nervousness during the first house on Monday night. He was of the old school – and looked it when conducting in his high stiff collar and white gloves, the latter a boon to the orchestra in dim lighting. I found every member of the orchestra most friendly and ready to give me the benefit of long experience in the world of variety entertainment. One piece of advice they forgot to give me was never to beat the Guv'nor at solo whist which was played when the orchestra left the pit during a 'patter act'.[1] Whether by luck or judgment I cannot remember, but I made a mistake during my first week by 'pipping' Sammy's dead-cert abundance with a 'misere'. These card games, which were friendly – or for very small stakes – were played during such acts as Gillie Potter's (Lord Marshmallow of Hogsmorton) which called for only 'intro.' and 'tabs': in Gillie's case eight bars of 'He's a fine old English gentleman'. For this epic Gillie carefully handed out at rehearsal small scraps of manuscript, though for what was heard of the orchestra through the tremendous applause given at the entry and exit of this superb artist, half the band could have played 'The Irish Washerwoman' and the other 'The Dead March'![2]

[1] Such acts were timed and the intro. music marked 12 minutes safe, and so forth.
[2] Gillie was equally fastidious about the *return* of his band parts after the second performance on Saturday night.

My First London 'Gig'

I soon learned that several of the fourteen players in the Holborn orchestra were well acquainted with Archer Street and the mode of picking up a Sunday 'gig' as these occasional engagements are known to musicians. 'Go down the street on Saturday afternoon and look for my friend Dave Musikant,' Sam Belafonti, one of the violinists, advised me. By that instinct which seems to go with professionalism I found Dave Musikant with whom I booked a gig for the following evening – a Jewish wedding at the La Boheme Rooms in Mile End – a pound for the job, and 'five bob for the gear', straight music from 8 p.m. to 10 p.m. with dance music until 1 a.m. The 'straight' music consisted of one or two musical comedy selections and a stab at an orchestral arrangement of The Mikado. When this rather lengthy Gilbert and Sullivan selection had finally ground itself to a halt, the tenor saxophone player – who seemed delighted with his performance of the B flat cornet part (which incidentally had swamped the six-piece band), turned round to tell me that he couldn't see why people made a fuss about playing symphonic music. Something after 1 a.m. I staggered, laden with equipment, to the nearby Colborn Road Station to catch the 'printers' train' from Liverpool Street (we had left a rather crummy bedsitter in Hornsey to lodge with my Aunt Lizzie) and reached home at Manor Park after a walk of a mile or so with a heavy case and bass drum as my only company. A walk back to Manor Park on the following morning, with a taxi from Liverpool Street to the Holborn Empire, saw my instruments back into the pit. This hard going for twenty-five 'bob' merely whetted my appetite for more. I did several Jewish weddings for Dave Musikant, a number of Sunday night deputy jobs at Brick Lane Palace and other East End cinemas and occasional Sunday charity concerts at the London Hippodrome with the Guv'nor. These charity concerts were the longest shows I have ever experienced. In addition to the appearance of the few famous variety artists whose 'engagements permitting' had permitted their appearance, there were the numerous deputies and small timers who were anxious to give their services for the sake of the 'shop window'. These seemingly interminable concerts always concluded with a raffle at which numerous well-worn jokes were cracked, and the curtain finally came down with those of us who were awake in the orchestra playing 'The King' without the aid of the Guv'nor, who was taking refreshment for the umpteenth time with the powers-that-be; whether or not at the expense of the charity I never did discover. With those Sunday engagements and my salary at the Holborn my income amounted to a little under six pounds a week – though it must be remembered that at this time many weekly earnings were less than two-thirds of that figure.

The news of the West End engagement had caused great excitement at home, and my father and Uncle George lost no time in paying a visit to the Holborn. 'It's a dress job of course,' said Dad, and Uncle George certainly saw me in evening dress playing in a London theatre. Truth to tell, both had formed a considerably higher opinion of my London engagement than I had. It was already clear to me that the Holborn must be regarded as a means to an end, though, from the point of experience, it was of course proving an education. One of my greatest thrills was Jack Hylton's band. This magnificent show band virtually took the world by storm, and staying in the pit to listen to it and to watch Harry Robbins play the xylophone (with six hammers: three in each hand), convinced me that there was nothing like show business, and playing in a band like Hylton's. The weeks sped by and in no time it seemed I was calculating my wordly wealth to see if I could invest in a pair of the latest pedal-tuning timpani as a Christmas gift to myself.

Christmas 1928

I am not certain whether I had cold rabbit pie on Christmas morning 1928, or whether it was roast beef or turkey for dinner. I am certain however that my mind was not altogether centred on what was on the table. It was more concerned with the ultimate safe arrival of the pair of Leedy (American) pedal timpani I had placed on order, and with getting a certain beat on a cymbal in the correct place on the following (Boxing Day) afternoon.[3] A great deal depended on my executing this stroke correctly – not the least my reputation. This cymbal beat was in no way connected with my duties as the Holborn drummer. It was concerned with my position as timpanist in the orchestra engaged every Christmas season by Roger Quilter for the production of his *Where the Rainbow Ends* which played each afternoon for two weeks at the Holborn. To my surprise only one or two members of the Holborn orchestra were engaged for these matinées, and at the outset I was not among them. More surprisingly – or so it seemed to me as a provincial – I was expected to lend my instruments to the visiting timpanist. To this I took strong exception. Again I had the help of George Black, who supported my contention

[3] These drums cost £60. The 1977 price is £1,100.

that I should be given the opportunity of playing these matinée performances. It was eventually agreed that I should do the first rehearsal and that if I played the work satisfactorily I would be given the fortnight's run. At the rehearsal a friendly bassoonist kept me posted about certain traps in the score, and cued me for the important cymbal beat which synchronised with the appearance of a huge mushroom from below stage. I did a satisfactory rehearsal for Roger Quilter, which led to a pleasant fortnight among many of London's illustrious free-lance players who forgave my ignorance of their etiquette in robbing a reigning 'monarch' (Stanley Beckwith) of what for some years had been his perk. It was during that fortnight that I became fully aware of London's famous deputy system; never an afternoon passed without my seeing one or two new faces. The conductor, frequently Leslie Woodgate,[4] seemed in no way concerned with the changes in the personnel (a reminder of the story of the London conductor who was told at a dress rehearsal to have a good look at the orchestra as it was the last time he would see them all together!).

Playing in that superb orchestra under the baton of either Roger Quilter or Leslie Woodgate was a great experience, as indeed was the experience at the Holborn in general. I learned a lot at that lightning variety house, especially from such single acts as George Robey who could capture an audience with a lift of his eyebrows, or double acts such as Naughton and Gold or Nervo and Knox with their rollicking fun.[5] Another of my thrills was to hear and see Teddy Brown. My efforts as a xylophonist compared badly with the incredible technique and showmanship of Teddy who, beneath a veil of vaudeville showmanship, and his apparent indifference to all around him, performed remarkable things including the closing of the single stroke roll on a side drum which today is a speciality in the presentations of some of our most famous percussionists. Teddy Brown was not above showing me a few strokes. I was thus encouraged to peg away on my practice instruments which now had a corner in a small place of our own – the lower rooms of a furnished house in West Norwood. Here there was sufficient room to accommodate my brother Tom who, after a summer season with Percy Bush and his Band at Bridlington, was working in a silent Picture House at Camberwell. Another clear recollection of that Norwood

[4] He was for many years Chorus Master for the BBC.
[5] Unless I am mistaken the famous Crazy Gang was inspired by the unrehearsed merriment that took place on the Holborn Empire stage at this period.

home is preparing for, and giving an audition on the xylophone at the Savoy Hill studios of the BBC where I remember being hustled into a rehearsal room, given over to an accompanist who, no doubt an excellent pianist, was neither *au fait* nor interested in accompanying a xylophone solo. After my audition I was told that they would let me know – a phrase at that time interpreted in the profession as 'give us your 'phone number, we'll write to you!' I did not get immediate work with the BBC, but a drummer friend of mine gave a more successful audition and became so associated with the instrument that he also collected the majority of the xylophone work in London at the expense of losing out on the more lucrative work as a studio drummer much of which eventually came my way.

My failure with the BBC, though disappointing, did not damp my enthusiasm, or that of my brother's, for we were both steadily becoming known as good all-round men. Tom had in fact received an offer of a plum: Gerald Bright's Hotel Majestic Orchestra. (Gerald Bright, already well known from his broadcasts from the Majestic, St. Anne's-on-Sea, became the famous Geraldo.[6]) Tom chanced to hear that Debroy Somers (of Savoy Orpheans fame) was looking for a drummer who could do a 'spot on the xylophone'. Tom lost no time in letting Debroy Somers hear him play. He suited 'Bill' – as Debroy was known – and was soon installed as Tommy Blades in Somers' newly-formed stage band. Tom's good luck was to prove a good thing for me too. Why not a period at St. Anne's-on-Sea with a small orchestra with a big reputation? The sea air would do my wife and myself good, particularly as Olive was looking forward, as I was, to an increase in our family. Tom put me in touch with Gerald Bright who, with his brother Sydney, then playing at the Savoy Hotel, auditioned me by coming to the Holborn – fortunately giving me prior notice, leading me to play so quietly that Sammy Richardson concluded I was unwell. My discreet performance evidently proved to Gerald and Sydney Bright that I could do other things than play for variety, for on the understanding that I purchased a vibraphone – the current rage in light music – it was arranged that I made a start as soon as possible at the Hotel Majestic, St. Anne's-on-Sea, salary £7 weekly with all meals provided; certainly my best job to date.

Submitting my notice to Sammy Richardson proved no light matter. I prepared a polite note with my thanks which I handed to the Guv'nor at the first suitable opportunity. 'What's this,' he said,

[6] Geraldo died in Switzerland on 5th May 1974.

'a present?' I replied that it was my notice. 'Your notice,' Sam bellowed, 'what do you mean, your notice. No one ever gives notice at the Holborn – they always get it.' He followed this by suggesting (rather more kindly) that I should give my decision second thoughts, and also discuss the situation with the manager (Percy Adams) and himself at lunch time on the following day (pay day). We met by appointment at the Ship Tavern, in Little Turnstile (one of London's oldest inns, dating back to 1549). The Guv'nor and Mr. Adams – who was as chic in his lounge suit as he was in his evening top hat, white tie and tails – did their best to convince me that I was making a mistake in leaving the Holborn, using as one argument the fact that it was nearing Christmas and they knew that I was to be asked to play again for the *Where the Rainbow Ends* matinée season. 'You've a job here for life,' said Percy Adams, to which I replied, 'Mr. Adams, that's just why I'm leaving.' He immediately put out his hand and said, 'James, I think you're right – the best of luck to you.' Mr. Richardson also wished me well, and having previously collected the band's money he paid me out in advance and in full, as he did to everyone, which was not the case with every conductor in those days. 'The Guv'nor – Big Sam', the man with the reputation of being something of a bully, showed nearly as much emotion as I did when we parted until evening. The following fortnight was an active one for me, for though there was no furniture to dispose of or a black retriever dog to find a home for, there was plenty to do before labelling my equipment for St. Anne's-on-Sea via Preston, and making arrangements for a somewhat larger conveyance to Euston Station than a barrow, and if possible a more salubrious vehicle than a coal cart.

It seemed strange quitting the Holborn Empire to join a provincial hotel band. What lay ahead at the end of this train journey? A bedsitter (with use of kitchen) had been arranged for my wife and I in St. Anne's, with a lady named Pickup, who had hurried home from evening chapel to be at hand to greet us. Mrs. Pickup was very much of a religious turn of mind, and was delighted to learn that my wife and I were abstainers. The blight of her life she explained was strong drink. The 'blight' we were duly informed was 'Pickup', her husband, who regaled himself on chapel nights and certain other occasions with a pint of mild ale in company with a pack of dissolute friends who, according to Mrs. Pickup, gave no thought to the hereafter. Pickup turned out to be a small and very meek man (a postman), a most agreeable little fellow with a keen interest in music – military marches in particular. From his conversation I concluded that he was of the opinion that I had come to St. Anne's to play the big drum at the 'Majestic'.

I rose bright and early on my first morning in St. Anne's and, fighting a gale force wind from the Irish Sea, made my way to the Majestic Hotel to partake of the first of the 'all meals included' – in this case a sumptuous breakfast. All subsequent meals were equally good, and in addition, a packet of delicacies was provided for 'supper at home'. Orchestral duties began at 4 p.m. – a programme of light music to entertain those taking tea in the lounge. The orchestra of five players was led by Gerald Bright at the piano. The violinist was Joe Cuvillier, twenty-five years with Messrs. J. Lyons and Co. according to himself. Joe (a Belgian), though a fine musician, was nervous about his job, as he explained he was 'no chicken' and it was an era of young men of good appearance. Joe was also concerned (as were hundreds of others) over the possibility of mass unemployment due to the ever-increasing threat of the talkies. The other members of the orchestra were: a clarinetist, doubling sax, and a 'cellist doubling banjo and guitar. Although many pianists at this time also played the piano accordion, Gerald Bright had no reason to double, for he was in any case the biggest attraction in the North-West. Apart from being a remarkably good pianist, he was quite the most debonair leader I have ever played under. The audience at the Majestic – especially the packed houses at the week-ends – included a large number of young ladies. There were also spinsters of doubtful age; married women; husbands who were musically inclined and those who were not and whose sole occupation was to keep an eye on their better halves and the other on the handsome Romeo at the piano. After my first afternoon session, Gerry expressed his satisfaction with my work in his salon orchestra. The evening programme included a few concert items, followed by a short period of dancing. I played a 'straight' xylophone solo as a concert item, and a rhythmic piece called 'Rainbow Ripples' as a dance number. 'Rainbow Ripples' was a tricky piece for the xylophone and the piano (the only accompaniment). Gerry took a great fancy to this piece and trotted it out as a challenge to us both, and particularly to me when he knew I was swotting up a new solo and likely to get a ripple in 'Rainbow Ripples' that really belonged to the piece I was breaking-in. (He also took a somewhat ghoulish delight in pouncing on me to play the opening of *Tales from the Vienna Woods* on my newly acquired vibraphone, knowing full well that the double stopping (chords), combined with the pedalling system – similar to the damping pedal on the piano – gave me trouble.)

Much of the time during my first week at the Hotel Majestic
was spent in preparing for a cabaret show which Gerry had devised
for Boxing Night and New Year's Eve. Each member of the orchestra
was to provide an item of entertainment, and as my predecessor had
on such occasions been in the habit of obliging with a stunt, I was
expected to follow suit. Now, during my fourteen months at the
Holborn Empire, I had memorised much of the patter of my favourite
stars. So what better, I thought, than a short monologue from the
repertoire of that delightful London comedian Jack Barty, who invariably rushed on the stage saying, 'Coo – I've just had a bit of
luck – went in Lyons and found fruppence under the plate!' The
gist of Barty's monologue was that he had a pal named Jim whose
fate was hard to bear, and whose swearing so oppressed him he vowed
he wouldn't talk, so everything he wished to say he wrote it down
with chalk. Poor Jim finished up in an asylum writing swear words
on the brick walls and being chased by a warder with a sponge. The
custodian evidently lost the day for as onward Jim did plunge he
shouted, 'I'm a couple of damns and a blast in front and the warder's
lost his sponge.' My rendition of Jack Barty's monologue went down
very well as a cabaret piece, and so did my making myself up as
a coon and playing a solo on the 'bones' (a feat which Gerry never
failed to remind me of when I played the timpani for him in his
Concert Orchestra). The seasonal festivities over, I settled down to
a pleasant routine of life at the Hotel Majestic. To keep body and
soul together I partook of three excellent meals each day (served in
the courier's room of the hotel) with a snack before the afternoon
session. This snack consisted of a cup (possibly two) of the Hotel
Majestic tea (specially blended to suit the water of the district) which
helped down one or two slices of the richest fruit cake I have ever
eaten.

Musical activity was by no means confined to St. Anne's. In
nearby Blackpool there were permanent orchestras, the most important being Laddy Clarke's Orchestra which made regular broadcasts from the Imperial Hotel. I became friendly with the drummer
in this orchestra, a young man named Steve Whittaker, a player
destined to become one of the best known of the world's percussionists. (He became principal percussionist of the BBC Symphony
Orchestra, and later of the Philharmonia Orchestra.) Stephen Whittaker came from a family of musicians who, like himself, were connected with the Hallé Orchestra in the days of Sir Hamilton Harty.
I also made the acquaintance of a genial character who styled himself
't'owd man'. He was none other than the father of the famous Jack

Hylton. George Hylton, in addition to promising to mention my
name to his boy Jack – which he did – introduced me to many of the
local musicians and to several of the Hallé players, including that
superb bassoonist and wit Archie Camden, and a timpanist named
Sammy Geldard, who did not become as well known to the laymen
as he should have been for, in my opinion and many others, he had
no peer. Archie Camden and Sam Geldard were among the Hallé
musicians who formed the small orchestra which played on the pier
at St. Anne's-on-Sea during Easter week. It is no surprise that Sammy
Geldard was such a fine player: he came from a drumming family.
He also studied under the renowned William Gezink, a famous
Dutch timpanist who came to England to join the Hallé Orchestra.
Gezink went yearly to play the Wagner operas at Covent Garden.
Here his playing, particularly of the Funeral March from *Götter-
dämmerung*, has become legendary. Of Sammy Geldard, Gezink is
reputed to have said, 'The young man has outstripped the master.'[7]
Easter came and went and so did Whitsun, but with Whitsun came
something of a bombshell: the news from Gerald Bright that his
contract at the hotel was not to be renewed. To the best of recollection I was not greatly shaken by this piece of information. The
summer season was approaching and with it the possibility of a good
job at a notable seaside or other resort. Charlie O'Grady (the clarinet
and sax) had already received the offer of a fourteen-week contract
from a London band leader: Al Davison who was taking his
Claribel Band[8] to the Villa Marina, Douglas, Isle of Man. Al duly
came to St. Anne's. He took tea in the lounge during the afternoon
session, after which I was introduced to him. He asked if I was
interested in the season on the Island followed by a good chance of
a winter's work in London. Of course I was interested. Eight pounds
a week was offered, added to which Al Davison's pleasant and
cultured manner had made an immediate impression on me. It
transpired that Al was a Mus.Bac., a Cambridge organ scholar and
in every way a profound man. He was in his early forties, had a
tendency to flat feet, possessed a delightful stammer, and though he
confided to me at a later date that he had perfected a permanent hair
restorer) he had a pate as bald as that of a medieval monk's. He had
been bitten by the jazz bug in the early twenties, and coming from
wealthy and indulgent parents had been able to abandon his career
as a church organist and follow his fancy as a band leader. He had

[7] At the Hallé Orchestra's concert following Gezink's death in 1928,
the timpani were draped (as at a military funeral).
[8] Al's 'clear as a bell'.

just concluded a winter season at the Hotel Metropole in London, and was making plans for his second summer season at the Villa Marina, Douglas. Al's only stipulation as far as I was concerned was that I added a marimba (a large deep-toned xylophone) to my outfit. I agreed: it was an investment in any case, as instruments of this type were becoming a 'must' in any progressive drummer's kit. Gerald Bright was delighted that his boys were finding no problems, and the last couple of weeks went by pleasantly. Gerry and I had much in common and chatted a good deal about professional life. I remember a conversation we had during our last week. The boys had gone off the stand for coffee whilst Gerry and I played our usual solos. It was a quiet night and during a pause Gerry said, 'Jimmy, what I want to see is my name in red lights in London,' to which I replied that my desire was to break into the London circle and get into the recording studios. We both made it. The season on the Isle of Man was preceded by three days of rehearsals in London. I made the journey south on my own – my wife going north to her Cumberland home in preparation for a 'happy event'. I despatched my equipment by boat from Fleetwood to Douglas and hired a few instruments for the London rehearsals. On a point of economy I travelled to London by night coach from Blackpool; a hair-raising experience in those days and one that could be compared to crossing the Sahara in a jeep.

The Claribel Band made their way en bloc to the Villa Marina, arriving in great style, all uniformly dressed in double-breasted maroon blazers, grey slacks, and two-tone brown and white shoes. Musically the band was a strong outfit and equally at home with the concert programmes played at the afternoon and Sunday evening performances, and the strict dance playing required in the ballroom every weekday evening. The concert programmes included overtures, concert waltzes, selections and solos from the 'corner men'. The dance playing was 'Palais' style, and to say the least, a 'four-hour slog' – particularly for the rhythm section.[9] In addition to the band's two performances daily, Al called a minimum of two morning rehearsals each week – one to keep the band up to scratch and one or possibly more for the Sunday evening concert which was the high spot of the week. The Sunday evening programme included solos form our leader Johnnie Cantor, Fred Hartley (the young pianist I had met in Dundee), a well-known concert artist, and a xylophone solo from myself. Al occasionally played a solo. He was a fine pianist

[9] Current pops included *Among My Souvenirs* and *Shepherd of the Hills*.

and was (as far as I can recollect) one of the first British pianists to play Gershwin's *Rhapsody in Blue*. My xylophone solos proved popular items (in those days xylophone solos usually did) and it was not long before Mr. Noah Moore, the manager of the Villa, included my name on the bill. I also got as far as being advertised on the side of the horse-drawn tram cars that patrolled the sea front. This was all most encouraging, but it kept me busy on my mornings off preparing for my next appearances. But there was always Al with his kindly encouraging manner. He was one of those people who could get every ounce out of a player without seemingly drilling him. He was also a tremendous teacher without giving a sermon. As for jazz, he simply exuded it. His contention was that if you can clap your hands quietly on the beat, and drop your knees on the off beat you can play jazz. He often gave me a session on chordal progressions: C, G7, C, G7, F, F7, B flat and so forth. 'Now fritter around in A flat on the vibraphone as I play "Dinah",' he would say, and away we would go on a busking session until our empty tummies reminded us of lunch time. To be correct I should say *my* empty tummy, for Al had little or no appetite, and would often pause in one of our many conversation to glance at his watch and say, 'James [it was always James], it's five hours since I obliged my tummy, my gold hunter tells me, so time to do something about it.'

During my first few weeks on the Island I was in constant touch with the mainland where my wife was in a nursing home in Workington. On 27th June I received a telegram: 'Congratulations – a boy. Both doing well.' In due course my family joined me in the furnished house I had rented for the season (at thirty shillings a week). My boy was christened on the Island and we avoided any possible family upset by naming him Douglas Hewitt. The baby thrived. So did I, on Manx lamb and green peas, with fish straight from the harbour by way of a change. Al did well too. He developed a liking for my wife's coffee and made a point of seeing me home most evenings, usually pausing at the corner of the street to say that he really should let me have an early night – 'but well, just one cup of your wife's delightful coffee and home to bed'. After the coffee Olive retired and then in spite of his promise of an early night Al would often keep me up as a fascinated listener to his tremendous flow of words and wit. He was a scholar, with all the polish of a University education, and in every way a most remarkable man. He had spent his spare time during the previous winter studying life insurance at the Sun Life Assurance Company's office in London,

and though he had no need of the money, was doing quite well selling life policies. He sold me one the day my son was born, and I
have never regretted taking out that policy on my son's life.

Al had some amazing theories: one concerned the 'yellow peril'.
Al's plan to deal with any possible menace from the East was
interesting to say the least. 'You know James', he said to me one
night, 'I could deal effectively with this yellow peril business and
enrich the world at the same time. Under the Ural Mountains there
is treasure beyond words – diamonds, gold, silver, precious stones and
rare metals, but they are locked away under impregnable masses of
ice, snow, and great rocks. But,' Al continued, 'I have a theory. If
the greatest cannon ever to be built could be exploded in the centre
of China it would, I am sure, turn the earth on its axis and in so
doing bring the Urals under the extreme heat of a tropical
sun. This would reveal and make accessible treasure untold. But,
you may ask, what of the millions of Asians who would be blown to
smithereens? No worry at all, for according to my calculations they
would fall on the Sahara Desert and fertilise it.' As a change of subject he would talk about Bach or 'Red' Nichols, or possibly Paul
Whiteman ('the king of jazz') and then with a glance at his watch
say, 'Good night, James, time for bo-bo.' So off went this remarkable
man puffing at a cigarette in an extremely long holder – 'to save
the peepers, James'. Back at his hotel he probably spent most of what
was left of the night pursuing some theory or other, or devising a
way of presenting a particular musical item in a novel way, though
not as novel as the way he presented the overture *Robespierre* on one
occasion – and one occasion only – for the guillotine that he had
assembled to typify the fateful drop of the knife almost severed the
arm of the stage hand who operated the drop handle. Another idea
of Al's, considerably less dangerous, was his method of amplifying
the instruments of the dance band. Each instrument had a microphone attached to it. The mikes were cunningly hidden or disguised
and were controlled individually from a main panel which Al
adjusted to suit conditions in the large ballroom, where the shuffle
of hundreds of feet could at times render a moderate-sized band
almost inaudible. The system was a brilliant piece of work for other
reasons, for however forte the brass were playing, instruments like
the violins were clearly audible. (Are the pop groups of today in-
novators?) There was no doubt about Al's popularity at the Villa,
though we were not without opposition. At the Palace, a rather
quieter type of establishment than the Villa Marina in certain
respects, there was an equally famous band under the baton of

Harry Wood (the brother of Haydn Wood of *Roses of Picardy* fame).
Wood's band – or orchestra I should really say – was composed
chiefly of Hallé men, and quite naturally was a quality orchestra.
Whilst we at the Villa excelled in our own style, Wood's orchestra
excelled in waltzes, Old Time, etc. What is more they had two
drummers, and what drummers they were: Sammy Geldard and
Steve Whittaker – a formidable duo if ever there was. My wife (when
she could get a baby sitter) sometimes spent an evening with friends
at the Palace, and she rarely failed to tell me of the beauty of
Wood's orchestra and how well they played her favourite music (the
waltz), and what fine performers Sam and Steve were. Sam and Steve,
however, used to hear from *their* wives about the drummer at the
Villa. Sam and Steve occasionally met me at the Villa after my
morning rehearsal. They had only one rehearsal a week – Sunday
morning – and worked only in the evenings. As a token of their
consolation for my marathon existence, I was taken to the Villiers
Hotel and over a pint of wallop (Sam and Steve – mine a ginger
beer shandy), I was told of the glories of the Island and how well a
kip for a couple of hours after lunch prepared one for the evening.
We of course discussed drumheads, xylophone solos, our respective
ambitions, and our immediate future, but ambitious as we were, not
one of us dreamed that we would really go places: Sam to be told
by Sir Hamilton Harty (the Hallé conductor) on his return from a
world tour that nowhere had he heard his expertise excelled. Steve
to be congratulated by Toscanini who halted the BBC Symphony
Orchestra to remark on his remarkable sight-reading on the glockenspiel; and myself? – but that would be jumping the gun. What we
did not know (and thank God for it) was that one of the trio was to
die too young.

Those days on the Isle of Man were pleasant days, even if (for me)
they were hectic days. My spare time, such as it was, was given to
home life, and it was a thrill to see young D.H.B. growing brown
and sturdy. But it was time to get down to sorting out something
for the winter. Al had one or two irons in the fire, but nothing
definite. His advice to us all was to fix up if possible, but to keep
in touch with him on our return to London. Word came my way
that the musical director, Mr. Ernest Grimshaw, of the P.C.T.
(Provincial Cinematograph Theatres) was looking for players 'of
good appearance and with stage experience'. Yes, with *stage* experience. The 'screen was talking' and the crash had come for thousands
of first-class musicians: those magnificent cinema orchestras had
been ruthlessly dispensed with in favour of the so-called canned

music.[10] However, a few organisations, such as the P.C.T., were considering supplementing the early talkies programme with a stage band interlude. The P.C.T. circuit was quite a big concern with several places in London including the New Gallery Cinema in Regent Street (the first cinema theatre to be wired for sound). I wrote to Mr. Grimshaw at his Regent Street office, and in reply received an offer of a six-months contract at £8 a week to play as a drummer and xylophone soloist, three performances daily, in any of the stage bands he was then forming for his company. My first few weeks were to be spent at the Finsbury Park Rink Cinema, with the option on Mr. Grimshaw's part to move me around as he desired. I accepted Mr. Grimshaw's offer and began to make the necessary plans for my next move. Fixing accommodation in London was then no problem, as all that was necessary was to decide on a district and answer any advertisement in *Dalton's Weekly* that looked interesting. There were plenty of bed sitters with use of kitchen and bathroom in the Finsbury Park area, and I rented a place near the Rink Cinema. It turned out as advertised : a large combined room – quite the largest and coldest I have ever lived in – and use of kitchen and bathroom, the latter if ever it was unoccupied.

The time came to quit the Isle of Man, which in many respects most of the band were sorry to leave. Apart from a few trifling squabbles (mostly domestic) all had gone spendidly. To the best of my memory Al Davison met with only one problem : the replacement at short notice of Fred Hartley, the pianist who, two weeks before the end of the season, asked leave to take up an appointment at the BBC. Al replaced Fred with another fine pianist who also became well known as a broadcaster : Sidney Davey who, in addition to having his own combination on the air (Sidney Davey and his Players), was for many years the pianist, and later director, of Harry Davidson's 'Old Time' Dance Band ('Those were the Days'). The Claribel Band left Douglas, I.O.M. *en bloc*, on a Sunday morning, and a foul morning it was as we boarded the Isle of Man Steam Packet boat for Liverpool. I wrapped D.H.B.'s cot and his linen in an old macintosh which made the bundle look like a corpse. This, together with one or two personal cases and my professional equipment, gave the Blades family the appearance of a travelling circus ! After one of the worst crossings in the history of the I.O.M. Steam Packet

[10] My brothers (like me) escaped this débâcle: Tom being nicely placed in Debroy Somers' Band, and Chris quite secure with a resident dance band in Weymouth. Blades No. 4 (Cecil) had entered the coal business, but continued with his drumming as a remunerative hobby.

Company, we reached Liverpool and finally Euston. These two interesting journeys – through the second of which the baby slept in the comfortable luggage rack above our heads – were followed by piloting D.H.B., the personal cases and the 'corpse' to our bed sitter at Finsbury Park. (I had made arrangements for my 3½ cwt. of equipment to be delivered to the Rink Cinema by a firm which specialised in theatrical transport – O'Leary's.) The following day witnessed my second onslaught on the big city, this time on the stage instead of in the pit; a step up if only in altitude, and the fact that a photograph of myself at the xylophone was displayed at the front of the theatre. The conductor – Van Dam – who, like Sammy Richardson, may have felt peeved at not being directly responsible for my appointment, coolly informed me that he did not want a xylophone solo in the week's programme. As my contract was as drummer and xylophonist I felt justified in pressing my case. Solo playing was a 'shop window' and I was anxious to sell my wares. Van eventually agreed to let me play one solo, but to gain his point, with piano accompaniment only *and* while he was off stage preparing his own violin solo. From what I remember we broke even on a matter of applause; a situation not entirely without problems, and a little depressing – though there was no time to be depressed, for after the tea-time performance I was met at the stage door by Al Davison. He told me he had fixed a six months' contract for the Claribel Band at the Carlton Cinema, Essex Road; three shows daily, 'doubling' two shows at a small cinema in Walthamstow. 'Hard work,' admitted Al, 'but every penny of ten pounds a week, with extra pay for Sunday concerts.' Al soon made it clear that he had not come to Finsbury Park merely to inform me of his good fortune. To join Al, however, presented me with as big a problem as trying to under play or over play Van Dam. After much discussion Al and I agreed that to cook up a dispute with my new conductor would be dishonest, and that a direct approach for Mr. Grimshaw's help was the only sane move. A telephone call early the following morning secured me an immediate appointment (at the Regent Street office) with the formidable Mr. Grimshaw, a smallish man with the reputation of being a martinet, and with a bark it transpired much worse than his bite. I made no immediate mention of the slight friction that had arisen between Van Dam and myself, but asked him outright if in view of the splendid offer made to me by Al Davison I could be released from my contract. Mr Grimshaw replied by saying that he had already been made aware of conditions at the Rink and that he was planning to move me to New Cross Empire. 'Now,' said Mr. Grimshaw addressing me in a stern voice, 'if you had come to me with some cock-and-bull story instead of the truth, I would have shown you your contract *and* the door! As it is,' he said, 'you can finish on Saturday week if it suits you.' Mr. Grimshaw's arrangement certainly suited me and my two weeks at the Finsbury Park Rink with Van Dam passed quickly and not at all unpleasantly.

A Job of Work

Al made certain of a good start at 'The Carlton' by choosing items that had proved dead certs at the Villa Marina. My spot was a solo featuring the xylophone and the marimba: both favourite instruments with Al and me. All went well at the first performance, and afterwards the whole band (fourteen players) tumbled into a coach and we were rushed to Walthamstow. Then back to Essex Road for the 5 p.m. performance, off again to Walthamstow and back to the Carlton for the final show of the day. (I arranged to keep a duplicate set of instruments at Walthamstow for which Al reimbursed me.) The four coach journeys each day were by no means dull affairs. The Claribel Band were a jolly lot and most of the time was spent in friendly banter; including current professional chat from Archer Street, and from the bachelors' tales of conquests with the fair sex – though if my memory serves me well, one or two of the married chaps could have recounted an escapade or two. The Claribel Band was a great success, and it needed to be, for we followed a fine stage band led by a real showman – Jan Ralfini. Jan had left the Carlton to take over a large suburban palais, although he retained an interest in the Carlton to the extent of giving a concert there every Sunday evening. Ralfini's drummer was a fine player but no xylophonist, so whenever possible I joined Ralfini's band on Sundays. As luck would have it Jan Ralfini had just started to record for Sterno records; in fact his Sunday evening programmes at the Carlton included 'flogging' the items to be recorded at any forthcoming recording session. My xylophone snippets were often included in Ralfini's discs, and by the following late spring when the Claribel Band were due again at the Villa Marina, Douglas, I was becoming known as a 'session man'.

My second season at Douglas went very much the same as that of the previous year. Rehearsals, concerts, and the work in the ballroom kept me well employed. In addition Al left much of the band management to me. Sam Geldard and Steve Whittaker were again with Harry Wood at the Palace. I occasionally joined them in a walk to the famous ginger beer house a few miles from Douglas, and we visited the famous Laxey Wheel, the Lady Isabella, said to be the largest wheel in the world, which with its three 'legs' was as typically Manx as was the novelist Hall Caine, or 'Kelly from the Isle of Man' – the song associated with that reigning music hall star and doyen of pantomime 'boys', Florrie Forde. Those morning strolls with Sam and Steve were the more pleasant for their rarity. One incident which was not so pleasant for many of those concerned, though at the time not without its humour, involved the Claribel Band and a large audience at the Villa Marina Sunday concert. Before the final item Al gave me the sign to play the solo roll to open the National Anthem. His signal was so direct that I concluded he had a valid reason for omitting the last piece on the programme, and the National Anthem was played, resulting in half the audience (those in the gallery included) making for the exit doors. The other half remained, hoping for their money's worth, during which time the manager had made his way to the front of the stage to question Al. It was eventually agreed that the final item be played, the sound of which prompted most of those who were going out to return to their seats; but in doing so they collided with a large crowd who had tired of waiting. The resulting confusion needs no description.

Mid-Sepember 1931 saw the exodus from Douglas, I.O.M. of a rather excited Claribel Band. We were bound for London, and due to make an immediate start at the Dominion Theatre, Tottenham Court Road, in a stage presentation featuring Jeannette Macdonald singing hits from *The Love Parade* – the film in which she made her début (co-starring with Maurice Chevalier). Only a six weeks contract, but really the West End. Things could happen in the next few weeks, I felt, and they did – and not solely connected with the profession of music. One activity in which I became involved was certainly far removed from music: I became Al's assistant in his manufacture of and marketing 'The A.D. infallible cure for baldness'. The scene of our labour in the preparation of Al's hair restorer was the back room of his flat in Store Street. This lower ground floor flat, which was only a stone's throw from Oxford Street, was Al's 'town house', and where he was occasionally visited by an auburn-haired lady friend of his own age and cultural inclinations. 'The A.D. infallible cure for baldness' consisted of a mixture of white vaseline and perfume, to which were added certain secret ingredients. The processing was done by Al who robed himself for the occasion in a surgical gown. For reasons best known to himself, Al concealed his own baldness (which had failed to react to a series of experiments with his discovery) beneath a gaily-coloured turban. My job was to pot the mixture in small milky-coloured glass jars and affix printed labels giving the directions for use and the virtues of this remarkable hair restorer. Al advertised his product (half-a-crown a pot including postage) in *Answers* – a weekly journal with a large circulation. Did we sell the stuff? I should say we did. After one insertion of the advertisement we were flooded out with postal orders. We despatched the first five hundred jars and ordered another batch of pots and labels. Enquiries continued to pour in, one, I well remember, from China. After the despatch of the second five hundred jars, both Al and I were obliged to admit defeat. It was either music or hair restorer, and music won and we both spent a lot of our precious time in returning the postal orders with an apology.

Busy as I was I found time to visit my friend Eric Little at The Premier Drum Company's showroom, and a good thing for me that I did. On one of my visits he told me that on the previous evening he had deputised for Rudy Starita in Jerry Hoey's band at the Piccadilly Hotel, and that Jerry was looking for a drummer to replace Rudy. I contacted Jerry Hoey immediately. His first question was, 'Do you play the vibraphone?' I said that I did, and he arranged to hear my 'solo spot' at the Dominion and to meet me afterwards. 'Sounded good to me,' Jerry said, 'but I must hear you at the hotel.' I played my party pieces (including 'Sally' on the vibraphone) in the quiet of a mid-afternoon in the Piccadilly Grill, and, unbeknown to me, gave an audition to the entertainments manager of the Piccadilly Hotel (Colonel Elwyn Jones) who had hidden himself behind a screen at the far end of the room. I was introduced to the Colonel, and over a cup of delicious tea served from a silver pot I was offered the job at the 'Pic': £12 a week to start, and to join the band as soon as possible. This was no problem, as the Claribel Band was approaching the end of its run at the Dominion and my friend Al was almost as excited as I was over my good fortune. Twelve pounds a week, evenings only, in a West End Hotel – and a super one at that.[11]

[11] Al quickly found an engagement for his Claribel Band. He engaged as his drummer an already well-known player – Jack Simpson. Jack was a fine drummer and an expert xylophonist, and subsequently became well known as a composer of xylophone solos. These include: 'On the Track'; 'On another Track': and 'Jet Propelled'. Jack became one of my closest colleagues and friends.

The Break

If getting into the West End signified being in the heart of London Town I was there – the Piccadilly Grill room being not more than 200 yards from the famous Eros. Jerry Hoey's band was already an institution at the Piccadilly Hotel. Jerry, who had worked for Jack Hylton, knew what the customers wanted: tuneful music, played with a lilt, and no playing for musicians. It was evidently the management's maxim also for, just before I joined Jerry, he had been asked to admonish his violinist (Benny Frankel) who had dared to play a 'hot' chorus whilst Jerry was off the stand. 'Tell him to do his practising at home, or he'll have to go', the manager (Mr. St. Jacoby) said.[1]

Jerry's motto, which was evidently paying a dividend, suited me admirably, and my style evidently suited Jerry, for after a few nights at the hotel he clinched my appointment and so began one of the longest and certainly one of the happiest episodes in my professional career. Not the most leisurely by any means if compared with certain other hotels, for unlike the 10 p.m. until 2 a.m. six nights a week at the Savoy, we in the Piccadilly Grill played 9 p.m. to 2 a.m. week nights, 8.30 to midnight on Sunday and for the weekend tea dance. Getting home in the small hours was no problem, other than waking up the baby in the region of 3 a.m. Transport was easy in those days, with plenty of all-night trams and buses, though to become a genuine West-Ender I invested in a car – a slightly-used Rover 9 costing £75, including tax and insurance. I had no parking problems (day or night), my season ticket at Lex Garage in Brewer Street costing six shillings per week (for anything from an Austin 7 to a Rolls Royce and a mechanic on duty day and night). On two or three nights a week (or to be correct early mornings) I arrived home with the milk, since to be in the fashion I joined the 'Lyons Corner House Brigade' and went from the hotel to Lyons Corner House in Coventry Street (then open all night) to talk shop over coffee and porridge. Here I met most of the leading dance drummers,

[1] Benny went, but of his own accord. He subsequently (as Benjamin Frankel of course) became one of Britain's most illustrious composers.

among them characters like 'Jack the Yank' or the redoubtable Alec
Cripps, who got the sack for pushing the Savoy hotel's best customer
into the forecourt fountain.[2]

On occasions a quick cup of Lyons coffee was followed by a visit
to such establishments as The Bag of Nails or The Hambone (night-
clubs), or the similarly late-closing Café de Paris. The bands in these
places were always interesting, particularly the resident band at the
Café de Paris – Teddy Brown's. Teddy was a great attraction, and
he certainly remained a constant inspiration to me. He did some remarkable things on the xylophone, and more remarkable if he sensed
the challenge of visiting 'pros', when he would play the 'evergreens'
('Dinah' for example) in any key requested. Once I saw him turn the
xylophone round and play the instrument back to front. Now, the
xylophone is an instrument that a lot of people find difficult enough
to play in the correct position, myself included, but I was obliged
on one occasion to tackle it in reverse, and those of you who are
acquainted with the pianoforte keyboard might try lying on the
top of an upright piano and playing 'Pop goes the Weasel' with a
drumstick, as I was obliged to do for a film called *The Magic Marble*.
(The shaft of the drumstick was specially treated so that only the
marble fitted on the end was visible.) I did a lot of things in the film
studios besides playing the xylophone lying on top of the piano, for
shortly after joining Jerry Hoey at the Piccadilly Hotel I heard – by
way of musicians' 'bush telegraph' – that a drummer was wanted
for Louis Levy's house band at the newly-built film studios
(Gaumont-British) in Shepherd's Bush.[3]

I lost no time in contacting Louis Levy's factotum (Emile Nacmanson), and it was arranged that I make a start on the following
Friday morning at the Gainsborough Studios, Islington, to be followed by the main studio ('The Bush') the following week to work
on the film *The Midshipmaid*, which featured Jessie Matthews. The
Friday morning session at the Gainsborough Studios consisted of
recording music for the Gaumont 'Mirror' and 'Gazette', and here I
met Louis Levy's second-in-command, Charles Williams, composer
of, among other successes, 'The Dream of Olwen'. Following Emile's
instructions I arrived in good time to assemble a prodigious array of
equipment. On observing my 'batterie' Mr. Williams said somewhat
caustically, 'Ah, I see we have a virtuoso with us this morning', to
which I replied, 'You'll be a better judge of that at the end of the

[2] Alec became Mrs. Meyrick's drummer at her famous and equally
notorious '43 Club' (43 Gerrard Street).
[3] Now the BBC's Lime Grove Studios.

session.' He shook hands with me and said, 'We're going to be friends – if you can play.' We became friends. After my first day at Shepherd's Bush with maestro Louis, he was similarly abrupt, saying as he towered above me (he topped my 5 feet 3 inches by half-an-inch), 'Well, you're not much to look at, but you can certainly play the drums!' So commenced another pleasant episode in my professional adventure, also a lengthy one, for I played for Louis Levy without a break for 27½ years. From 9 p.m. to 2 a.m. at the Piccadilly Hotel and from 10 a.m. onwards at least four days a week in the film studios; it may well be asked: how did I manage it? Working up to eighteen hours a day with little more than four to five hours sleep did not worry me; so many men have worked harder and slept less.

My biggest problem was fitting in one job with the other, for the sessions in the film studios were rarely guaranteed to finish at a certain time. The call quite often was 9 a.m. for make up, followed by a day on the set, or 10 a.m. until 5 p.m. (or later) in the 'post-sync' theatre, where background music for the finished film and sound tracks for the set were recorded.[4] These sessions on the set and in the studio would often run late, on occasions until midnight, or, as on one notable session recording a tricky sequence with Jack Hulbert for the film *The Camels are Coming*, from 10 a.m. until breakfast time the following morning (still with somewhat negative results). Though my previous experience in Workington and elsewhere had almost taught me how to cut myself in half, to be in two places at once was quite beyond me. I was not overtaken by disaster for several reasons – chiefly the co-operation of Jerry and Colonel Jones at the Piccadilly,[5] and a comfortable mind due to the fact that my wife and son were snug in a house of our own in Mitcham. Our Framfield Road home had many advantages: it was backed by a large open green which made an ideal run for young Douglas; it was within easy reach of the shops, the Underground, an all-night tram route,

[4] The call, 10 a.m. until 5, Emile Nacmanson abbreviated 'ten to five' until one new man failed to arrive at 10 a.m. thinking the call was 'ten minutes to five'. Emile who, in addition to fixing for Louis, played the double bass in his house orchestra, eventually made punctuality more certain by adopting his famous 'quarter to ten for ten', a phrase almost as well known as his saying at the conclusion of a session: 'one more and one less'.

[5] I also had a friendly arrangement with Gibilaro, the pianist in Leonardo Kemp's Salon Orchestra which the dance band relieved at 9 p.m. Gibilaro – known to his brother-in-law John Barbirolli and of course Evelyn Rothwell as 'Fof' (Alphonse) – would prelude a little if I was a minute or two late. (Leonardo Kemp succeeded de Groot.)

and equally important, it was on the telephone. I prided myself on the manner of acquiring this Mitcham house, having bought it off my own bat as a surprise for Olive on her return from a holiday with her father, who was continuing to support his political party by giving the Workington Conservative Club his constant custom. I also prided myself on striking something of a bargain by getting £50 off the original quote of £625. The vendor, however, was perfectly satisfied, having increased her price when she learned that I I was a West End musican. At the same time, having quickly assessed my knowledge of household matters, she persuaded me to purchase a few trifles in the way of fitted carpets, and one or two pieces of 'antique' furniture, which included an ancient electric cooker.

In addition to the work in the studio and the hotel, I deputised for my predecessor Rudy Starita at such gramophone recording studios as H.M.V. and Decca. I also played at H.M.V. for George-Scott-Wood, one of their permanent conductors. George was the pianist at the 'Pic' for a short time, taking over from Bill Thorburn. After George left the hotel to give his whole time to the studios, Jerry engaged a 'young man' by the name of Tommy Hinsby. I say a 'young man' because Tommy was several years senior to us all, but did not look it, in fact he so retained his youthful appearance that on reaching the age of 65 and applying for the old age pension he was obliged to return to his native town of Nottingham to get a church dignitary to qualify his birth certificate. (Tommy's father designed the famous Boots name plate trademark.)

Life at the Piccadilly

The Piccadilly Grill was certainly a place to meet the great. Our regulars included leading lights in the entertainment and sporting world (the leading jockeys included) and such film stars as Charles Laughton. One great favourite with the band was George Robey, who occasionally brought in a violin which he had made. He usually left the instrument for a week or two with 'Tich' Poster (the violin and tenor sax who had replaced Benny Frankel). As well as violin makers we numbered among our pet customers some violin players and famous ones at that, as for example Fritz Kreisler, to whom I was introduced. He kindly autographed my drumhead, and I remember him saying, as his pen slipped on the drumhead, 'Ah it is a good skin, it's alive – like a good fiddle string'. (See Plate 19). Other well-

known musicians included Pouishnoff – the concert pianist who was internationally known for his Chopin recitals – and Charlie Kunz.
Pouishnoff was quite friendly with the band, particularly with Tommy
Hinsby, whom he occasionally allowed a respite by playing a waltz
for him. I was not permitted a similar relaxation, for Pouishnoff
insisted that I accompany him – possibly to check his natural urge
to play *rubato*. There was no need to check any *rubato* on the part
of Charlie Kunz if he gave Tommy a break. Here was a strict tempo
pianist if ever there was, and never a better loved man into the bargain. Charlie, who had his band at the *Chez Henri*, dined and danced
at the 'Pic' on an occasional Sunday evening, usually in company
with his wife Ninette and her sister Trudy (Mrs. Jerry Hoey). On
the Sunday evening I first met Charlie, Jerry delayed introducing
me to him until I had played the then-popular Heykens' *Serenade*
as a vibraphone solo. This piece, played as a waltz, had made a great
hit with the Piccadilly clientele. Charlie's first words to me after
a friendly handshake were, 'Are there any more at home like you?'
It so happened that there was another at home like me: my brother
Tom who, after a year or two with Debroy Somers (a good part of
the time on tour) felt the need for settling down in Town. It was
not long before Tommy let Charlie Kunz hear *him* play Heykens'
Serenade on the vibraphone. Within a few weeks he was settled in
with Charlie at the *Chez Henri* and moved with him to the Casani
Club. The broadcasts from this élite club (founded by a renowned
ballroom dancer, Santos Casani, and Charlie Kunz) became famous,
as did Charlie himself and his well-known tune 'Clap hands – here
comes Charlie'. In saying that Charlie Kunz was a darling of a man
I do not exaggerate. He was kindness itself, typified for example in
his annual Christmas tree which was loaded with presents for his
wide circle of friends. It was traditional to collect the presents on
Christmas morning, and always by the side of my gift was one for
'the Blades Boys'' father. To some extent I was considered one of
Charlie's 'boys', for on a few occasions Tommy and I played a
marimba duet on Charlie's broadcasts, which resulted in a friend of
my father's informing him that he had heard his two boys 'de-
nounced on the radiograph'.

Happy memories – and none more vivid than the occasion of
Charlie Kunz's début as a solo pianist at the Alhambra, and how
Jerry and I escorted him – a bundle of nerves – from his dressing
room to the stage, and in spite of his attempts to abandon the project,
pushed him on to the stage as the 'tabs' opened! He was a tremendous success from the first chord he played and remained so

until his death in 1958. Due to my brother's absence abroad I played
in Charlie's rhythm trio (string bass, guitar and drums) on one of his
final batch of Decca recordings which, because of his frail state of
health, were recorded in short sequences. He was the only Decca star
for whom the red light and the recording bell (which followed the
steady red light signal for a take) were never used.[6]

Our regulars at the 'Pic' included those who, if not public characters, were decided characters in their own right. One was 'Old
Bressor' – as a wealthy North Country business man was known to
us. Among Old Bressor's delightful idiosyncrasies were his liking for
kippers, preceded by oysters which had to be brought in specially
from Bentley's oyster bar, in Swallow Street, and his unique manner
in ordering a grilled steak from the silver grill. Though his consumption of the kipper presented no problem to Mr. Bressor, his manner
of draping himself in a tablecloth and throwing his head back and
lowering a whole succulent kipper saturated in butter into his mouth
placed the management in a difficult position. But being an easy-
going sort of a chap Old Bressor raised no objection to being placed
in an extreme corner of the Grill Room where, surrounded by a
screen, he could enjoy his banquet in isolation. Even then he occasionally popped his head round the corner of the screen to show
the band how adept he was at lowering the best part of a fish into
his mouth and doing a flourish with his enormous serviette after he
had wiped his moustache. Old Bressor was however permitted to
consume his steak in public. His first request was for the raw steak
to be brought to his table in order that he should measure its length
and depth with a six-inch rule which he boasted that he carried in
his breast pocket for that express purpose. The steak was then grilled,
and on its return again carefully measured; and woe betide the chef
if in the basting or the grilling the shrinkage was greater than the
amount permitted by Mr. Bressor. People like Old Bressor, though
difficult customers to handle, were gold mines to the hotel: they
spent their money like water and were most generous to the whole
of the staff. Rarely did the band fail to get a drink from Old
Bressor, and if he had chanced to forget us, I invariably caught his
eye, and would give Tich Poster, who sat directly in front of me, a
seemingly heavy blow on the head with my drumstick whilst giving
a concealed woodblock (known as Bressor's joke block) a heavy

---

[6] 'Wilkie' (K. E. Wilkinson), Decca's senior recording engineer, reminded
me of this on a recording session at The Maltings, Snape, at which
Benjamin Britten and the English Chamber Orchestra were recording his
and Imogen Holst's realisation of Purcell's *Fairy Queen*.

135

stroke at the same time. There was a chair in the Grill Room which could have been called Bressor's chair, for he was one of its most frequent occupants. It was an armchair in which a customer who had reached the 'nodding stage' was discreetly placed, and on his complete collapse carried (in the chair) to the head waiter's office or, if a resident, to his bedroom. (In some cases a bedroom was engaged merely as a means of defeating the licensing hours: at the 'Pic' in the thirties until 2 a.m.). One night Old Bressor got so much under the influence that the head waiter was obliged to stay with him until the morning. But it was worth his effort, for the following evening he showed the band a gold watch that Old Bressor had given him in gratitude. Another regular with whom the band was a great favourite was a certain Major H., whose blonde 'moll' hailed from Nottingham, and who as a girl had been an old flame of Tommy Hinsby's. She was a real sport and rarely failed to convince her wealthy patron that the boys in the band had earned a drink.

Whenever a drink was ordered for the band, the wine steward would be informed and he, resplendent in tails, with his badge of office – an imitation grape as a buttonhole – but with a black bow to signify his being one degree less than a head waiter, would enquire at the first opportunity what each of us wished. The order was then handed into the still room where it was entered on the slate. In many cases these drinks were negotiated for cigarettes[7] or given to members of the kitchen staff in return for a choice leg of chicken (or similar titbit) to be served with our interval coffee – for me a modest change from my farinaceous diet. If the fish cook had his thirst quenched with one from the slate, a nice piece of fresh salmon found its way into a secret niche in the bandroom (for home consumption). Such 'perks' were winked upon rather than being frowned upon by the management; it was all good for trade. (In any case who were they to throw a stone?) One form of perk which we all found amusing was to watch the spots grow on a new 'commis' boy's face – a sure sign that he was helping himself too liberally to the petit-fours, the serving of which was usually the first responsible duty allotted to him.

I can recall only one occasion on which Tommy Hinsby's Nottingham sweetheart let him down, and this she did rather badly, as it cost him the price of a nice semi-detached house in Streatham. It happened that Tommy and I were chatting in the lounge one evening whilst waiting to take over from the straight trio led by

[7] As I rarely smoked I regularly posted supplies of the best brand to my father.

Leonardo Kemp. Actually Tommy was asking my opinion about his taking out a mortgage for £750. I, rightly or wrongly, was not too happy about Tommy's venture, the property being leasehold. As we were chatting, the Major made his way to his table and in passing bade us good evening, and at the same time enquired of our welfare. Knowing him to be an astute man of business, I asked his opinion about freehold and leasehold, to which he replied that there were many aspects to be considered. 'Best to buy outright if you can,' he advised Tommy, to which I suppose Tommy replied that he wished that he could do so. Whatever else may have been said, the Major pulled out his cheque book and was just about to put 'a roof over Tommy's head' when up came the blonde. 'What's going on,' she said and, rather meekly for an astute businessman I thought, the Major put back his cheque book and was led to his table. So Tommy took out a mortgage which was on a freehold property among the élite in Streatham.

Tommy's place in Streatham had many advantages over his flat in Marylebone, chiefly because he left behind his mother-in-law and her parrot. The parrot and the mother-in-law had lived with Tommy far too long for his liking, particularly the parrot, whose vocabulary included all the known swear words, plus a few of the creature's own invention. Tommy was completely dominated by the mother and the parrot and, to use Tommy's words, 'It was difficult to say which could bawl the loudest'. The mother-in-law prided herself on knowing what was good for her. She also boasted of knowing what was good for her son-in-law, and what was more, what was bad for him – strong drink in particular. Not even a bottle of Pilsner as will be seen.

Tommy Hinsby's Pilsner

It was not an unusual thing in a hotel restaurant for a customer to wish to conduct the band. In most cases the customers were slightly tiddly and harmless enough, as the band, whilst giving the appearance of following their beat, took not the slightest heed of it (a situation not entirely without precedent in symphonic circles). On a few occasions we in the Piccadilly Grill Room Band were conducted by customers who knew what they were about, none better than a certain gentleman who asked to be allowed to conduct *The Blue Danube*. If he had asked to conduct the overture to *Tannhäuser* we would not have refused (at least not point-blank). Our conductor for the famous Strauss waltz certainly knew his score, and we played up to his superb direction. The 'guest conductor' received spontaneous applause, and after bowing himself back to his table, sent a waiter to the bandstand with a request that one of us should speak to him. It was usual for me to deal with such matters (I kept a 'tip book' which built up our Christmas fund), and after a discreet bow to the gentleman, I asked how best we could next serve him. He replied by asking if all in the band were fond of Pilsner. I must have replied suitably for he asked for the address of each member. It transpired that our conductor was one of the 'Pilsners' and a few days later two crates of Pilsner lager were delivered to each of our doors. The door was as far as they got at the Hinsbys' flat in Marylebone, we afterwards learned. The drayman's knock was answered by Tommy's mother-in-law, who shrieked at the amazed bearer of goodwill, 'What! the . . . has been ordering himself some liquor has he? Take the stuff away.' It was never discovered where it went, but perhaps the drayman's horse had *its* thirst quenched with Pilsner as well as its driver's.

Some may say those thirties were the 'good old days', others the reverse. W. H. Auden described them as 'a low and dishonest decade'. Perhaps so, but I like to think those days were (to quote Dickens) 'the best of times, the worst of times', or they were good days for some people, but without doubt bad days for lots of others. I saw many down-and-outs on the Embankment whilst waiting with other dance musicians for the all-night tram; and I for one cannot believe that every one was there by choice. To see them 'bedding down' for the night (as they still do in this welfare state) by wrapping old newspapers round their chests, and eating ravenously of any food we had scrounged at the hotels, was puzzling if not convincing. There were of course exceptions, one in particular: 'Piccadilly Jim'. This character was a heavily-built man, well past his prime, who 'lived' between two telephone booths at the Jermyn Street end of Eagle Place leading into Piccadilly.[8] A few of us from the 'Pic' 'adopted' Piccadilly Jim and for several years kept him supplied in clothing – he wore a thick overcoat and scarf summer and winter – and in food, and pocket money. He was an educated man with the most cultured voice and never to my knowledge abused our generosity (sixpence was the limit he would accept at a time). Piccadilly Jim told us quite openly that he had no desire to work or to be shackled down, and that he enjoyed every moment of his life, waking and sleeping – the latter on a small padded box in which he kept his worldly belongings and which had a permanent place between the above mentioned booths.

[8] They are still there.

138

Life in the Film Studios – and Elsewhere

By the end of 1932, in addition to my work at the Piccadilly Hotel, the Gaumont-British and Gainsborough Film Studios and various gramophone studios, including the Highbury Studios recording with Jerry and the Piccadilly Band on the Piccadilly label, I had become a member of the London Film Symphony Orchestra (directed by Muir Mathieson) at Denham Film Studios, and the house orchestra at Elstree Studios (directed by Idris Lewis or Harry Acres). On sight a formidable undertaking, but rendered negotiable by a simple factor: the orchestral managers for Muir Mathieson and Idris Lewis were also members of the Gaumont-British and Gainsborough Orchestras. So, quite naturally, many clashes were averted, and although I was expected to give priority to the hotel and Louis Levy I was able to spend many pleasant days at Denham and Elstree. I played in fact at the first music session at Denham, in one of the main studios, and a little later at the test session in the specially-built recording theatre. The G.B. Studios at Lime Grove were then by far the busiest of the British film studios, and it was here that I met Gordon Walker (then principal flautist of the London Symphony Orchestra) who 'fixed' for Muir Mathieson, and Gerry (Geraint) Williams, principal 'cellist in the L.S.O., who arranged musical matters for Idris Lewis at the Elstree Studios. Although I know it was whilst I was playing for Louis Levy that I first met Gerry Williams, for the last forty years he has contended that it was my buying him a threepenny port at Henekey's wine lodge in the Strand that, to use his expression, 'made me famous'. Gerry proved such a good friend and delightful companion that I have long since forgiven him his 'threepenny port' quip. In addition to being a fine musician, he was a wit of the first order, and, with his voluble Welsh repartee, a foil for any man. A book could be written about the 'Welsh Wizard' as Gerry was affectionately known, as indeed it could be of W. E. Gordon Walker, one of the gentlemen of the profession and a true friend to me from the time I met him until his death. The musical profession may not fully realise what it owes to people like Emile Nacmanson, Gordon Walker and Gerry Williams, for example, who in those early days of recording for the talkies cemented a system of honest payment. In the hands of people of less integrity, a system of graft could have made conditions intolerable.

The shooting and recording routine was similar in all film studios. No studio was without occasional chaotic conditions, such as lamps burning out on the set, recording machines breaking down, to say nothing of scenes between producers and temperamental stars, all of which led to a considerable amount of overtime and all adding up to a tidy wage packet – a three-hour session being worth £3 on an average. Almost unthinkable situations arose and incredible things happened. On one of the early pictures at Elstree, a small brass band with myself on drums was required to play in the middle of a large field, for what reason – if there was one – I have forgotten. The band included George Eskdale (principal trumpet with the L.S.O.) and a few 'recording angels' as the 'session boys' were known. In due course (a few hours in the canteen or, in fair weather, on the cricket pitch, were not unknown) we were given our music and instructions as to where and when. As we left the studio George Eskdale said in a joke, 'What do we do for an A?' After some considerable time on the field we noticed a trolley being drawn laboriously towards us by two men. On the trolley was an upright piano of doubtful vintage. On recovering his breath one of the men said to George Eskdale, 'The producer has sent this piano so you chaps can tune up'. George thanked the man and then tried the A, which was at least a full tone down. We resorted to a tuning fork. George had a slight physical problem: he suffered from bad circulation in his feet (or at least he said he did). His condition was the more grievous in cathedrals, and at such affairs as The Three Choirs Festival he surrounded his feet in a blanket. His circulation was helped externally and internally because inside the blanket was concealed a couple of bottles of Guinness. For reasons best known to himself George did not like the sound of drums, and whenever we played together I did my best to arrange my instruments some distance from him.[9]

Those early thirties were pioneering days in an industry that had revolutionised the entertainment world. Film studios were erected at top speed, and in a space of two or three years there were, in addition to Shepherd's Bush, Islington, Denham and Elstree, well-equipped studios at Isleworth, Shepperton, Ealing and Merton Park. During the early years of the talkies industry the largest studios were those controlled by B.I.P. (British Instructional Pictures – later A.B.P.C., Associated British Picture Corporation). They were huge

[9] George was one of the greatest of trumpeters – a fact not entirely accepted by one small boy, for after he (George) had given a brilliant rendition of the Haydn Trumpet Concerto at a school concert, he said when addressing the audience that there were only one or two people in the world who could play that piece well, prompting the boy to ask, 'Are you one of them?'

corrugated iron structures which had excellent acoustics, but at the same time certain disadvantages, as every extraneous sound was magnified, particularly that of the dozens of sparrows nesting in the upper girders and inner roofing. Until a permanent remedy was found for this menace, a temporary silence was obtained by the floor manager (Sam Grossman) who would fire a blank shot from a huge revolver pointed towards the roof. This became a ritual before every 'take'. Many of those early Elstree films (such as *Goodnight Vienna*) featured or were directed by Jack Buchanan. The musical background was provided by orchestras consisting of well-known free-lance players, or on occasions by such famous bands as the Savoy Orpheans directed by Carroll Gibbons. Due to a heavy schedule, bands of this calibre occasionally recorded in the film studio from 3 a.m. to breakfast time. I clearly recollect joining Carroll Gibbons' boys on three successive night sessions, and after breakfast at Elstree going straight to Lime Grove, Shepherd's Bush, for the day, and thence to the Piccadilly Hotel until 2 a.m.! With the special rate for the night sessions, my earnings for that remarkable week amounted to ninety pounds, with which I bought a new Morris Minor, taxed and insured, and it proved to be one of the most faithful cars it has been my pleasure to own.

It is not at all easy today for a professional orchestral player to purchase a new car with a week's earnings, or for that matter a three-bedroom house in less than twelve months, as did Harry Wild, who played second trumpet to George Eskdale in the Gaumont British Studio Orchestra. Harry – a typical Northcountryman – was a friendly, home-loving man who took astute advantage of being among the musicians who were 'making hay': he was a fine trumpet player, as was his brother Albert who was equally shrewd, and who had the reputation of always buying the right shares. Albert often spoke of outwitting his broker, but Harry was more fond of talking about the good jobs he had done, his conversation invariably opening with 'Corse I was playing principal tha knows'. Some said the Brothers Wild played a little on the bright side, which was a polite way of saying they were inclined to play slightly sharp. Sir Henry Wood (the indomitable 'Timber') may have had that opinion, for at a rehearsal in York Minster he stopped the orchestra and said to the Brothers Wild who were playing off stage in a gallery, 'Trumpets, you're sharp.' Harry, as indignantly as politeness would allow replied, 'But Sir Henry we haven't played yet!' 'I know you haven't,' Timber barked back, 'but you'll be sharp when you do!' I am sure that Harry and Albert enjoyed Sir Henry's wit as much as the orchestra and the choir. Dear old Timber (a darling among 'carvers' with his tree-trunk like baton) overcame tremendous difficulties with an almost unrivalled fortitude. In building up his famous Prom concerts – a heritage to the musical world if ever there was one – he constantly fought the lack of rehearsal time. It is well known that he conducted at every performance throughout those early seasons at the Queen's Hall and later at the Albert Hall. Little wonder that he got exasperated with one or two players who found the lunch time atmosphere of 'The George' in Mortimer Street so inviting that they were often late back on the stand for the afternoon rehearsal at the nearby Queen's Hall. One afternoon when two players crept in some few mintes after the 'down' beat, Timber yapped, 'There you are, late again – you get stuck in that "George" like flies in a glue pot.' And 'Glue Pot' the George has been named and known to the profession ever since.

Life in the Gaumont-British Studios was also not without incident, humour, and the wit of such players as Cedric Sharpe, the principal 'cellist, who always described his family (himself, wife and daughter) as 'a trio in A major'. The long days were also rendered less arduous by situations that might seem incredible if compared with the less exciting routine of today. For my part, I had solved the lack of night time sleep to some extent by sleeping on the job, and on a bed at that – one I purchased for five shillings in Shepherd's Bush market. This small bed the dubbing theatre property man stowed behind the screen, and during the frequent long breaks due to various hold-ups I snoozed at the expense of the firm. I never missed a cue, due entirely to Props[10] (who attached himself to me much as John Henry Wright had done in Workington) acting as my 'scout' and awakening me, often with a strong cup of tea, when he felt the cue was approaching. What Louis Levy would have said to me had my chair been vacant I dare not contemplate. He was a martinet who brooked no nonsense. He paid well and demanded his pound of flesh, though beneath his veneer he had a kind heart, which I had reason to remember. Rarely did he crack a joke, though on one occasion before tapping the stand at 10 a.m. and giving his usual summons, 'Settle dahn', he said. 'Look here, you so-and-so's, I rarely give anything away, but I'll give you a tip – *buy Decca shares*.' We all ignored his advice and missed a fortune. Whilst Louis did not appear to have any particular friend in the orchestra we all appreciated that he did have a soft spot for Freddy Wood, the first bassoon. Fred

[10] An abbreviation for 'Property man'. An electrician was known as 'Sparks' and a carpenter as 'Chippy'.

Ernst Minges Weingut

RHEIN

Weinbau in der Familie seit 1285

Edesheimer Ordensgut
Scheurebe Kabinett
Qualitätswein mit Prädikat

Amtliche Prüfungsnummer 5 021 218 31 77

PFALZ

Edesheim Weinstr. Weinkellerei

and his bassoonist brother had cornered most of London's free-lance bassoon work. To maintain this they spent most of their free time at the London Orchestral Association (The Club) in Archer Street: one it is said in the bar, whilst the other was in the 'phone box either negotiating a date or keeping the telephone available until his brother had quenched his thirst.

'Growing Up'

Whilst I was 'settling dahn' at the film studios and the Piccadilly Hotel, my family had settled down very comfortably in our Mitcham home. Though I saw very little of my small son, he had evidently formed his opinion of me, for about the time of his fourth birthday he asked his mother what he would be like when he grew up. On being told 'very much like your Daddy, I suppose' he commenced to cry and said, 'Oh dear' – proving maybe his wisdom at an early age. He had grown wise in another direction. On two consecutive Christmas Eves I had brought Father Christmas to his bedroom in a rather novel way. On my arrival home soon after midnight, I quickly robed as Father Christmas and then spent a few minutes in the front garden shaking some sleigh bells, the crescendo of which awakened young D.H.B., who had been told that Father Christmas would come in his sleigh. I placed his present at the foot of his bed during which time my wife kept the reindeers pawing with inter- mittent shaking of the jingles near the foot of the stairs. After waving goodbye to the boy I made my way into the front garden and 'disappeared' to a diminuendo on the sleigh bells. These noctur- nal visits of Father Christmas ceased when my son began to wonder why the man with the white beard never spoke to him. Another sure sign that he was growing up was his way of getting some peanuts in return (in his own mind) for running an errand. The shopkeeper evidently had his doubts about my boy being a George Washington, for on one occasion he sent the lad back home with a note reading, 'Dear madam. Your little son said he could have one pennyworth of peanuts. Hope this is in order, E.R.H.' Master B. also had his own ideas regarding theatrical entertainment. As a special treat he was taken to a matinée performance of *Where the Rainbow Ends* at the Holborn Empire. I told him to watch how St. George killed the dragon and to shout and cheer like the other children. At the first opportunity I asked him what he had enjoyed most, and his reply was, 'What I liked best was the man outside drawing funny faces on the smoky plate'. I well remember this man, and his kerbside friends, who included orators and conjurers, many of whom were real artists. One regular who always took my fancy was the chap who played the spoons. His daytime pitch was in Oxford Street. He did more with his spoons than some drummers did with their drumsticks, and I remembered him on the occasion Louis Levy asked me if I could play the spoons. I said that I did, but not like the fellow in Oxford Street. 'Go and pick him up', Louis said; which I did, though judging by the fee he asked I concluded that spoon playing in Oxford Street was not a badly paid occupation.

Perhaps I saw too little of my family in those busy days, but such free time as I had was given to them. Our trips included an occasional spin to sample 'Dr.' Brighton's fresh air, and to bring back some fresh plaice for tea. The forty-odd mile trip from Mitcham to Brighton was done comfortably in little more than the hour (no traffic jams en route or parking problems on the front). Another trip we made was to see dear old Auntie Lizzie and Cousin Lil at Manor Park. 'Our Lil' was now quite an invalid.

It is no overstatement to say that almost every ambitious drummer in the late twenties and early thirties had a common goal: Jack Hylton's band.[11] To be in Hylton's band meant having a good time and earning big money. It also meant hard work, for Hylton was ruthless: 'Death is the only excuse' was his motto. It was not until I had been at the Piccadilly Hotel for some time that I had the opportunity to become a 'Hyltonian'. I met the maestro, who offered me a job in his band. When I told him how well I was doing in London, he advised me to stay with Jerry Hoey and Louis Levy.

Exciting and enjoyable days those early thirties. On reflection I have concluded that a good deal of fun has gone out of the profession. Where in the musical world of today is there the like of Ernest Irving? People with far more skill with the pen than myself have spoken of Ernest Irving as a character. Derek Hudson in his prologue to Ernest Irving's autobiography[12] says: 'But he was something more than an accomplished theatre musician. He also enjoyed the privilege – and this of course partly explains his success – of being known as a "character" – a distinction as refreshing in these days of uniformity as it is rare.' At the time I met Ernest Irving he was

---

[11] These show bands were not without their critics. One famous London band leader when extolling the virtues of his band to an acquaintance said, 'People come to London regularly from Brighton to hear my band.' 'What a waste of time,' his friend replied. 'They could hear it just as well from Brighton.'

[12] *Cue for Music*, Dobson, London.

musical director of the Ealing Film Studios – a position he held until his death. I was engaged to do a day's recording for him (as a timpanist doubling jazz kit) by his henchman Jimmy Crawford. Jimmy was Ernest's shadow, and woe betide him if, at the shout of 'Crawford' he was more than a yard away from the Boss. I remember only one occasion on which Jimmy did not respond to Irving's first bark of 'Crawford'. Within seconds he was located and made his way hurriedly to the podium. He had manuscript paper under each arm, a pencil above each ear, and a quill pen in his mouth: he had only been completing at top speed a set of parts; Ernest had threatened him with dire consequences if they were not at hand when required. 'Where the —— have you been?' roared Ernest, to which Jimmy made no direct reply, having long since learned that only a fool crossed swords with Mr. Irving. 'Props', yelled Ernest, and a 'Props' (possibly the same man who had brought a bucket of water to the double bass player because he had heard Ernest say, 'We shall have to damp the bass down') appeared as if by magic. 'Draw a circle in front of my rostrum,' Ernest said. This was done. 'Now get inside that,' said Ernest to Jimmy, 'and if you stir one inch outside of it I'll break your bloody neck.' When booking me Jimmy Crawford warned me of the 'old man's irascibility' and begged of me to be fixed up ready to kick off when the baton was lifted. I fixed up as advised and stood armed with my sticks behind three cauldron-like kettledrums awaiting Ernest's downbeat. Glancing round – to check his corner men and assess any strange face – he said on observing me, 'Ha! when shall we three meet again,' to which I replied, 'In thunder, lightning or in rain'. 'When the hurly burly's done', came the retort, to which I ventured, 'That will be 'ere set of sun.' 'Thank you,' said Mr. Irving, 'I'll see you afterwards' – ominous words from a conductor in certain circumstances. I saw him afterwards and the first thing he said to me was, 'You're fond of Shakespeare', to which I replied, 'Not altogether, sir, but my schoolmaster was.' He said, 'Young man, we're going to be friends' – and like a good many others I profited both materially and otherwise by my long contact with Ernest Irving.

At chess and at repartee Ernest Irving had few worthy competitors. He could play two games of chess simultaneously and conduct (or mis-conduct it has been said) an orchestra at the same time. His repartee was like the thrust of a snake's tongue. On one particular recording session the saxophonist (Frankie Johnson) exclaimed excitedly, 'Mr. Irving, I've just noticed that when I'm playing the E flat alto [saxophone] the chap on the screen is playing a tenor' [saxophone]. 'Don't worry, my boy,' Ernest fired back, 'we'll have leaflets printed to that effect and hand them out at the door.' Among other things, Ernest Irving was an encyclopaedia of knowledge regarding train travel. He could quote from memory the times of departure of every main line train from London, and the best way to get to any place in the United Kingdom. His own numerous train journeys were normally spent in winning a game or two of chess, or engaging his fellow passengers in lively conversation. He rarely (if ever) met his master in debate. It is also said of him that he was involved in the terrible train disaster on Shap Bank on the night of 23rd December 1912. He and his fellow coach passengers were unharmed, but Ernest could not be accounted for among the immediate survivors. Small wonder. He had made his way in the darkness to the nearest village and earned himself a couple of guineas by telephoning details of the accident to the press !

Mr. Irving's amazing personality was such that he could be forgiven almost everything, though I am not certain whether I should have forgiven him from awakening me from my beauty sleep at 4.30 a.m. on a dark winter morning to tell me of a nightmare he had just experienced. He had, he informed me, dreamed that a large gong I had loaned him for a show he was conducting at the Haymarket Theatre had fallen with a terrible crash into the orchestral pit during a dramatic silence on stage. 'James my friend,' he said, 'do promise me on your honour that you will test those cup hooks on which you suspended the gong before this evening's performance.' His fears were quite unfounded and I forgave him, as I did Louis Levy, who telephoned me at the Piccadilly Hotel at 1.30 a.m. to tell me he had forgotten to mention that 'the pony trotting along in tomorrow's film had a loose shoe', and that I was to bring along a suitable 'effect'. I got to work and by 5.30 a.m. had produced what proved to be successful by loosely inserting two or three nails and a strip of metal into one half of a coconut shell. This I used in conjunction with the other half of the shell in 'clippity-clop' rhythm on a small slab of marble. Finishing this job of work by 5.30 a.m. gave me just 4½ hours for repose and refreshment before being in the studio at 10 a.m.

Though by no means as explosive as Ernest Irving, Louis Levy was considered by his staff to be no turtle dove. 'Looey' or 'L.L.' as he was known to 'Woodie' (his amiable and efficient secretary) and Tommy Kottaun (his chief copyist), kept a Scrooge-like eye on these two most faithful servants. Louis often got rid of the effects of a contretemps in the studio or on the set by taking it out of one or both of them – a situation that secretly amused Woodie and Tommy. On an average Tommy Kottaun was sacked twice a week – a fact that worried him little as he said to Louis each weekend, 'See you on Monday morning Guv'nor', and Louis would growl, 'There'll be trouble if you don't.' Woodie and Tommy were a great help to me: Woodie kept me informed of forthcoming dates which helped me to juggle my many commitments, and Tommy let me browse through the scores a day or two before they were to be recorded, and copied out for me snatches of what I felt would be as well to have at my finger-tips. Louis Levy's three staff composers Hubert Bath, Bretton Byrd and Jack Beaver, were equally helpful. All were first class men and equally at home with the baton as they were with the pen. Hubert Bath (the composer of *Cornish Rhapsody*) was responsible for the 'heavy' scores. Among them was the score for the epic film *Wings over Everest* – a film story of the first flight over Everest. During the recording of this score I remember him asking me for some sort of workshop effect in the sequence where the building of the plane was featured. After trying various sounds I struck on the idea of lightly tapping on the copper kettles of my timpani with coins, bringing a shout of 'Bravo' from Louis Levy in the sound box. Hubert Bath's sense of pitch was remarkable. At the first run-through of the title music for *Wings over Everest*, he stopped the orchestra (an unusually large one) and said, 'I'm sorry chaps, there's a written error in bar 9. The D sharp in the second violins should be E flat.' (The players in sight-reading would naturally play the D sharp slightly 'bright'.)

Hubert's colleagues, Bretton Byrd and Jack Beaver, though as far apart as two poles temperamentally, were both superb musicians. Bretton Byrd was one of the jolliest and most lovable conductors I have had the privilege to work under. As a minor diversion (if Louis was out of the way) he would give a realistic impression of Rach-maninoff, with a life-like impersonation of Art Tatum – complete with grunts – as an encore. On one occasion when Bretton and I were working alone in the studio, he entertained me by playing a tune on the piano in waltz time, whilst whistling another tune in 6/8 and doing a step dance in 2/4 on the piano pedals at the same time.

Bretton's keen sense of humour led to many a quiet leg-pull and the Guv'nor's leg was not excluded. It is possible that I was not entirely without guilt in this direction, as it stands to my credit or otherwise that, for more years than I care to mention, whenever Louis asked me how I was playing, I replied (with poker face),

'Medium, Mr. Levy', at which I would be told, 'Just a little more, Jimmy' – or a little less as the case might be. Whether Mr. Levy was ever suspicious I cannot recollect, but I do know that it would have been a great disappointment to the orchestra if I had replied otherwise. A similar situation arose regarding the 'J.B.' signature tune. This was a simple three-toned motif followed by two 'drum' beats. It was not a subject intended for posterity, or one that came after deliberation on the part of a creative mind. It was an impromptu effort on the part of two instrumentalists who became composers quite unexpectedly. The tune was a sudden inspiration on the part of an oboist, Jack Brand, and myself whilst working on the set with Jack Hulbert in the film *The Camels are Coming*. Our purpose on the set (or to be exact, as we were out of vision, off the set) was to provide music whilst Jack Hulbert – who was a spy disguised as an Arab – sat cross-legged outside a tent supposedly playing a shawm which he held to his mouth with one hand, whilst he beat on a small drum with the other. After several hours (or it might have been days) the time came for the sequence to be shot. The background music, however, was still undecided. At a most inconvenient moment Louis Levy pounced on Jack Brand who was fiddling about with his reed and said, 'Play something Eastern.' Jack hurriedly put his instrument to his mouth and played

to which I added 'pom-pom' on a tom-tom and the 'J.B.' signature tune was born.

'Keep it going', said Louis. Jack Hulbert immediately got into the swing of it and Jack Brand and I spent several pleasant and profitable hours recording (off set of course) this musical masterpiece. Perhaps it would be more precise if I said I enjoyed the situation, for Jack Brand in his hurry to 'play something Eastern' picked on a most awkward fingering, and in a key which had a curious Eastern timbre and which he realised he must maintain as it had met with the approbation of the powers-that-be.

The 'J.B.' tune caught on, and it was expected of me to put in the 'pom-pom' whenever it was played, so much so that it developed into a challenge. It was played on every conceivable instrument at some time or other in the most ridiculous rhythms

and at the most inappropriate times (for me): at Denham, for example, my dear friends Gordon and Eddie Walker would trot it out (quite discreetly) when I had been called to the rostrum to speak to Muir Mathieson about an effect in the score or for the screen. I counteracted these challenges by never being without my drumsticks which enabled me to tap one lightly on the other whenever I heard Jack Brand's 'something Eastern'. Gordon Walker always said that the theme should be engraved on my gravestone if I maintained my reputation and was never caught out. (The 'J.B.' tune is no longer heard and there are few professionals left (alas) who remember it.)

'Buggering-about' Music

A strange title it may seem, but befitting a strange piece of music: a magnum opus that Bretton Byrd and myself secretly dedicated to Louis Levy. It was a work that had many performances and was equally well received on each occasion. It was essentially film music and was used as background music for scuffles, disturbances in cafés and rumpuses of every description. It entailed only Bretton and myself and was trotted out each time Louis told us to 'stay behind' and fit a given film sequence with sound effects, a job he always left entirely to us. As soon as his back was turned out came the 'music' which Bretton solemnly handed to me, saying, 'Here's the part I've written for this particular sequence'. Neither of us needed spectacles to follow the part for the simple reason that, with the exception of the title 'Buggering-about music', the manuscript was blank. After seeing the film through a couple of times we gave Slim, the sound man, the cue to roll for a take and 'buggered about' around the whole of my equipment with rolls and crashes, etc., as the situation demanded. After hearing the playbacks the following day Louis invariably said, 'Good show, you two – keep the score, Bretton, it might be useful another time.' A great pity the 'score' was not retained, and a greater pity those sound tracks are lost in the limbo of the past, for perhaps they would have made a fortune for us as avant-garde compositions. Certain percussion scores occasionally written for me by Hubert Bath could not have claimed such a distinction, as in the case where I had only a few quiet triangle strokes to play throughout a whole week's recording. Hubert always apologised to me on such occasions and made it clear that the triangle strokes were not really necessary but 'he did not want to be responsible for his little friend Jimmy being out of work'.[13]

My work in the film studios called for varying aspects of musical activity. On one occasion I was called to Shepherd's Bush to play a barrel organ. I found Louis Levy and Hubert Bath struggling to record a strain of *The Blue Danube* in the time of forty seconds. What was defeating their timing was that they were finding it difficult to wind the handle out of time with the rhythm of the music. I made a small joke about their sending for a percussion player and not a musician, which was well received – at least by Hubert. I then set to work experimenting with a given number of turns at a certain speed. After a few trial runs I felt ready for a take and to make certain that I was not disturbed by the waltz rhythm I asked for large pads of cotton wool to be strapped over my ears. I got a good take and Louis expressed his gratitude by saying, 'Why the hell didn't we think of bunging our ears up?' The next time I made music by turning a handle was many years later and under rather different circumstances. It was not in a studio with my efforts timed to a second, but to a delighted audience in the open air at the front of the Opera House in Amsterdam. The instrument was one of the famous Dutch calliophones, the sound of which had intrigued me as I made my way to the stage door prior to a performance of Britten's opera *The Turn of the Screw*. I paused to admire the skill of the performer and was reminded of my performance on the barrel organ. I ventured to ask if I could 'have a go' at which the organist laughed and said, 'Not possible.' I showed him five guilders and was given the handle, which I wound at the relentless pace I had observed he maintained. I received an encore, possibly because I was in evening dress, and the admiring organist did very well at the same time.

My Sound Goes Round the World

If I had received a royalty for every stroke heard on my largest Chinese tam-tam (large gong) since 1935 I could have made a bonfire of my instruments years ago. But as I recorded the gong strokes that heralded the Rank Organisation films throughout the world as part of my orchestral duties – and have similarly recorded them on

[13] Film studio orchestras were engaged as the score demanded.

several subsequent occasions – I have been obliged to work for my living and keep my drumheads in good condition. The instrument concerned with the original recording remains one of my greatest treasures. It is thirty inches in diameter and is a superb specimen of Eastern craft; not only tonally but visually as can be seen on Plates 19 and 20. The engraved dragon which is resplendent among storm clouds and other phenomena of nature is to the best of my knowledge 'Sir Earthquake'.[14] (Similar noble creatures adorn the two skins of certain Chinese drums: a dragon on one skin, and a phoenix on the other.)

My 'Rank gong', as it became known, was imported in the early thirties by The Premier Drum Company of London. Word came to me regarding this importation during an afternoon recording session at Lime Grove. That evening I got my first sight of the instrument through the keyhole of their shop door in Golden Square. My wife, whom I had 'phoned to meet me, was as excited as I was, and I slipped a note through the letter-box asking for the instrument to be reserved. Being good friends of mine, Premier reserved it. I was also shown two others, which at the price of £18 each including a stand (modest specimens are now up to fifteen times that amount), I asked to purchase too; but to my disappointment I was told that the BBC were considering acquiring one of the instruments and the other had been promised to some other organisation. I was allowed however, the choice of the three, and if I chose the best I have not lost any sleep about it. The BBC secured their gong and the other went North as far as I can remember. It is now in the possession of Norman Del Mar. The BBC instrument came to a sad end: it was struck forcibly with a hard beater, as marked in the score, and was damaged beyond repair. As well as being dangerous, this in my opinion renders the tone of a gong of any description quite uncharacteristic and certainly not more powerful. It fell to my lot to record the famous film trademark in a quite uneventful way whilst working at Beaconsfield with Benjamin Frankel. When giving me the list of percussion instruments he required, Ben asked if I would include the largest gong I had, as the Company – General Film Distributors (then controlled by Mr. C. M. Woolf and subsequently by J. Arthur Rank) wished to experiment with a trademark. I took along my Chinese tam-tam and at the end of the day's work I recorded strokes of varying volume and length. When the desired sound was established I then synchronised three strokes with the miming of that gentle-

[14] A feature no longer retained: the instruments exported today have a uniform and less arresting appearance.

man of heavyweight champions, Bombardier Billy Wells, who, stripped to the waist, struck a dummy instrument most elegantly.[15] (See Plate 17.)

Those early thirties were good days for me and mine. Hard work on my part and good management on the part of my wife was leading to a comfortable bank balance and a feeling of security, and I was thankful to the Lord that my wife did not have to ponder on Saturday night how to find the rent for the following Monday, as my mother had done so often. By 1936, Olive and I had promised ourselves that if the year continued prosperous we would move to a larger house and let young D.H.B. start his junior schooling in the (professionally) much-favoured district of Hendon. The year 1936 remains in my memory for many reasons. It was at a film session in that summer that I first met Benjamin Britten, and as I played the percussion parts, so ably written and conducted by the slim, shy young man who, at the time, was to me – and the rest of the small orchestra – just a newcomer, I little thought that here was the musician who would subsequently exercise the greatest influence on my career. One thing I vividly remember about that day at the G.P.O. Studios at Blackheath working on the film *Night Mail* is the fact that every member of the orchestra (of somewhat blasé session men) which Henry Bronkhurst had assembled for the occasion, found plenty to keep them busy and interested in young B.B.'s score.[16]

Earlier in this eventful year for the British public, I had been greatly saddened (as had thousands of others) by a more solemn sound than film music or music for dancing. On the night of 20th January, due to the grave condition of King George V, our music for dancing at the Piccadilly Hotel stopped at 11 p.m. Shortly before midnight I entered the front door at my home and heard coming from the kitchen loudspeaker the calm voice of Stuart Hibberd saying, 'The King's life is slowly drawing to its close'. These sorrowful words were shortly followed by Sir John Reith's announcement of the King's death. It was arranged that during the days of mourning, our little band at the Piccadilly should play quiet orchestral music. We made an attempt at suitable items, such as *In a Monastery Garden*. This piece I knew to be a favourite with the late King, as my colleague Jack Simpson had told me that, along with 'Sing me

[15] Two strokes are currently used.
[16] Years later Ben told me that this, one of his earliest commissions for recording, proved to be one of the most difficult he had ever encountered, as the prepared score had to be tailored on the spot to suit the slow pace of W. H. Auden's commentary.

to Sleep' and the main theme from *In a Persian Market*, it was one
of the constant requests made for him to play on the vibraphone
whilst appearing at Windsor Castle with the Horse Guards (The
'Blues') Band.[17] Although Jerry Hoey forsook the saxophone for
the 'cello and the rest of us made various efforts at solemnity – which
included some rather sombre rolls on the bass drum for me – our
efforts to play 'symphonically' may not have been as successful as
when playing 'Tea for Two' or 'Clarinet Marmalade'. It is possible
that we 'started badly and fell away', as Harry Gerrard, the second
alto, said at times of our dance playing. But whatever the reason,
after the first night of serious music the manager said that he felt it
would be more respectful to the situation if we had a few nights
off.

A New Home

The summer of 1937 found the Blades family on the move once more;
though only from the south to the north and no great distance,
merely a trip (in style on this occasion in a swell removal van) from
Mitcham to Hendon. Our new home in Hendon was delightfully
situated domestically and professionally. The rear garden backed on
to Sunny Hill Park, over which young D.H.B. scuttled to his new
school, or to be precise scuttled home from it! To date he had not
proved a great scholar, but nevertheless he was a happy and interesting little chap. From a glance at his school books I learned that,
like myself at his age, he was being impressed by the fact that apart
from the British, all nations of the world were a poor lot, and that
the Gulf Stream kept our island warm. I cannot remember whether
or not he asked me what the Gulf Stream did in the winter, but I
can say with confidence that he never forgot that he was due to have
sixpence each Saturday, or the way to the shop near Hendon Parish
Church where they sold peanuts. He also brought many of his young
friends to meet me: invariably when their bicycles needed repairing.
The professional advantage of our house in Southfields (off Hendon
Way) was that it was better placed for the West End and the
majority of recording studios than our old home at Mitcham, although I clearly remember that my first date after taking up resi-

[17] At the age of 17, because of his reputation as the showiest mounted
drummer, Jack was put in front of the Royal Artillery Mounted Band at
a Royal review. He was subsequently chosen as a model cavalry man for
the Military Manual. (He became an internationally known xylophone
artist.)

dence in the north-west of the metropolis was at the studios in
Merton Park!

There was some excellent work done in those small studios at
Merton Park, in fact everything from a musical to a documentary.
Merton studios were particularly associated with 'shorts' and cartoons. The music for many of the latter was composed and directed
by a superb musician named Leo Croke who, like Beethoven, grew as
deaf as a post, but could detect the slightest flaw in his music. Composers such as Francis Chagrin and Gilbert Vinter were also frequent
visitors to Merton Park. Other 'notables' I played for in those small
and friendly studios included Debroy Somers and Matyas Seiber.
Matyas became internationally recognised as a composer with a flair
for everything from jazz to symphony, as for example his string
quartets, *Improvisations for Jazz Band and Symphony Orchestra*
(with John Dankworth) and the music for one of the finest cartoon
films ever to be made in the U.K.: *Animal Farm.*

Cartoon films were particularly interesting to me if only for the
cunning use made of percussion instruments, never more so than
in the famous Disney cartoons, which were outstanding examples
of the skill of the animator, the composer, and the instrumentalists.
It may not be well known that the Gaumont British Studios at
Shepherd's Bush might well have became a second 'Disneyland' had
they not been so actively engaged in other directions. The opportunity arose because of Studio 8 (the dubbing theatre) at Lime Grove
being allocated for two days to record music for a foreign cartoon.
The composer (a German) brought along one of the cleanest scores
I have ever played. He also brought along a small black box into
which he fixed a few lengths of electric cable, each terminating in a
green bulb. The 'lights' were placed in the centre of each section of
the orchestra, and the clock face apparatus in the black box set at
$\downarrow = 120$; $\downarrow = 80$ etc. as each sequence demanded. Therefore, in
addition to the conductor's beat we had a flashing light ensuring
dead accurate tempi, in fact a 'silent' but visible clicktrack or metro-
nome if you wish. This small and somewhat rotund German composer was indeed a master, and I for one was sorry to be told by
Louis Levy that Gaumont-British were not able to take up an offer
to record more of his scores. So the little black box and its owner
went to the U.S.A. to become – as Walt Disney later told me – one
of the king pins of the Disney Organisation. I shall never know
whether or not I did right in declining the invitation to take a
chance along with the little black box for after all I might not have
done as well in emigrating to America as did that superb horn

player Alfred Brain, brother of Aubrey and uncle of Dennis; William Primrose, the eminent viola player, or Arthur Gleghorn – a flautist without a peer, and who had such a photographic memory that on one occasion, after the first rehearsal of the title music for a G.B. film, he (as a challenge) tore up his manuscript and played everything correctly no matter whether Louis Levy took it from the 'top left hand corner' or from any particular part of the work. (Arthur could also play a flute or piccolo part upside down or from back to front.)

Of one thing I feel certain: I might not have found the U.S.A. any more rewarding or exciting than my native land, and London in particular. Where in the U.S.A. might I have played a quite important part in the film *Sanders of the River* disguised as a heap of straw; tutor a prominent military official who wished to play *The Blue Danube* on a vibraphone because of a wager with a famous artist; spend a considerable time with Arthur Bliss (he was knighted in 1950) deciding how many iron girders I should play on to augment the background music for the workshop scene in the film *Things to Come* or, together with Muir Mathieson, make many experiments with a large gong, bass drum, two tubular bells an octave apart, and the bass of the piano (struck simultaneously) to get as faithful an imitation as possible of Great Tom of St. Paul's. (This great bell only chimes outside its duties as a timepiece at the death of a monarch.) Prior to the experiments in the studio, abortive attempts had been made to record this famous bell 'live'. The recordings were taken at midnight, but every effort on the part of those in the recording van was ruined by outside interference such as a passing taxi or newspaper van. The studio experiments were successful: the deep sound of my large gong and bass drum added the required depth to the pitch of the tubular bells.

To be disguised as a heap of straw has not fallen to the lot of many professional percussionists, but I enjoyed the experience, if only for the privilege of supplying a 'bass' to a group of pukka African drummers. My task presented no great technical problems: all that was necessary for me was to pound away on a big drum in time with the magnificent (though somewhat frenzied) drumming of a group of African players, not one of whom would condescend to be seen performing such an unspectacular action as beating the solid bass ostinato that the film sequence (and the director) required. Hence my being completely camouflaged as a heap of straw and taking my place in a genuine African ensemble without the risk of being questioned about my somewhat European deportment.

Teaching a somewhat irate and distinctly unmusical military gentleman to play *The Blue Danube* on a vibraphone proved a more difficult business than playing a big drum in a heap of straw. My first failure was to convince the military gentleman (a regular customer at the Piccadilly Hotel who I will call Colonel 'Strauss') that a vibraphone was an expensive instrument to purchase and a difficult instrument to play. 'Nonsense,' he said. 'Get me one of those darned machines and teach me to play it. I've wagered my friend Belcher that I'll play *The Blue Danube* at a garden fête in my village.' Belcher (Colonel 'Strauss's' dining-out companion) was none other than George Belcher the artist, who may be best remembered for his picture 'I dreamt that I dwelt in Marble Halls', portraying a cornet player whose wont it seems was to play his cornet to himself after his frugal supper. From my assessment of Colonel 'Strauss's' musical accomplishments, Belcher was on a winner, but the Colonel felt otherwise, and demanded his machine. By a stroke of luck I picked up a decent second-hand instrument which I let the Colonel hear at the first opportunity. 'Get that contraption to my place near Sheringham,' he ordered. A pretty tall order, but as it happened I was able to oblige him on the following Monday morning after spending Sunday with my folk in Peterborough. Finding the place near Sheringham from the rather sketchy information given me led me to some queer-looking establishments, and it was as well that I had made an early start on my devious return journey to London. I finally identified 'the place near Sheringham' (a shooting lodge) by a wall of empty liquor bottles that partly barricaded it. My rat-a-tat on the front door resulted in a rather superior-looking flunkey enquiring what the hell I wanted knocking on the door at that time in the morning. I replied equally forcibly to the effect that I had urgent business with the Colonel. Further parley was immediately interrupted by the shriek of Colonel 'Strauss', 'I know that voice,' he yelled, 'It's the young man from the Piccadilly – bring him and the machine upstairs.' I gave the 'machine' to the flunkey, whose looks could have killed me when I told him to be very careful with it as it was a musical instrument. I found the Colonel in bed, and he seemed in no way embarrassed by the fact of having a charming young lady as a bedfellow. With the help of the perspiring flunkey I assembled the machine, and at the Colonel's request I played 'something'. My listeners were delighted, particularly the Colonel, who said I was to spend a fortnight at the lodge: shooting and tutoring him on the machine. My protests led nowhere. 'Get me Luigi on the 'phone,' yelled the Colonel. I managed to convince him that Luigi and most of the Piccadilly Hotel staff would still be abed, and in the end it was agreed that we should meet each week in the 'Pic' bandroom, where I would prepare him for his début as a vibraphonist at the garden fête. I was escorted to my car by the Colonel's lady friend, who in a charming French accent expressed her regret at my inability to sample all that the 'place at Sheringham' had to offer. She told me she was helping the Colonel in his study of French culture. Whatever she was teaching him it was certainly not music, for he was about the dumbest case I have ever encountered. After many attempts with crotchets and quavers and the normal notes of the scale, I finally drilled the rhythm and the tune into him by rote, employing the scale of C with each note numbered and using figurations, i.e. 1, 3, 5, 5, 5, 5, 3, 3, etc. with X for the semitone below the keynote and Y for the one semitone. George Belcher lost his £50 and I subsequently received half of it in crisp white fivers – plus the 'darned machine' as the Colonel had no desire to extend his repertoire.[18]

I was also reasonably successful as a tutor with a well-known film actor who played the part of a dance-hall drummer in a Hitchcock film.[19] It was arranged that this gentleman should receive a series of six weekly lessons from me, all for our mutual convenience to be given in the Piccadilly band room. He was an apt pupil, which was fortunate for he insisted that his lessons should be short ones in order to give us more time in Bentley's oyster bar in the nearby Swallow Street. He played his part as an instrumentalist admirably, and no one who saw the film would have imagined that he had insisted on my being placed in a position out of shot where he could follow my every movement; a subterfuge decided on over a bottle of wine in Bentley's. My most brilliant pupil (among film actors, I hasten to say) was the boy Sabu, whom I taught to play the side drum in the film *The Drum*. This young Indian boy had (not surprisingly) an impeccable sense of rhythm and quickly mastered the Western style drum beatings required for marches in 2/4 and 6/8 time. I remember the film *The Drum* for another reason. At the conclusion of a music session the producer, Sir Alexander Korda (who

[18] Some years later I had scheduled to relate this story during a BBC broadcast talk, but the producer (Arthur Langford) decided that it must be omitted lest the BBC be accused of plugging an unusual method of determining musical notation.
[19] To work under Alfred Hitchcock was an education, and unforgettable. I remember politely pointing out to him, during the filming of *The 39 Steps* in 1935, that a mantelpiece clock was at the wrong hour, and his reply 'Jimmy, give up the drums and be a continuity girl'.

built Denham Studios and founded London Films), asked me if I had
a pair of Indian tabla. On learning that I had, he asked if I would
bring them along on the following day. I replied that I would on
one condition: that I would not be asked to play them. 'How right
you are,' Sir Alexander replied, 'but all I need is a tremolo on the
higher-sounding drum to imitate a rattlesnake.' Other famous people
I met at Denham included Gabriel Pascal, George Bernard Shaw,
Betty Balfour, Gracie Fields, and of course composers such as William
Walton[20] (he was knighted in 1951), Miklos Rozsa and Richard
Addinsell. In *Goodbye Mr. Chips* I played, at Richard Addinsell's
request, a roll on a timpano with coins to intensify the drama of
Mr. Chips' deathbed sequence (an effect closely associated with
Variation 13 in Elgar's *Enigma Variations*). Gabriel Pascal I associate
with lighter moments; not all pleasant ones for him, however, for
on one occasion when taking part in a crowd scene in the film he
was directing, he was bitten by a camel and had to be taken off the
set. Pascal was most fastidious regarding the background music to
his films, and was rarely absent from a music session. Some of his
suggestions led to interesting situations, one of which involved that
queen of harpists, Marie Goossens, who, however hard she tried,
could not get a glissando on her harp that was fierce enough for
Gabriel. 'More vicious,' he cried. So Marie tried again but with no
more success. 'I know,' shouted Gabriel, 'think of your husband –
fight with ze harp.' As Marie was not the fighting sort I made the
take by scraping the harp strings with a triangle beater. Gabriel
Pascal was greatly admired by George Bernard Shaw for whom he
produced (or directed) *Major Barbara*, *Pygmalion* and *Caesar and
Cleopatra*. Shaw was as critical of the background music to his films
as was Pascal. If he was not able to attend the recording, he insisted
on hearing the whole score privately, and on such occasions we in
the orchestra were treated to some typical Shavian comments, myself
in particular, for on one occasion I was challenged to request that
he autograph the skin of my side drum. Towering above me he
growled, 'Young man, of all the instruments in the orchestra you
bring me the drum to autograph'; to which I politely replied, 'Sir, it
is often the best seller.' 'Give me your pen,' he barked.

[20] I took part in a performance of Walton's *Façade* given in the Aeolian
Hall in 1938. The performance was conducted by the composer with
the narrators (Dame Edith Sitwell and Constant Lambert) speaking from
behind a screen. Both spoke into large megaphones which protruded
through the backcloth.

Calm in a Storm

Though some of the most highly temperamental people I have ever met were connected with the film business, I also met some remarkably cool customers – none more so than Tim Whelan, the American director responsible for, among others, *It's a Boy*, *The Thief of Bagdad* and *Badman's Territory*. Tim Whelan was a genial, kindly man, who got the last ounce out of everyone on the set without seeming to drive them. He remained placid however disturbing the emergency, as, for example, the afternoon at Denham when without rising from his comfortable chair (an elaborate type of deckchair with his name on the back – one of the first of its kind I ever saw) he halted a 'take' and called all around him – including myself as I was supplying (out of vision) the sound of the mouth-organ which Alf Goddard (one-time heavy-weight boxer) was supposedly playing whilst reclining in a slowly swinging hammock. (The tune, I remember, was 'Rock-a-bye-Baby', one of my 'party' pieces when playing to my mother.) When we were all clustered around Tim's chair, he slowly lit a huge cigar, and after one or two obviously satisfying puffs, he quietly asked if we had observed a white-faced youth whisper a message into his ear. 'Possibly not,' drawled Tim, 'but my information is that for the last two weeks we have been printed on stock we shot in the two weeks prior. Waal,' he continued (after a few more slow puffs at his cigar), 'according to my calculation that puts us a month behind schedule; we'll start shooting backwards – from now !' And we did, and, like Alf Goddard I did quite well out of 'Rock-a-bye Baby on a Tree Top'.

Compared with some people's escapades, my own adventures may seem a trifle commonplace, but nevertheless they were hectic ones as far as I was concerned. Playing on the roof of a swell establishment in Mayfair as a Magyar was not one of the most uneventful moments in my career, nor was sweeping the remains of a custard tart from a red carpet in India House to permit Royalty to pass without incident. My debut as a Magyar musician proved to be my one and only performance as a Hungarian musician. Somewhat against my will, I was persuaded to deputise for a professional colleague who had agreed to take the place of a famous cimbalom soloist (from the Hungarian Restaurant) at an élite Mayfair gathering. The fact that I possessed no cimbalom was, according to my professional friend, no problem. 'Take along a vibraphone,' he said, 'no one will know the difference.' So dressed as a zigeuner musician I performed elaborate variations – based on current jazz formulas –

on a vibraphone discreetly veiled in blue velvet. My expertise was highly applauded by the assembled guests – few of whom were sober, though the members of the orchestra (none of whom spoke English) were by no means so enthusiastic and viewed me with grave suspicion.

In March 1939, I took part in a concert given in India House in honour of the State visit of the French President, M. Lebrun. The musical arrangements for this famous concert were in the hands of Ernest Irving. Three days were spent in rehearsing the various items of entertainment which were timed to within a few seconds – even the delightful fragment which was played whilst a bevy of small girls distributed programmes to each of the assembled guests (of whose regalia a member of the Household staff told me he had never seen the like in his long career). The programme included such artists as the Poet Laureate (John Masefield); Edith Evans; John Gielgud; Peggy Ashcroft; Ivy St. Helier; Sacha Guitry; Seymour Hicks; Cicely Courtneidge and Jack Hulbert who, as they were currently appearing at the Palace Theatre, were given a straight run from the theatre in Shaftesbury Avenue to India House (near Downing Street) – the traffic lights being set in their favour. Despite the most elaborate preparations, minor things went wrong such as Ernest Irving missing his gold watch after being presented to Their Majesties and then finding it in his back pocket, and a slight mishap during the introductory narration which followed our overture, caused by the chatter of the police and various officials who were refreshing themselves in a room just below the well in which the orchestra was playing. For what reason I have never discovered, as I had no more chance of making an exit than anyone in the band, Ernest beckoned to me to do something about it. As luck would have it there was a slit in the flooring which allowed me to 'post' to those below, the last page of the overture on which I hastily scribbled, 'Keep it down, you're ruining the show.' My missive proved successful, possibly more so than my effort to 'spring-clean' the red carpet that led from the ladies' powder room to the concert hall after sprawling on it with a custard tart in my hand. Part of my interval had, as is so often the case with drum players, been spent in making various adjustments to my equipment, and by the time I had snatched a cup of coffee and a sandwich it was time to make a dash back for the second half. As I passed the custard tarts I grabbed one 'for later', but whilst crossing a passage I tripped on the carpet and finished full length on it together with most of the tart, just as the Queen and her retinue turned the corner on their way back to the hall. What

Her Majesty saw was a small man in tails brushing away at the carpet in an endeavour to tidy things up. I stood as she passed and bowed in my best manner. This she gracefully acknowledged. So on that splendid and somewhat momentous evening I not only justified my printed card 'Played before Royalty' (connived with the help of my chum Frank Hitchborn some seventeen years earlier), but actually received the approbation of Royalty for a performance of a minor domestic duty.

In addition to my work in the various film studios and at the Piccadilly Hotel (which included regular broadcasts), I had become a member of such broadcasting combinations as the Richard Crean Concert Orchestra, Peter Yorke's 'Sweet and Lovely' Players, and Louis Levy's famous 'Music from the Movies' Orchestra. I also deputised (for my brother Tom and others) in small combinations such as Harry Leggett and his Players, the Charlie Kunz Casani Club Orchestra, Walford Haydn's Café Colette Band and the Alfredo Campoli Orchestra. Occasional calls came from Decca and H.M.V. Studios, and a great experience it was recording under the direction of superb musicians such as Joe Batten and Walter Goehr, and to meet such personalities as Peter Dawson, Richard Tauber and Count John McCormack. Tauber, who invariably wore blue overalls (a form of siren suit) and carried a walking stick (with which he used to give my drum a tap) always bubbled over with good humour. As is well known, Tauber was a fine conductor and he liked nothing better than to conduct the first run through of the orchestral accompaniment of the work he was to record. John McCormack was always good for one or two pleasant anecdotes – perhaps a spicy one if there were no ladies present. Peter Dawson was such a fine sight reader that he could afford to spend rehearsal time telling us about his dahlias, or a cupboard he was building. They were great singers, for it must be remembered that in those days there was no editing of tapes and taking out a 'bum' note and substituting it with a good one, or picking up again at a given point and joining up the best portions of a series of takes to build up a master tape. The musicians were also on their mettle, for there was always the risk of a slip on any one player's part spoiling what so far had been a perfect recording, and I for one can recollect anxious moments whilst awaiting a solo entry towards the end of a three-minute disc.

It is possible that in comparison with the tension in the gramophone studios, my work at the Piccadilly Hotel, and quite often in the film studios, acted as a safety valve. This could certainly be said of the Piccadilly Hotel, where our quiet 'West End drone' – in view of the management's request – a little on the corny side maybe, continued to keep the customers happy, and our job intact. Jerry Hoey's maxims 'Give it 'em aleish' and 'play the cabaret better than the band up-stairs' and 'the customer is always right' continued to pay a dividend, and in spite of the rumours in the profession to the effect that the Piccadilly Grill Room Band was due for the sack, we stayed put and became known as the 'Dilly Veterans'. Jerry and I had become (and have remained) firm friends. He did all in his power to help me cope with my outside work, such as allowing for brother Tommy to hold the fort for half-an-hour or so at night when I was delayed in the studios. I did my best to justify Jerry's interest in my welfare by keeping up to scratch with a xylophone solo for our broadcasts, and as an item in the nightly cabaret. My 'Daisy Belle' and similar medleys continued to do well, and invariably received an encore, which meant putting on my top hat and playing a nippy galop with dessert spoons on my tablecloth-covered xylophone. Great fun, and after my 'spot' I relaxed by enjoying (and learning from) such cabaret acts as Giovanni, one of the greatest of card manipula-tors, who could strip a customer of his entire belongings whilst shaking hands with him – or alternatively remove his waistcoat without taking off his (the victim's) jacket. As a diversion I watched 'Abdul' our 'Gippo' coffee king, complete in fez and robe, sell cups of coffee to customers at one shilling a time out of which he paid the Piccadilly Hotel ninepence. He was able to send his two sons to Oxford, mainly because a dining out party of four rarely took the change out of a ten bob note. Abdul's personality was as genial as his rotund shiny face. His coffee was a marvellous pick-me-up, and he was quite generous as far as the band was concerned with any of the 'makings' left in his small flame-heated silver crucible. He was, according to himself, British to the core, and on one occasion when, during the announcement of election results, an Italian and a Greek waiter came to blows, Abdul coolly remarked, 'These bloody foreigners – they get me down.' Small wonder that with being so involved in activities of such varied descriptions, people like myself were taking little heed of international matters, and the threat of the rasping voice of Adolf Hitler. We in the Piccadilly Grill Band for example little thought that giving an occasional hour of our own time to support the musical functions of the Italian Club would eventually involve us in a somewhat tense interview at Scotland Yard, endeavouring to prove that whilst our names were on the books of the Italian Club, by no stretch of imagination could we be termed Fascists.

Though my circle of acquaintances was widening, I kept in touch with many of my old friends. Nothing pleased me more than to spend an hour or so with Al Davison, who still seemed anxious to test the possibility of bringing the ice-bound Ural Mountains under the burning heat of the tropical sun, or to give me the benefit of his superb musicianship. Like many others, I was greatly saddened to hear of his sudden death whilst conducting his Claribel Band at the White Rock Pavilion, Hastings. I missed him greatly, particularly the occasions when he dropped into the Piccadilly Grill for a snack, and the pleasant wink he gave me if I played 'hot vibraphone' based on the famous busking formula he had expounded to me on the Isle of Man. Others to pay a friendly call at the Piccadilly Hotel included my father, Uncle George, 'Pop' Hewitt, and my boyhood pal, Den Leach. Den, a successful bookie, occasionally dined in the Grill Room after a visit to White City, and a great thrill it was for me when he lifted his glass to wish me well, and drank with obvious satisfaction the sparkling champagne he vowed as a youth his lips would taste. My father and Uncle George had no great love of champagne, but nevertheless enjoyed all that the famous Piccadilly Grill had to offer. Uncle George never tired of saying how pleased he was to see me in the West End – in evening dress and really playing from my music, though with due respect to my first teacher it must be said that on such occasions I was playing mostly by ear or from memory. 'Pop' Hewitt, although too deaf to pass an opinion as to my progress musically, was delighted to see me in such swell surroundings, and more than enjoyed his bottle or two of stout and juicy steak – the 'Pic' being no place to order Walls pork pies!

New Year's Eve 1938

Our 1938 New Year's Eve presentation was, to quote Jerry, 'to be the best to date'. A change he said from Tommy Hinsby dolling himself up as a baby and jumping through a paper hoop, or Tommy and I doing our ventriloquist act with me sitting on his knee as his dummy. Alf Edwards[21] our saxophonist doubling trombone, concertina and bandoneon (among other things) would of course play 'Auld Lang Syne' on his bagpipes, but the band's New Year's Eve cabaret was to be something quite special. After much discussion it was agreed that Bill Whinnie the bass player should dress up as Father Time and announce the New Year as I struck the hour of

---

[21] An exceptional musician who became internationally recognised for his rare talents.

midnight on my tubular bells. As luck had it, whilst browsing around Shepherd's Bush market during a break at the Gaumont British studios I came across a grandfather clock – minus the innards but with a presentable face. This I purchased for a few shillings and for a similar amount had it delivered by taxi to the Piccadilly Hotel. It was decided that Bill, complete with a beard and wig, and armed with scythe (made to fold) should be secreted inside the clock which was to be shuffled to the front of the band rostrum at a little before midnight. It was also planned that Bill should work the hands of the clock from the inside, and that 12 on the dial should be my cue to play the chimes of Big Ben. On the twelfth stroke Bill was to emerge, and whilst opening out the folded scythe announce the New Year. At the afternoon rehearsal the whole thing went like clockwork, and we were all certain that we were on a winner. At a few minutes to midnight the lights were lowered and the clock was duly placed in position. The head waiter, who had a full view of the clock face, gave me the tip as the hands reached midnight. I chimed the four quarters and started to strike twelve; but then the trouble started. Instead of the door opening slowly we heard Bill scratching about inside the clock, and it soon became obvious to us that he had either got hooked up or could not find the catch in the dark. I slowed the strokes on the bells far beyond the great clock's *nobilmente* and hoped for the best! As I struck twelve, the door of the clock burst open with a terrific crash and Bill shot out halfway across the ballroom floor falling on his scythe and breaking it in half. Here was disaster – or so it seemed, but Bill was a resourceful chap. Up he shot and shouted, 'Out with the old', and dashed the remainder of his scythe on the floor. 'In with the new,' he yelled as he threw his beard and wig to the 'customers'. It was a riot. Bill took umpteen calls. I then nipped in with a drum roll, and off Alf went into 'Auld Lang Syne' on the bagpipes, followed by the band's medley, starting (traditionally) with 'Happy Days are Here Again', during which the manager grabbed Jerry's hand and said, 'Jerry my boy, that was the best ever – how did you think it all out?' And so 1939 dawned in the Piccadilly Hotel Grill Room. On the following New Year's Eve, with thousands of others I was engaged with material of a sterner nature.

⚓ 11 ⚓

War!

The morning of 3rd September 1939 found me peacefully engaged at Teddington Film Studios recording for my friend Bretton Byrd. Soon after 11 a.m. however, we were informed of the Prime Minister's dramatic broadcast statement that Britain was at war with Germany. The announcement was soon followed by an alert: an unidentified plane, causing one dear lady known to me to exclaim as she closed the windows with a bang, 'The devil – he's here already.' We in Teddington Studios were quickly marshalled into the nearby B.P. Country Club (Lensbury) air raid shelters. The unidentified plane proved to be French, so the scare was a short one and the all clear was sounded. Further recording was abandoned and I lost no time in getting home. Here I learned that a telephone call had come from Jerry Hoey telling me that dancing at the Piccadilly Hotel was to be abandoned until further notice. I made hurried preparations for evacuating my wife and boy, being under a promise to 'Pop' Hewitt to get them to Workington if and when war was declared. I had also promised my brother Christopher to deliver my two young nephews and their mother to her parental home in Cockermouth. Fortunately we were none of us large people, so three adults and three nippers were squeezed into my trusty Morris Minor, and with the boot and roof rack laden with sundry apparel and temporary provisions, and after a hurried goodbye to Mabel Hewitt, my wife's sister who held a staff appointment at the Euston Hotel and who had agreed to keep an eye on our Hendon home pro-tem, we headed north to Peterborough as our first and only night halt.

At my old home we were greeted by my father who, temporarily overcoming his now slight stoop, drew himself to his full 1914–1918 military height and glancing into the darkening sky and then eyeing me somewhat sternly said, 'You've left it rather late haven't you?' To which I could find no suitable reply. There may have been descendants of that Star Road oracle, Matty Goodley, who had already predicted that the war could last up to a twelvemonth, and those (holding the opinion of my grandfather in 1914) that it would be over by Christmas, arguing that this time there was no Kaiser Bill to fight. My father, like me, was not optimistic and agreed that in any case my first care was to get the children out of harm's way. This meant an early start on the following morning to complete the 250 miles to the Lake District by the evening. All went according to plan, and after depositing my cargo at their respective destinations and taking a night's rest in 'Wukkin'ton', I returned to London to find all intact, but in the throes of feverish preparations for what might arrive from the other side. As nothing happened we were back in harness at the Piccadilly Hotel within a week and, in view of the continued lull my family soon returned to London. Apart from being called to Scotland Yard to prove that the members of the Piccadilly Grill Band were not Fascists even though our names were on the register of the Italian Club, work at the hotel took on a peace-time swing. After a brief period of inactivity work was resumed in the film and other studios, and in due course with the call-up and the movement from London of the BBC orchestras and the increasing provincial touring of orchestras such as the London Symphony and the London Philharmonic, free-lance London players were as busy (or even busier) in war as in peace.

One place that was certainly busy in various ways was the Theatre Royal, Drury Lane, for it became the headquarters of ENSA (Entertainments National Service Association).[1] This association was not, as many consider, a product of the 1939–45 war. ENSA (or its equivalent) flourished in the 1914–18 war, but it became a more influential organisation from 1939 onwards. In the early stages of the war three of the people prominently concerned with ENSA arrangements at Drury Lane were Sir Seymour Hicks, Basil Dean and Ernest Irving. With their wide theatrical experience, they quickly organised a small troupe to France, for though the war was only a few weeks old, the B.E.F. were beginning to feel the boredom of inactivity. I was invited (or should I say requested?) to join the first party, which included Gracie Fields, Sir Seymour Hicks, Claire Luce, Tom Webster, Dennis Noble, a trio of girl dancers (The Exquisite Ascots), and a conjuror (Deveen). A pianist, William Walker, and myself as drummer and xylophone soloist formed the 'orchestra'. Our courier was Peter Stewart (a celebrated columnist), and our batman a lively Cockney, Percy Newman.

We assembled on the evening of Sunday 12th November on the Drury Lane stage to meet and be wished God Speed by Their

[1] ENSA became known to the troops (affectionately) as 'Every night something awful'.

Majesties King George VI and Queen Elizabeth. On the Tuesday following we had a rough crossing to Boulogne. On arrival at Boulogne I accompanied Sir Seymour to the post office from where he sent a telegram to Lady Hicks (Ellaline Terriss). At his suggestion I sent a telegram home for which Sir Seymour insisted upon paying. Our destination was Arras – a distance of 80 kilometres from the coast. A pleasant enough journey even if taken in an army truck. We halted for refreshment en route, and I remember that Deveen our conjuror puzzled (and scared) a group of French children by producing flames from his mouth, at which the children exclaimed 'Le diable'.

At Arras the troupe was billeted at the Hotel Carillon. Here a splendid dinner was served over which arrangements for the rehearsal and the concert were discussed. The performance was to be given in the nearby town of Douai. Basil Dean, who had spent some days in France making the necessary plans for this inaugural concert and subsequent tours, told Sir Seymour that the party would be conveyed to and from Douai in an army truck. This, however, did not please Sir Seymour, who promptly called Basil Dean's attention to the fact that there were ladies in the party and that he himself was no chicken! Basil then pointed out that, chicken or no chicken, there was a war on. A heated argument developed between these two excellent friends and I had visions of us all walking to Douai. Eventually Sir Seymour turned to me (he had already begun to insist that I be near his right hand) and said, 'Jimmy, what would you do in these circumstances?' to which I replied, 'Sir Seymour, I would call for another bottle of champagne'. 'My gad my boy I'm sure you're right,' said Sir Seymour and promptly called for more wine, and so harmony was restored in the dining room of the Hotel Carillon.

The concert at Douai, which was broadcast and heard throughout Britain and was given to a capacity audience, was an unqualified success: Gracie Fields delighted the troops and the French guests with such items from her repertoire as 'Sally', 'The Biggest Aspidistra in the World' and 'Walter'. Tom Webster caricatured reigning nobilities and various regimental characters. Dennis Noble raised the roof with 'On with the Motley' and Sir Seymour and Claire Luce (with my help handing in a telegram) played the second act of the sketch 'Sleeping Partners'. The three Exquisite Ascots showed a trifle more leg than usual, and Deveen enthused and confused the audience with some remarkable sleight-of-hand. William Walker and I provided the orchestral background, and as a diversion I played a xylophone solo, followed by a medley of tunes as a sing-song. These tunes included 'Daisy Belle', 'Run Rabbit Run' and 'We'll hang out the washing on the Siegfried Line' – the latter occupation taking rather longer to complete than was envisaged in 1939. (See Plate 19.)

We returned to the Hotel Carillon at a late hour, but not too late to be greeted by Madame the hotelier, who was anxious that none of the party went to bed hungry. Unfortunately in carving a cold joint she cut her wrist. The immediate loss of blood was sufficient to warrant a tourniquet. This I applied. The doctor who was called explained to Madame that my first aid had probably saved her life, and I was immediately dubbed *le docteur*. Our stay in Arras was not long enough for me to extend my medical practice, but as we were held up for a day awaiting permits to return to London I decided to take a trip to Paris. I had, however, overlooked the fact that there was a war on, and that the whole population of France was already under suspicion. My knowledge of French amounted to the few phrases I had memorised from a phrase book *All you want in France*; but with the help of an interpreter and my ENSA badge I was allowed to join a small queue of locals. My *'si vous plaît un billet Paris retour'* was received graciously. The episode which followed my being granted leave to board the Paris train was described in a London newspaper as follows, 'Today, when the troops leave for Somewhere in Europe, they will still have to brave discomforts, as Jimmy Blades, the trap drummer, found when he, Seymour Hicks, Claire Luce and the rest were held up for a day at the base, after the Gracie Fields' concert, waiting for their permits to return. Jimmy took a train to Paris, armed with the four phrases written down – "Where is the Eiffel Tower?" "What's the time?" "How much to go in?" and "Where is the Gare du Nord?" He thought the train would leave him two and a half hours in the French capital. But it was not the Blue Train he expected – instead, an ill-lit one which arrived so late that he had exactly 22 minutes in which to see "the sights of Paris" before the return journey. . . . Just then a gendarme[2] grabbed him and pushed him into an air-raid shelter, for a warning was sounded, and there he stayed until, shouting *"Où est la Gare du Nord?"* he came out again.'

My brief glimpse of the somewhat deserted French capital was in fact taken at top speed in a French taxi. Back at the Gare du Nord I found that my return to Arras that evening seemed doubtful, but again with the help of a red cap and my ENSA badge I was allowed to board a troop train. The train was packed with young soldiers on

[2] With true press licence: I have no recollection of the gendarme.

the way to the line. I found the behaviour of those boys very similar to that of our Tommies: the same jokes I felt certain, the sharing of a bottle of *vin rouge* possibly in place of a bottle of beer, but certainly similar pranks and card games, even to the playing of the latter leading to the removal (with the point of a bayonet) of a portion of the blue (blackout) paint on the electric light bulbs; proving, to me at least, that fundamentally we are much the same and would act so if the powers-that-be would allow us to express our true selves.

With the exception of the anxiety of the Channel crossing, the return journey of the ENSA concert part was uneventful. I resumed my duties at the Piccadilly Hotel and elsewhere, but for a short period only, as a return to France was quickly arranged – on this occasion for a complete tour of the front. The crossing was a tense one, and made after a twenty-four hour delay at Folkestone, as magnetic mines had been discovered in the Channel. We crossed at slow speed headed by a flotilla of mine sweepers. The French schedule involved a visit to fourteen areas in as many days, and for this trip the party was enlarged to include Dorothy Ward, still a Queen of Pantomime, and Billy Russell, 'the working man's comedian'. By this time several parties had been mustered, including a troupe led by Leslie Henson with whom we travelled as far as Arras. Leslie Henson's troupe boasted of a small orchestra in which my brother Chris was the drummer. A gala concert was given at Arras at which the Leslie Henson troupe and our own combined forces. My brother and I were greatly intrigued by the drummer in the resident orchestra who played (remarkably well) on the vellum of a banjo in place of the normal side drum. We were also intrigued by his performance on his improvised drum the following morning, this time as a pukka banjo on which he was busking in one of the main streets of Arras. We toasted (with his help of course) this ingenious musician in a nearby estaminet where it was obvious that the banjo and its master were well known. Chris and I then parted company to make a start on our respective tours.

The following fortnight was one of feverish activity, but nevertheless a most pleasant experience. We played a concert every evening and occasionally matinées, in some cases travelling up to 200 kilometres a day, visiting such places as Lille, Rheims, Le Mans, Nantes and Brest. Incidents in these various places are clear in my memory. At Le Mans an officer, in thanking me for our visit, said, 'Your party has certainly given us pleasure, but I wish it had been as many tanks'. Remarkable foresight bearing in mind the speed of the German advance after the break-through some months later. One camp on our schedule was so remote that it was accessible only on foot. This meant no props but, between Tom Webster, The Ascots and myself, we managed something in the way of a concert. I supplied The Ascots' musical accompaniment on a mouth-organ which also proved an adequate alternative to the xylophone in my sing-song medley.

Though not strictly a member of His Majesty's forces, I certainly donned khaki in 1939. The uniform was not my own and it was worn but briefly. It happened this way. During the concert I had the best part of twenty minutes' *tacet* (rest) whilst Tom Webster amused the audience with his cartoons and witticisms. Tom was a remarkable man in every way. A wizard with a piece of chalk and a raconteur par excellence. He may be best remembered for his famous cartoon of 'Tishy' the prime favourite for the Derby who arrived last at the post, which prompted Tom to illustrate him with his legs crossed. At the troop concerts, one of Tom's jokes was to caricature the oddest-looking chap in the regiment. After the first three strokes on the blackboard the fellow would be recognised and amidst a roar of guffaws made to mount the stage and take a bow. One evening whilst Tom was busy with his blackboard and his anecdotes (he seemed to know everyone in the world of sport and entertainment) I left the hall to collect a piece of equipment from the transport lorry. It was a dank late November night, and so must have thought a Tommy who was sitting disconsolately in front of a small spirit stove on which a can of water was being heated. He was obviously on fatigue and not very happy about it either. I greeted him with, 'Hello Tommy, rotten job, eh?', to which he replied 'What wouldn't I give to get in there instead of boiling this water for the ladies to wash their dials with. No hope,' he continued, 'the tickets are drawn by ballot anyhow.' I said, 'Look here, I'm not due back for a quarter of an hour. Give me your cap and overcoat and get inside – through that little door which leads to the side of the stage. Tell them you're keeping an eye on the time for Jimmy the drummer, and be back in ten minutes, honour bright'. It worked like a bomb. Clad in the King's uniform, I mounted guard until the genuine member of H.M. Forces returned, dead on time. As I disrobed the Tommy thanked me briefly – but to the point – 'Coo, mate, he said, 'you've made my war'.

Sir Seymour, finding me reasonably reliable and willing, adopted me to some extent as a batman cum stage-manager. Nothing pleased me better than to assist him and listen to his vivid descriptions of his remarkable and colourful career. On one occasion he gave me an insight into the club life of London at the end of the nineteenth century by telling me that, as a young member of the Athenaeum Club, he had plucked up courage to ask a certain nobleman why he had taken to 'cutting him', to which the nobleman replied, 'Hicks, some months ago I was playing whist with your brother and he had the damned effrontery to tell me to hurry up!' Sir Seymour's advice was as golden as his anecdotes. One morning when he was suffering to some extent from the effects of the previous night's party, he said, rather sadly, 'Ah! Jimmy, *anno domini* I fear' (he was 68); but suddenly brightening up, he added, 'Remember this: when you reach the age of forty never take yourself seriously before midday, even if on rising you do as I am prone to do and collide with the bedroom wall'. I think I may be permitted to say that Tom Webster also took an hour or two to thaw on more than one occasion when we were obliged to make an early start on the day's journey. But whatever Tom's early morning condition may have been, or the length of the journey, he was always as fit as a fiddle for the show, and would often find time to draw a few strokes on a theatre band-room wall which could be taken for no one but me playing the xylophone and at times adding the caption: 'J.B. – he does everything with a xylophone but look at it.'

The days were so full of pleasant incidents that it seemed hard to realise that we were at war. All was certainly quiet on the Western Front, but never more quiet to me than the dark and foggy December night when, after a performance at a camp near Bethune, we were given a grim reminder of what war was really like by a glimpse (at midnight) of a 1914–1918 battlefield, and I for one felt I could smell death and see ghosts among the barbed wire entanglements. From the Bethune area we made our way to Nantes, St. Nazaire, Quimper and Brest, calling at Paris, where the whole troupe was wined and dined by Maurice Chevalier and given a run round the city on the following Sunday morning.

The delightful Breton town of Quimper was seething with excitement: a German spy had been caught, the first of the war we were told. At Brest almost everyone seemed to be wearing French naval uniform or to have some connection with the sea. Our audience in the local theatre that evening was half British and half French. Here, to make certain that they did not lose a night's pay, the resident orchestra, most of whom were in naval uniform, played the French and the British National anthems whilst we all stood at attention on the stage. The orchestra – and the audience – made a splendid job of *The Marseillaise*, and not to be outdone, we replied with a lusty rendering of God Save the King. Unfortunately, the French orchestral parts had not been marked 'no repeat of the first eight bars'. This resulted in our singing 'Send him victorious', whilst the orchestra was playing a repeat of 'God save our gracious King' and I am afraid a rather strange performance of our anthem was given. This farewell concert, however, was a tremendous success, as was our buffet supper that followed, and I have a hazy memory of helping Percy, our batman, to bed. My recollection of the journey to Cherbourg on the following day is also hazy, but I do remember being told that there were 'tin fishes' in the Channel again and that we made a zig-zag crossing to Southampton that took every bit of eighteen hours to complete; and that during the night – to ensure a blackout – an armed guard was mounted to see that no one went on deck with a lighted cigarette. The blackout on shore was so complete that, though we lay within a short distance of Southampton for some hours, not a glimpse of the port could be seen until dawn.

On my return to London I resumed duties at the Piccadilly Hotel and elsewhere. 'Elsewhere' included concerts with Sir Seymour's party, in some cases at army camps or stately homes in the provinces. On one occasion, soon after our return from France, we played in Welbeck Abbey, where we were given a private view of the Portland art treasures, some of which were temporarily stored in the subterranean passage (the Horse Corridor) leading from the Titchfield Library to the underground ballroom. The Duke and Duchess of Portland autographed the drum I used at the concert. (I little thought that my drum and xylophone would pay a return visit to Welbeck Abbey; but they did: as part of my lecture-recital equipment on two occasions when I addressed the Musical Society of this military college.) At the Piccadilly Hotel, the Christmas and New Year's Eve arrangements were dull affairs if compared with earlier celebrations. Jerry Hoey, like me, found difficulty in accepting the dreary routine of tea dances each afternoon, with the 'mixture as before' in the evening, and it was not long before he confided to me that he had offered his services to ENSA.

He was invited to join ENSA as leader of a small troupe of entertainers. I was sorry not to be able to continue playing the drums for him, but apart from my occasional duties with Sir Seymour's ENSA party, I was busy with the BBC, various film companies, the London Symphony Orchestra (of which I had become an associate member) and as a deputy with such large orchestras as the London Philharmonic. In fact I had reached the rung of the ladder which was leading me to the concert hall.[3] It was with these symphony orchestras that I gained an insight into the works of the Classical and Romantic masters. These works I grew to love, as did many thousands of others who, prior to the days of concert programmes in factory canteens, Naafi camps, garrison theatres and aeroplane hangars, had never heard, or at least never taken heed of a note of serious music. For example, I rarely hear the slow movements of the Grieg Piano Concerto and the Rachmaninoff Piano Concerto No. 2 without having a vision of Eileen Joyce or Moura Lympany and a massive audience clad in khaki, blue, or overalls, sitting enthralled, and temporarily relaxed by artistry, in composition and performance, that opened a completely new world of sound for them. It was at a rehearsal for one of these ENSA concerts that the orchestra was confounded by finding Dr. Malcolm Sargent momentarily lost for words.[4] The early part of the morning rehearsal was constantly interrupted by preparations in the hall: a large mess room. Sargent, always a stickler for decorum, finally seized on a rather elderly and weedy-looking little man who was operating a vacuum cleaner near to the temporary platform. 'Cease that dreadful noise while we are rehearsing', bawled Sargent. The man stopped his machine and, in the curious silence that followed, faced the Doctor somewhat pugilistically and in a querulous voice said, 'You can't stop me working, I've got my bit to do.' After what seemed to us in the orchestra hours of silence on the part of our conductor, he splurted, 'Yes, yes, good for you, my man.' Such occasions were rare, for as is well known Malcolm Sargent was a master in the art of repartee, and with all due respect to him, any comeback on the part of a player rarely led to the good humour that followed a neat reply to Sir Thomas Beecham, for example.

My work as a deputy in the London Philharmonic Orchestra brought me in touch with Sir Adrian Boult. My first concert with Sir Adrian was in the Sheldonian Theatre, Oxford. The work was

[3] As an associate member of the London Symphony Orchestra I was granted privileges such as occasionally remaining in London when the orchestra was touring. On many occasions I acted for Gordon Walker and booked a substitute London Film Orchestra for Muir Mathieson. My instructions were that the first two players to be certain of were Dennis Brain and Norman Del Mar and to comply I was frequently obliged to switch a session to suit the free time of these two fine young horn players, or persuade the band sergeant (Mick Sotheran) of the R.A.F. Central Band to release them from a duty.
[4] Malcolm Sargent was knighted in 1947.

Elgar's *Falstaff* and in this I was obliged to read at sight at the performance, as I was a last-minute deputy. With Sir Adrian's kindly
direction and the prompting of the principal percussionist, 'Bonzo'
(Fred) Bradshaw,[5] who knew the percussion parts of every work of
note inside out, and what is more, exactly how Sir Adrian wanted
them played, I managed my bass drum part to Sir Adrian's satisfaction. Bonzo's prompting helped me on another occasion, when I had
to play without rehearsal the tambourine part in Elgar's *Wand of
Youth* Suite No. 2. He whispered in my ear just before my entry,
'Not a close roll – shake it awkwardly'; and explained to me afterwards over a drink (Bonzo knew the shortest cuts to all the locals)
that the sound of the tambourine was to represent the chain on the
tame bear as it lumbered along. My early concert hall experiences
brought me in touch with many other notable conductors including
Basil Cameron, whom my L.S.O. colleagues, the timpanist Harry
Taylor (father of Alan, the timpanist at The Royal Opera House,
Covent Garden), Gilbert Cobbett and Reginald Barker, regarded with
great affection; and one whom we agreed had a profound knowledge
of percussion, George Weldon, who at a morning rehearsal would
glance at his watch and say, 'Boys, they're open – interval'; and Sir
Henry Wood, for whom I played the xylophone in the first performance in this country of the Shostakovich 'Leningrad' Symphony.
Sir Henry's friendly squint at the first run-through was a compliment
in itself. It was also a 'port in a storm' when playing the tubular
bells in the *Overture 1812*, for he would give a squinty wink when
it was time to dry up. Considering that nothing can be heard of the
orchestra when playing those double forte scales, and that I felt as
though I was virtually performing behind prison bars, Sir Henry's
recognisable sign, as well as a thrust from his huge baton, was most
welcome. 'Timber' was certainly a character, and what mattered if
his tuning machine – his old 'Wind Chest' – which he made himself
and wound with a handle gave a doubtful A (A = 439, strings,
A = 435, wind), or that he may (or may not) have known that
when checking and criticising the pitch of violins brought to his
dressing room, the same instrument was trotted in by each player in
turn?

On 10th May 1940 the unreal placidity of life in Great Britain
received an abrupt shock. With Hitler's invasion of the Low
Countries and France and the subsequent evacuation of the B.E.F.,
the war lost its appearance of a phoney war and became reality.
Even the church bells were silent, as they were to be sounded only

[5] Brother of James and William Bradshaw, the celebrated timpanists.

174

if our island was invaded. But Hitler struck from the air, from August 24th onwards, and on Saturday 7th September with intensity (the first mass raid). From the London Docks the bombing crept westwards and during the evening a crunch in the vicinity of Oxford Circus brought down the curtain at the London Palladium where I, with the 'corner men' of Peter Yorke's Concert Orchestra, was playing the first week of a musical (called *The Top of the World* I think). To say that I was playing the first week of a musical show may seem surprising to some, but such orchestras as Peter Yorke's Concert Orchestra were made up of free-lance players who gave full attention to the orchestra's broadcasts and recordings, but should the leader undertake a long run in the theatre would, by mutual arrangement, often help to get the show under way, making no exaggeration the story I mentioned earlier of the conductor who, at a dress rehearsal, congratulated his factotum on the number of well-known faces in the orchestra and was promptly told to have a good look at them as it was the last time he would see them together! Peter Yorke, who was a fine pianist as well as an ace arranger, made certain that he saw all *his* favourite faces on special occasions. He demanded loyalty and received it, even though his dates invariably seemed to clash with better offers. To borrow an expression from the well-known clarinet and saxophone player, Frank Reidy, 'Putting a Peter Yorke date in your diary is like putting a cart horse in the Derby – it gets in the way of everything.' As it happened, Peter Yorke's run at the Palladium got in the way of very little for me. This musical, which was the only one I ever played and my one and only engagement at the London Palladium, was also my briefest engagement: a public dress rehearsal, a matinée and half-an-evening performance, the nearby explosion speedily emptying the theatre.

To remove my instruments from the theatre on that Saturday evening was impossible, as was getting on the Underground at Oxford Circus. I made a dash to the Cambridge Theatre where my brother Chris was playing, to make certain that all was well with him. I found him waiting for a suitable moment to get to Leicester Square Station. As one moment seemed as good or as bad as another, we took a chance, and apart from taking shelter once or twice in shop doorways, we reached the station without serious incident. Here we parted: he to Kenton and me to Hendon, and I can remember the feeling of anxiety and sadness felt by my wife and myself, as from the bottom of our garden we gazed at the red glow in the night sky – and glancing at our boy's bedroom window thought – where? and who next? Early the next morning my father telephoned to the effect that I was 'leaving it rather late again' – meaning of course that it was high time I got the family out of London once more!

Getting my wife and boy out of London meant evacuating them to either Peterborough or Workington, where homes were awaiting them. As it was not politic for me to be out of touch with London, Peterborough was the more convenient, and after spending a few weeks at my old home I was able to rent a furnished house for my wife and D.H.B., and my wife's sister, who had undergone some harrowing experiences whilst in London. For my part, I 'commuted', as it was often quicker to go from King's Cross to Peterborough by rail than to my Hendon home by car or public transport. For the first months following the September blitz there was little musical activity in London, particularly in the film and recording studios. To be idle at such a time was unthinkable, so I made arrangements to work such days as I was free in a small engineering firm in Peterborough (Burdett's). Now, though I had forsaken my engineering apprenticeship to join a travelling circus, I had kept an interest in mechanics to the extent of owning a small lathe. I was therefore put on a lathe with an old school friend as my foreman. The twelve hour day was no hardship to me, neither did I suffer any ill effects from catching the 4.20 a.m. from Peterborough North to King's Cross on the days I was required in Town. This, if on time, arrived in most cases before the all-clear had been given, resulting in a very uncomfortable wait among the shelterers in the overcrowded and ill-smelling tube station. Like many others I had some narrow shaves during alerts, and I witnessed some dreadful sights, but I jogged back and forth with no worse injury than occasionally returning to Peterborough with a sooty face, and once whilst driving from Shepperton Film Studios to my Hendon home I struck an object on the Chertsey Road. On investigation, however, I found my 'victim' to be none the worse as my front off-side wheel had merely struck a portion of a coffin that had been blown out of a roadside cemetery.

I made many good friends in Peterborough, as indeed had my son. He had solved the problem of my finding him a suitable school by getting (off his own bat) into the Cathedral Choir, under Dr. Henry Coleman, and consequently into King's School. Like my wife, he had quickly become accustomed to the even tempo and safety of my home town, for in comparison to London and many other places, Peterborough was little affected by enemy action. Admittedly the dreadful drone of the enemy bombers making their almost nightly flight over the city, en route to Coventry and elsewhere, was an awesome experience, as was the sound on the return of these massive planes, the engines of which emitted a completely different note. My factory workmates were intrigued because I could 'pitch' the drone of plane engines, or the clank of a metal bar, and nothing seemed to please them better during a tea break than for me to rig up a scale of metal objects and play such tunes as 'The Bells of St. Mary's.' I fear, however, that I was never able to convey to them what was really required of an orchestral percussionist or that only practice made perfect. This fact was brought home to me quite forcibly on the occasion I invited one of my shop friends to have Sunday tea with me. (That he had a smallholding and kept chickens which laid brown eggs was no incentive I assure you.) After tea and a rather lengthy chat I told him that I was due to play in London on the morrow and must get down to some practice. 'What music have you got to play?' he asked, to which I replied that I did not really know. 'Then what the hell's the good of practising?' he exclaimed!

· · · – V For Victory

The close of the year found Britain in a serious position, but we had a man at the helm who gave no thought to defeat. Victory was Churchill's maxim, and V for victory the symbol by which he may best be remembered. I have reason to remember this famous symbol, for I was concerned with the early experiments and the subsequent recordings of the aural signal that the BBC adopted as an overseas signal and call sign, as a means of identification and for announcing their news bulletins. This signal became a symbol of Britain's encouragement and promised support for the resistance movement. As early as midsummer 1940 the rhythm of the morse letter V had been adopted in the occupied countries as a fraternal call sign and as a symbol of determination to resist oppression. It is not surprising that this rhythm of the four units comprising the morse V ($\cdots$–) suggested the theme of a large number of symphonic compositions, notably the opening theme of Beethoven's Fifth Symphony – occasionally given the title 'Destiny knocks on the door'. This ominous and arresting pattern was used in various ways in the Underground Movement to boost morale. It was heard – surreptitiously and otherwise – in the knock on the door or café table, applause in cinema or theatre, the whistle of railway engines and the pealing of church bells. It supported in every way the avalanche of the visual 'V' which was chalked or painted on walls, doors, pavements, telegraph posts and similar places. The defiant victory sign was also seen in

Britain, and in addition to Churchill's historic portrayal of the letter
V with his first and second fingers, its melodic counterpart (used by
generations of symphonic musicians to hail each other) was encountered in various ways, including an occasional use 'on the air',
for, whilst broadcasting, orchestral players would slip in the 'V'
rhythm or melodic structure during a holding note or in other applicable places. Drummers (myself included) became adept at finding a
suitable opportunity to give four easily-discernible strokes, particularly if the broadcast was concerned with the European service.

From the middle of 1940 onwards representatives of the BBC and
Belgian Radio worked together on the 'V' symbol campaign. The
date of 28th September 1940 (the anniversary of the commencement
of the final offensive in Flanders in 1918) was chosen by Radio Belge
for the first broadcast in which direct reference was made to the 'V'
campaign and the value of its continuance. In Britain, the 'V for
Victory' campaign – perhaps the best known of the Government-
promoted propaganda activities during the war – was launched in
January 1941. The co-operation between Belgian Radio and the BBC,
with other factors, led to the decision to put the letter V into some
sort of signal that could be used in broadcasting. It was at this time
that the BBC requested my services at their studios in Bush House,
Aldwych, to make certain experiments with percussion instruments.[6]
It was explained to me that attempts had already been made to put
the morse code pattern of this letter to music. The experiments with
orchestral ensembles and sections of woodwind, brass and strings
with such themes as the opening of the Beethoven Fifth Symphony,
had proved unsatisfactory. What was required, I was told, was a
form of signal that was completely different from anything else on
the air at the time and one that, in spite of the prevailing jamming
of the BBC's wavelengths, could be easily distinguishable at low
level by overseas listeners. To me there seemed no more suitable
instrument for transmitting a clear signal than a message drum, such
as those used in Africa in the bush telegraph, or possibly a drum
similar in sound to Drake's drum, which legend has it drummed the
enemy up the Channel so effectively in the sixteenth century, and
which it is said was heard in the English Channel during the fateful
month of August 1914, and when the Kaiser's fleet came in to sur-
render in 1918, and again on the first night of the blitz on Plymouth
in March 1941. (See Plates 21 and 22.)

[6] Due to the telephones in the area of my home being blitzed, the
BBC's representative, Geraint Williams, finally contacted me by Post Office
courier.

After many experiments it was agreed that, when struck with a normal kettledrum stick, the tone of one of my African membrane drums, which incidentally gave off the note B, was ideal (see Plate 22). The ···− rhythm was produced by me holding a folded handkerchief on the drumhead whilst I struck the three short notes, and lifting it from the drumhead for the long note. The rhythms were timed to the movement of the studio clock – the first three beats taking a second, the long note (the dash) taking another second, with a gap of two seconds before a following identical pattern was played:

A recording consisting of a number of recurring patterns was made and approved by the 'V' Committee. Though there was controversy regarding the value of the 'V' campaign, due to possible German reprisals, the 'V' Committee finally backed Douglas E. Ritchie's ('Colonel Britton' – head of BBC propaganda) plans to extend the campaign, and on 27th June 1941 the recorded signal was broadcast, followed by the opening theme of Beethoven's Fifth Symphony. From 28th June the sound on the drum became the station identification and interval signal throughout the BBC's European Service. Every few months – sometimes under difficult circumstances – I made further recordings of the signal, always in lower ground studios and in conditions of secrecy. Owing to the pitch of the African drum varying somewhat under certain atmospheric conditions, it was substituted on occasions by two European drums of different size that could be tensioned to the required pitch, the larger and more tightly tensioned drum being used for the short notes. These recordings were made on wax discs and were four minutes in length, and it was therefore something of a technical 'tour de force' to record the numerous recurring rhythms in dead strict tempo, with every stroke of equal volume. It has been said that the impact of the 'V' signal lay to some extent in its aural simplicity, and its defiant rhythm, plus the fact that it could be identified under difficult circumstances: for instance on the small radio sets concealed in the mattresses of prisoners of war in German camps. To the best of my knowledge, though the German propaganda machine decided to appropriate the letter V for themselves, the sound of the BBC signal was never imitated.

In the spring of 1945, with the fall of Hitler certain, I was approached to record a victory signal. For this it was unanimously agreed that the regal sound of kettledrums be recorded in V rhythm. I tuned a pair of drums to the interval of a fourth and played the three short notes on the lower-sounding drum, and the long note on the higher-sounding drum. This gave the signal an impression of finality. For the first week or two, as the signal was to be a symbol of rejoicing, the sound of the drums was backed by a recording of the bells of St. Margaret's, Westminster. To conform to the pitch of the bells I tuned my kettledrums to the notes B flat and E flat.

For the purpose of clarity on this extremely delicate recording – where the touch of my hand in controlling the vibrations of each drum would have been audible – I had the assistance of my brother Tom, who, sitting opposite me, checked with a silk handkerchief the reverberation of one drum as I was about to strike the other. The sound of the kettledrums without the bells is still used as an interval signal (or spacer) on the BBC European Service. It is possible that this and the original signal are (not forgetting Big Ben) among the most frequently heard sounds in the history of radio.

Like many others, I suffered material loss during that year of 1941. Fortunately, though occasionally shaken, my Hendon home suffered no damage from the blitz and the subsequent sporadic bombing. I was not so fortunate with my instruments, for on the night of 10th May, my entire kit that was housed at Denham Film Studios was totally destroyed, due to a stray incendiary bomb falling on the stage of the recording theatre. This loss I learned about on arrival at Denham on the following morning where I was due to record with Muir Mathieson and the London Film Symphony Orchestra. Muir and Leslie Howard, who was directing, had lost no time in coping with the prevailing chaos. Fortunately the film stock and recording apparatus were sufficiently intact for work to be undertaken in one of the several studios. The problem with the orchestra was the lack of percussion equipment and such instruments as a double bass which, like my drums, had at that time a second home at Denham. Hurried arrangements were made to have instruments brought from London. To replace my equipment was no problem; my brother Tom (who was on the session) and I each had a garage full of 'spares', and I immediately telephoned my brother Chris to hire a van and bring the required equipment. Whilst I was talking to my brother, George Yates, the principal double bass player, whispered in my ear, 'Ask him if he will call at the Queen's Hall and pick up my double bass.' Chris certainly called at the Queen's Hall – but there was no spare bass, and very little left standing of that noble building, which, due to the initiative of Sir Henry Wood, had seen the birth of the 'Proms' and resounded to the sounds of so many great artists and orchestral ensembles. (The Henry Wood House – a BBC establishment – stands on the original site.)

I had by this time ceased to combine engineering with music-making. Professional playing in London and elsewhere was keeping me fully engaged, often to the extent of a seventeen-hour day, as it was not unusual to begin with a 6 a.m. rehearsal for a 9 a.m. broad-cast, followed by other studio engagements, and concluding with a late-night 'Music While You Work', finishing at 11 p.m. Due to the scarcity of musicians, players like myself were exempt from Civil Defence and similar duties. Certain of us frequently played for the 'Music While You Work' programme three times in one day, broad-casting for example as 'Apaches' with Lionel Falkman and his Apache Band from 10.30 to 11 a.m.; as 'Bessarabians' with Michaeloff and his Bessarabian Orchestra from 3.0 to 3.30. and as members of the Arthur Dulay Cameo Players, or the Richard Crean Orchestra from 10.30 to 11 p.m. The late night 'Music While You Work' broadcast was frequently interrupted by the alert sirens. In these circumstances the studio red light went off and the orchestra and staff were obliged to go to the shelters until the all clear. The problem of these breaks in transmission was soon overcome, however, for the first complete run-through of the programme was recorded and used to 'shadow' the actual broadcast.

In addition to being an Apache or a Bessarabian, I had become – to coin a phrase – a 'Bartókian', due entirely to the persuasive powers of Dr. Alfred Kalmus, who convinced me that there was a need for the music of Bartók to be played and that I should join Louis Kentner, Ilona Kabos and William Bradshaw in performances of the Bartók Sonata for Two Pianos and Percussion. Saying that I was *persuaded* to play the music of Bartók may seem surprising, but to be truthful I must relate that I knew little about the music of this Hungarian composer and what little I did know about it did not fill me with enthusiasm. In the first place I was extremely well employed playing the music with which I was better acquainted, and secondly my brief acquaintance with Bartók's Sonata had convinced me that it was a difficult piece to play, and whilst no doubt culturally re-warding, certainly not financially rewarding if compared with my normal remuneration. The latter I deduced from my colleagues, Sam Geldard and Bill Bradshaw, who during the summer of 1939 had shown me the percussion parts of the piece, and had also informed me that their fee for a performance of this work, at a concert of new music given in Broadcasting House, was 37/6d. They had the satisfaction, of course, of playing the first performance of this Sonata in England (20th June 1939) and the distinction of appearing as percussion soloists with the composer himself and his wife. They were (and I quote them) also given a cup of coffee after the performance which they drank in the passage behind the Concert Hall in Broadcasting House while the powers-that-be regaled themselves in the Green Room.[7] Dr. Kalmus however was as astute as he was persuasive. He arranged that I should meet Louis Kentner and Ilona Kabos, and I could not refuse the proffered assistance and companionship of these charming artists, or of becoming the partner of that superb timpanist William Bradshaw. I quickly learned to appreciate the beauty of this sonata and the subtleties of the composer who, to make certain that the final strokes on the side drum and the cymbal which conclude the work would sound *pppp* gives instructions for the drum to be played with thin wooden sticks and the cymbal with the fingernail or the blade of a penknife. As with many other great composers, Bartók's music did not meet with the immediate approval of everyone: for instance after one of the broadcasts of the Sonata during the early years of the war, Elizabeth Poston – the eminent composer and director of music of the BBC's European Service – showed me a postcard from an irate Yorkshire lady which read, 'Surely, with bombs and ration cards we have enough to put up with without having to listen to the music of such people as Bartók!' Not all, however, including the critics, shared the opinion of the Yorkshire lady, and many performances of this splendid sonata were given during the war and post-war years, and continue to be given. I played it in London and elsewhere with Louis Kentner and Ilona Kabos, and later with Ilona and Noel Mewton-Wood on the BBC and at the Aldeburgh Festival, John Ogdon and Brenda Lucas at the Edinburgh Festival, and with Louis Kentner and Hephzibah Menuhin at the Bath Festival. At the Edinburgh and Bath performances my percussion partner was my colleague Steve Whittaker. These performances of the sonata were challenging, but at the same time gratifying experiences. After the Edinburgh performance the quartet was introduced to and congratulated by Shostakovich and Rostropovich. The majority of the performances in which I was concerned remain

[7] A situation unheard of today.

clear in my memory, one particularly so: at a performance at a Saturday afternoon concert in Wigmore Hall in June 1943, during one of the impressive moments of silence in the second movement a bomb fell in the vicinity, emitting a sound uncommonly like a beat on a bass drum; so realistic that I sensed some severe glances in my direction from members of the audience, who I fear were of the opinion that I had played a 'domino' (that is, made a mistake).

In contrast to the tension of playing the music of Bartók with the possibility of enemy action augmenting the score, I played under considerably more relaxed conditions at Evesham, with the BBC Salon Orchestra under Leslie Bridgewater (as a deputy for Sam Geldard, whose health was causing concern). I also made occasional journeys to Coventry and Bristol, strange-looking places in those days, and as in London during the blitz, it was not unusual to spend considerable time in finding a way along debris-strewn and often unrecognisable streets. I went to Bristol to take my brother Tom's place in Charlie Kunz's 'rhythm trio' for the Monday Night at Eight broadcast. Charlie travelled with us, and as we were not able to get refreshment on the train, he promised us a slap-up tea on arrival at Bristol. On one occasion, due to the blitz of the previous night, our slap-up tea consisted of a cup of tea and a slice of bread and jam in the one café we found open between Bristol (Temple Meads) Station and the BBC Studios in Whiteladies Road. The café proprietor, who was coping manfully with the lack of normal services, heated a kettle over a spirit stove, and in spite of the gloom served us with a cheering smile. As Charlie was leaving the café he gave me a crisp white 'fiver' saying, 'Jimmy, pay the bill and tell our friend to keep the change.' But 'our friend' did not wish to keep the change. 'What do you take me for?' he said to me. I replied, 'Do you know whom you have been serving? The frail-looking gentleman was Charlie Kunz.' 'Charlie Kunz!' our host ejaculated, and he immediately pinned the £5 note on the dartboard and wrote in chalk underneath 'From Charlie Kunz'. Getting to Bristol in the middle of the day was one thing; getting back to London in the middle of the night was another, and it was imperative that the 'trio' returned on the overnight train. According to the timetable there was sufficient time for Charlie (never a strong man, who consequently rarely travelled at night) to give us supper at his hotel before we joined the train. But we did not join the train as per schedule. On arrival at Temple Meads we learned to our dismay that there was no night train to Paddington that evening, and in view of prevailing conditions, there was very little hope of alternative transport.

A ticket collector gave us the cheering information that the only train to London was 'that fast goods in the siding over there', but that we could sleep in the (cold) waiting room if we wished. Whilst speaking to us he caught sight of the name Charlie Kunz on the label on Frank Davis's double bass. 'Do you chaps know Charlie Kunz?' he enquired. We told him that we not only knew Charlie, but that we had just finished broadcasting with him. 'What wouldn't I give for his autograph', came the ticket collector's reply. I took a good look at him *and* at the train and asked what chance there was of getting on the 'fast goods' if one of us nipped back to the hotel and obtained Charlie's autograph. Need I say more? The ticket collector got the autograph – and a couple of bottles of beer – and we boarded the 'fast goods' and a nightmare of a journey it was, as my two companions, who had reached that maudlin state after an overdose of liquid refreshment (stirred up by the constant buffeting of our conveyance), spent most of the night trying to stop the train by pulling on the emergency chain, or endeavouring to open some wooden cases which Frank the bass player was convinced contained black market butter. We arrived at Paddington at 6 a.m. and, as the tail end of an air raid was in progress, managed to slip away unnoticed.

A *Change of Address*

With my time fully taken up in London I saw far too little of my wife and son, and after several months of separation my wife rejoined me, leaving D.H.B. in the choir (now under Dr. Douglas Hopkins) of Peterborough Cathedral and as a boarder at King's School. In the meantime, I had sold my Hendon home and had rented the upper part of a house in Wembley Hill. After some months in Wembley we became house owners again, this time a house near the lake in the delightful Canons Park, Edgware – so delightful that Master D.H.B. begged to be allowed to return to London. Our Dorset Drive home was near to the site of the smithy that is (quite erroneously) said to have inspired Handel to compose the set of variations now nicknamed *The Harmonious Blacksmith*. It was also a short walk from the home of the Duke of Chandos for whom Handel was chapel-master and composer-in-residence, and the St. Lawrence (Whitchurch) Church where Handel occasionally played the organ. I have reason to remember this church, not only because my son became a chorister there and I was given the privilege of playing a few chords on the console of the original organ, but also because it was in this delightful church that I came very near to joining the ranks of Handel's admirers in the next world. This narrow escape was not from an enemy bomb or similar wartime mishap, but from a blow from a cross that was dislodged from the altar as my kettledrums were being removed after a performance of Handel's *Messiah*. Fortunately I did not receive a direct hit, and was sufficiently conscious to remark to the Rector that if I had met death by the blow from the cross I might have been given unquestioned admittance into Heaven – a remark he included in the following issue of the church magazine.

Our new home, in addition to being ideally 'rural', was well sited for getting into and out of Town. It was also handy for 'The Bush', Elstree and Denham, and the BBC Maida Vale studios. The Delaware Road studios at Maida Vale were originally a skating rink, which had in 1934 proved acoustically ideal for the newly-formed BBC Symphony Orchestra, and other orchestral ensembles. Its comparatively quiet and unobtrusive situation led to its being used during the war years for many programmes concerned with propaganda and overseas broadcasts, in addition to such Home Service and Forces Network programmes as 'Music While You Work'. My activities in the Maida Vale studios were decidedly varied. They included recording (with Francis Chagrin) programmes of French songs especially for the French Resistance movement; playing the timpani in Chappel's Queen's Hall Light Orchestra conducted by Charles Williams, being a (supposedly carefree) Bessarabian with Mischa Michaeloff in a 'Music While You Work' broadcast, and in complete contrast (1945) playing the theme of Chopin's *Funeral March* on three muted kettledrums whilst an announcer read the names of German dead, and extracts from letters found on them – a macabre style of propaganda used for a time by the Germans but which in our case was soon abandoned.

There were, however, many light moments in those Maida Vale studios, as for example the broadcasts with the genial Mischa Michaeloff who during rehearsal rarely failed to tell us quaint stories (in even quainter English). Mischa's stories were always those we had heard before, and in most cases in the same order; but what mattered? No one complained of listening to them instead of rehearsing Bessarabian music, and Mischa (a splendid musician) had many interesting things to tell of his early experiences as a boy in Southern Russia. How for example as an 'apprentice' in a small gypsy orchestra it was part of his job to go among the audience with a plate for the tips, but before leaving the rostrum he was obliged to catch a fly in his free hand, and on returning to the rostrum open his hand as proof that he had not 'rifled the till'.

Other BBC studios used for orchestral purposes included the Concert Hall and Studio 8 at Broadcasting House; the Camden Theatre; the Monseigneur Theatre, Marble Arch; and the Paris Cinema, Lower Regent Street. The Monseigneur and the Paris were below ground. One of the most important weekly broadcasts from the Monseigneur was the regular Thursday evening programme 'Marching On' which reported the progress of the war with items linked (or backed) with incidental music. The orchestra – quite a sizeable one – was conducted by Walter Goehr (known during the war years as George Walter).[8] Walter Goehr also composed the special music for this programme, sometimes at lightning speed, as it was often necessary for an item to be replaced at very short notice with a more immediate bulletin, but whatever the situation, Walter was undisturbed. On one occasion whilst recording at Denham Film Studios he received a call from the the producer of 'Marching On' (Leonard Cottrell) telling him that a sequence was to be changed in that evening's programme. Walter merely asked for a description of the new material. He completed the film session and, whilst on the way to the Monseigneur Theatre in my car, he scribbled out a set of band parts.

In some cases a last-minute bulletin would be inserted during a relay. In such cases Walter (in contact with the programme engineer by means of headphones) would fade out the orchestra whilst beckoning to me to carry on playing, controlling the speed and character of my improvisations by hand signals and facial expressions. This superb musician's only failing (if it could be judged a failing) was his fiery temperament, and his difficulty in remembering that all minds were not as brilliant as his own. (He could play a melody on the piano with his left hand whilst writing a different theme with his right, and chat about something quite different at the same time.) His quick temper would in some cases lead to fun, as for instance when he quarrelled with his composer friend Alan Gray (a fellow German). Walter always conducted Alan Gray's film scores. After almost every rehearsal or 'take' there was a violent quarrel, with Walter invariably having the last word. On one occasion however Alan Gray was the victor: as he reached the rostrum after listening in the recording room to a particularly exacting 'take', he waved his score at Walter and said, 'Valter, shall we have ze row now instead of after?'

[8] His Christian name (Walter) was retained among his associates.

Walter Goehr (the father of Alexander Goehr) was a pupil of Schoenberg. In the post-war years he became a recognised authority on the music of Monteverdi. I for one will remember his musical skill, also his friendship and advice, even though he endeavoured to enrage me on occasions and delighted in calling me 'Doctor' or 'Professor' if I seemed to be in difficulties with a part. If I attempted to combat his repartee, he would threaten to include his composition *Orient Express* in which there was a fierce part for the marimba, on the next occasion I deputised for my colleague Jack Collings in the Orchestre Raymonde.

A temporary outburst on the part of a temperamental conductor rarely disturbs or is taken seriously by the average musician. Was Toscanini feared because of his irascibility? – certainly not. Even Louis Levy's 'Bomb Alley' in the Regent Street Paris Cinema, though a dangerous place for musicians – particularly fiddle players – had no real terrors. And where was 'Bomb Alley', it may be asked? It was to the right hand of Louis Levy during rehearsals for his 'Music from the Movies' broadcasts. No matter what went amiss (and where) it was 'Bomb Alley' that got Louis's spleen. The fiddle players, who caught the full impact, used to take it in turn to sit at Louis's right hand. The only man, however, who had any real concern about Louis's outburst was his factotum (Gerry Williams after Emile Nacmanson's death) who, in addition to trying to keep a straight face at Louis's requests for 'more morendo', feared a scene if there was a comeback from one of the orchestra.[9] Such occasions were rare, and the one I best remember was when Louis told Cyril Stapleton (a popular band leader) to go home, and then called him back to his place before he reached the foot of the exit stairs (an experience Cyril enjoyed as much as Louis and the members of the orchestra).

Played before Royalty

Louis Levy's Orchestra was a fine and popular orchestra. In addition to regular broadcasts, the combination recorded for Decca and played at many concerts including those at the Royal Albert Hall and at a special wartime concert given to the troops in Windsor Castle. Here, with the rest of the orchestra, I was presented to the King and Queen and the two Princesses. Louis Levy told His Majesty that though I

[9] Louis Levy was beholden to no one. When he was conducting Honegger's score for the Shaw film *Pygmalion* in addressing the distinguished Swiss composer over the inter-com he said, 'Honeggar, this is Mr. Levy speaking.'

was the smallest member of the orchestra, I could if needed make the most noise. The King remarked on the orchestra's rendition of Ravel's *Bolero* (a special 'Music from the Movies' arrangement) and said that it was a favourite piece of his, and that there was a record of it in the Castle Library. He also asked me how I knew when to stop playing the repetitive drum rhythm (the two-bar phrase is played 168 times). When I told him that eight bars from the end of the piece the three trombones all played the melody and that I had 'cued' my part to that effect, he asked me what would happen if the three trombone players did *not* play as they should. I replied, to His Majesty's amusement, that I felt sure there would be four new faces in Mr. Levy's orchestra at the next concert. That evening at Windsor Castle was a splendid one, my only moment of anxiety being whilst leaving, when I was questioned by a member of the household about the contents of a bag I was carrying (it contained the metal bars of my vibraphone). After inspecting the contents my interrogator said, 'It sounded to me as if you were getting away with the Royal plate!'

Playing in Windsor Castle was not only a great experience, but also a reminder of how far I had come since my days with the circus band at the not too far distant Henley-on-Thames. Was I halfway up the ladder? I had certainly reached the concert hall and met many notabilities in the world of music. Playing with the London Symphony Orchestra under Muir Mathieson's baton brought me in touch with composers such as Sir William Walton and Vaughan Williams – 'V.W.' to all who knew him well. V.W., and his amanuensis Roy Douglas, knew exactly what was wanted on the drum, and I remember V.W. giving my kettledrum a light tap with his walking stick whilst we were experimenting to produce a particular sound in the music for the film *49th Parallel*. Sir William was also keen to experiment with percussion sounds, though perhaps he had forgotten the occasion at Denham Studios when he became my assistant and played (remarkably well) on my set of tubular bells. I was doing my best to imitate the clash of a great number of church bells, an effect required by Sir Laurence Olivier (now Lord Olivier) for the film *Henry V*. To produce what Larry wanted from my array of tubular bells needed several pairs of hands, so I enlisted his help as well as that of the composer. I am certain that these two Noble Knights enjoyed their experience as orchestral campanologists, particularly Sir Laurence, who practised diligently to obtain the correct clash from a row of eight bells when struck (simultaneously) with a length of broom handle.

I am quite fond of the sound of bells.[10] So was my friend Ernest Irving. For the film *The Life of Handel* (the music for which was recorded at Pinewood Studios in 1943), he asked me to provide as many tubular bells as I could muster, among them some high-sounding bells. All were to be used in the background music covering one of Handel's walks around London. To make certain that Ernest got his high-sounding bells, I shortened a set of tubes which I remember tuning in the boiler room of the Albert Hall (with the assistance of that grand timpanist Clarence O'Neil) during the lunch break between a morning rehearsal and afternoon concert with the London Philharmonic Orchestra. Mr. Irving was delighted with my muster of chimes and with my tintinnabulation in the *Handel in the Strand* and other scenes. My playing of a single bell in the title music for the film did not please him, however. For reasons of acoustics I was placed with the choir – away from the orchestra. After considerable rehearsal we got down to the business of 'taking'. My first bell stroke occurred on the 25th bar of the piece. I had no sooner struck the bell than Ernest stopped the 'take' with a shout that nearly shook the sopranos off the platform. He turned to me and said, 'You came in a bar too early with the bell'. Though I knew that my entry was correct I apologised, but Ernest was in one of his moods. 'You're not convinced,' he said. I made a non-committal reply. To this he barked, "Too expensive to hear the play-back now, we'll make another take, but see me at 9.30 in the morning in the cutting room.' 9 a.m. found me in the cutting room. 'Bunny,' I said to the chief recorder, 'Let's hear that first take.' The bell was in the right place. 'What do we do now?' I asked and Bunny replied, 'You know the old man as well as I do', and he struck a match and applied it to the short length of film which disappeared in a flash. At 9.30 in sturmped Mr. Irving. 'Let's hear that play-back Bunny,' he said. 'Sorry, guv'nor,' said Bunny, 'there's been a mess-up. The boys thought the take was a wash-out and have scrapped it.' Ernest passed due judgment on the boys and turning to me said, 'I was going to bet you a fiver that you were wrong. We'll call it even – two pounds ten apiece to the Musicians' Union Benevolent Fund.'

Tuning tubular bells for the Handel film was one thing. Tuning a Burmese gong to match the pitch of the Vichy gong used on the French radio was a different matter. This I was asked to do by the Director of the BBC European Organisation (H. A. Dunkerley). The

[10] I was delighted when Decca invited me to join Charles Smart in recording two albums of *Organ and Chimes*: Xmas Album and 'Sweet Hour of Prayer'.

gong was required by the European service to announce certain French propaganda and news bulletins. It was necessary, therefore, that the sound of the instrument approximated closely to the French Vichy gong. For experimental purposes I was given a recording of the original instrument. It sounded in the region of E flat in the tenor register. Burmese gongs sounding E flat in the tenor register were (at least in 1942) rare in this country, and the only instrument I could find that was in any way near to the required sound was a Burmese gong in my own collection. As the instrument was slightly flat in pitch I raised the sound by filing a slot in the rim. The 'doctored' instrument proved satisfactory and was used throughout the remaining years of the war.

I am Called Up

My varied activities did not give me exemption from National Service and in due course I presented myself for my medical. Though I felt remarkably fit, my examiners passed me Grade III, and I was told to carry on with what I was doing until further notice. Further notice to the effect that I was to report for duty in the 22nd Middlesex Battalion Home Guard came a year later. Though I had no objection to joining the Home Guard, I appealed against this decision as I felt that my time could be better spent elsewhere. At the Court of Appeal, I showed my diary as an example of my activities, my wife swore an affidavit that she had made the entries, and the chairman (who thought that all professional musicians played in theatres) recommended my exemption. The summons to the Home Guard with withdrawn, and I was permitted to carry on with my 7 day, 90–100-hour week, playing with, in addition to the orchestras already mentioned, such units as that conducted by Arthur Anton (whose orchestra recorded a weekly programme for ENSA); regular weekly programmes for the BBC, as for example 'Marching On', 'Corporal Wilf' and a programme for South Africa; occasional deputising for colleagues such as Charles Botterill with Mantovani at a public concert, or on one of 'Monty's Hospital Programmes', or recording at the Drury Lane Theatre for the Forces Network with Jack Leon's Orchestra.

Grim Days

The close of 1944 brought grim days to those in No. 9, Dorset Drive, Edgware. Our concern was not the fear of doodlebugs, dangerous as those beastly things were with their menacing zoom after cutting out and the awful moments waiting for them to land, but with the low state of my wife's health. Nevertheless, we made as much of Christmas of 1944 as the war and circumstances would allow, although we did not bring in 1945 with the pealing of church bells or any form of jollity. Olive and I quietly toasted each other and went to bed, but as so frequently now, to sleep little; she in pain and me stunned by our doctor's report. I called in a Harley Street specialist – Mr. Horace Evans (later Lord Evans, the Queen's physician) – who arranged for my wife to be admitted to the London Hospital to receive deep ray treatment. Olive said 'goodbye' to her Edgware home (the one she loved the most) quite bravely. It was goodbye, for at midday on 18th April I wiped the last tears from her eyes, just a few hours after she had grasped my hand and said, 'Jim – it has been lovely'. And it had been lovely. A slog perhaps, but no one better rewarded in her own mind than Olive who, as my comrade for eighteen years, had so helped my feet to step firmly on the rungs of the ladder in my climb from the circus to the concert hall. Feeling that our Edgware home without his mother was no place for my son, I arranged for him to return to King's School, Peterborough, as a boarder, for by now, being fourteen years of age, his voice was no longer that of a boy chorister. Bearing in mind the number of hours I was away from home in the course of a day, I decided that I could fend for myself. This I managed remarkably well. After putting moth balls among the furniture in all but one bedroom and the kitchen, reducing my culinary equipment to one cup and saucer, one porringer, one dinner plate, and a similar economy in other tableware, I fell into a steady if monotonous mode of domesticity by breakfasting on corn flakes, and a hard-boiled egg (when there was an egg), keeping alive during the day on canteen meals, and if not too tired or depressed supping on a bowl of thick soup from the stock I purchased at odd times from a friendly grocer in Cricklewood.

With the coming of peace, or, to quote Robb Wilton 'the day peace broke out', I had the satisfaction of hearing on the air the Victory signal that my brother Tom and I had recorded some time earlier. However, my professional activities did not diminish in any way with the cessation of hostilities. This in many ways was a good thing for me, as I was certainly in a low state. My mental condition had led me to ponder on many things, spiritualism included. I took a friend's advice and sought comfort among those who genuinely believed in the possibilities of contact with those beyond the grave.

191

I did not experience the contact I desired, but nevertheless I felt comforted by the thought that my wife was (according to those who profess psychic powers) beyond the 'third dimension'. I had experiences, however, that went a long way to convince me of the possibility and powers of clairvoyance. The most remarkable of these occurred in the modest North Harrow home of a non-professional clairvoyant. During a deep trance this lady medium told me that she 'had someone for me' and then gave me a vivid description of a youth who was pushing himself to the front of a crowd of boys and excitedly pointing to his well-formed teeth and going through various forms of physical exercises with his nimble limbs. Now, I was a complete stranger to this lady: how could she have known of my boyhood friend Harry Cottom, whom I took turns to wheel to school in a pushchair, and who was so conscious of his ill-formed teeth that he never spoke without covering his mouth, and (even on the hottest of summer days) kept his sadly crooked limbs covered with a blanket?

My Housekeeping

As a housekeeper I was a dismal failure. As 1945 proceeded I got into a real muddle, but I had friends; and who better at housekeeping than 'dear old Auntie Lizzie', with whom I had long been a favourite? So Auntie Lizzie locked up her Manor Park home and came – with her black bag containing her little bit of money and her pension books[11] – to sort me out, and for several months this stalwart (she was then approaching her eightieth birthday) sustained me physically, and with her iron will did much to improve my low mental condition. But there was a snag – the telephone. She could not cope with the numerous calls from people, some of whose conversation, due to their foreign accents, was almost unintelligible to me, as for example, my good friend De Wolfe who, on begging me to do a Pathé Gazette session for him that my colleague Jack Simpson had turned down on account of a dispute concerning the porterage, said, 'Jeemy, your friend Jaak Zimpson, he tell me keep my zession and stuff ze porterage up my vestcot.'[12] Quite often on my

[11] Her own and her son Jim's – a 1914–18 war victim.
[12] Porterage was paid to percussionists for transportation and provision of equipment. Arguments over the amount to be paid were numerous, as for example, Gerry Williams who, until his retirement remained one of London's most influential orchestral managers, was so convinced that I did very well out of transport fees that he christened my home 'Porterage Villa'.

return home and asking Auntie what of the day, she would say, 'Now let me think. Yes, six people 'phoned; I did not quite catch their names, but I told them that you would 'phone them when you came in.' Bless her heart, she worried over this sort of thing much more than I did – to such an extent that Auntie and the little black bag returned to Manor Park and I returned to frugal breakfasts and nightly thick soup, and of course my depression and muddle, though the last-named did not cause me as much concern as it did my friends.

At this time I was going through a period of depression with the future apparently having little to offer. My health seemed to be deteriorating due to worry and scrappy meals taken at irregular intervals, but a friendly Harley Street physician, a lover of music, assured me that there was nothing physically wrong. I have always been fortunate in my friends, and none failed to do their best to brighten my life and outlook, particularly Wally Morris, a fine double bass player who, in his capacity as 'factotum' for such composers as Hans May (who always called me 'Chimmy' and the cymbals 'chims') did more for me than booking me for film and recording sessions. One day at H.M.V. Studios he suggested that after the best part of a year of introspection I should come out of myself a bit and take someone out for a good meal. 'Why not one of the ladies of the orchestra, there's a very nice one over there,' he said as he glanced at a young lady who was packing up her oboe before going to lunch. I knew her of course. It was Joan Goossens. She accepted my invitation to lunch and she has lunched with me a few times since, for some two years later she honoured me (and delighted my son) by becoming the second Mrs. James Blades.

12

Halfway

By 1946 I was halfway through the fifty years of percussing that have so far been given to me. My father had retired and my half-sister Margaret had married a young (and brilliant) engineer. Their problem, like that of many young married people, was to find a suitable house. I solved their problem and my own for the time being by letting them take charge of my home and my domestic needs, and that friendly grocer at Cricklewood lost a good customer – at least as far as tins of thick soup were concerned. Perhaps my sister Margaret's Yorkshire pudding was not as good as Auntie Lizzie's, but Auntie would have been the first to admit that in answering the 'phone Margaret was a 'little cough drop'.[1] And the 'little cough drop' (known affectionately to the Blades Brothers as 'a bit of a harum-scarum') took over my desk diary and managed my professional affairs in the same efficient and diplomatic manner as they had been managed in previous years.

A Trip to Switzerland

I could not refuse an invitation to spend a fortnight in Switzerland in early May, receiving top Musicians' Union rates (plus) for playing a programme of symphonic music, including Brahms' Symphony No. 4 and Richard Strauss's Symphonic Poem *Don Juan* with the National Orchestra, conducted by Sidney Beer. The members of the orchestra included David MacCallum (leader), Douglas Cameron ('cello), Dennis Brain (horn), Alec Whittaker (oboe), Jack Alexandra (bassoon)[2] and a host of London's top players, all as keen as myself for a change of air and diet. My colleagues were William Bradshaw (timpani) and Fred ('Bonzo') Bradshaw and Frank Kennings (percussion). The journey to Switzerland was made by rail and boat. On

---

[1] My half-sister was at least six inches taller than Auntie Lizzie.
[2] Alec and Jack were members of that superb group of woodwind players known to all professional musicians as the 'Royal Family': Alec Whittaker (oboe), Arthur Gleghorn (flute), Reginald Kell (clarinet) and Jack Alexandra (bassoon).

reaching Basle (at 5.30 a.m.) the whole orchestra descended like a pack of wolves on the superb fare on the refreshment trolleys. Thoroughly fortified, we proceeded (one or two somewhat unsteadily from an overdose of 'strong coffee' taken in the famous Basle buffet) to the Basle City Hall for a short rest before morning rehearsal which, as we were already well rehearsed, was more of a *'sitzprobe'* (seating rehearsal).

For the first two days of the tour it was arranged for the orchestra to be accommodated in the delightful spa of Rheinfelden – which was within easy reach of Basle. After the rehearsal we were driven to Rheinfelden and introduced to our hoteliers by Tony (Anthony) Baines, whose fluent German (among other languages) made up for the fact that the linguistic talent of most members of the orchestra including myself was limited to *'ein dunkles Bier'* and *'Auf Wiedersehen'*. Being in a spa hotel, Bill Bradshaw and I decided to take an after lunch brine bath. After a certain amount of splashing about I heard Bill shout, 'Oh! I feel so frisky.' He certainly was and for a very good reason. He had used the rejuvenating mixture in treble strength and came out of the bath a deeper pink than when he went in. Bill was not the only one who sampled the remedial powers of Rheinfelden Spa. Alec Whittaker, for example, who was staying in a nearby hotel, lost no time in refreshing himself externally and internally, the latter to the astonishment of his landlord who – not being aware that, in addition to Alec's rarely equalled powers as an oboist, he had few rivals as an experienced drinker – challenged him to a drinking contest. Alec accepted on condition that the bout commenced after the evening performance. He needed no rehearsal for a rhythmic intake of his favourite brew, and so the Rheinfelden landlord and Alec got down to business soon after midnight. At 3 a.m. the landlord slumped under his chair and Alec was one of the team who helped to carry him upstairs to bed. Alec's prize was free board and lodgings whilst in Rheinfelden and as much as he could drink by way of a bonus.

That Swiss tour with Sidney Beer was a pleasant experience. The orchestra met with a splendid reception in each of the cities visited: Basle, Berne, Lausanne, Zürich and Geneva, and in all cases we were almost overwhelmed with true Swiss hospitality. Whilst in Berne a trip by train and boat to Interlaken was arranged as a present from our conductor. It included a funicular ride to the summit of the Harder. Although the season had not yet started, the funicular was expressly opened as a gesture of friendliness to the visiting British orchestra. From the top of the Harder I got my first unimpeded

view of the Jungfrau, the Eiger and the other peaks of that part of
the Bernese Oberland, a part of Europe that has become dear to me.
The weather throughout the tour was glorious and many winter
vests were cast. Other things were cast, including utility suits and
footwear. New suits (and new suitcases) and wrist watches appeared
daily. Those at home were not forgotten and a great deal of fun
occurred in ladies' wear shops with the married men (and some
bachelors too) searching for a lady assistant whose vital statistics
tallied with 'the wife's'. There was no lack of news from home,
much of it indirectly, for rarely a day passed without one or more
players being called from the lunch or dinner table to take a long-
distance call from Walter Legge, who was then forming the Philharmonia Orchestra – in fact the fine orchestra that Gerry Williams
recruited for that Swiss tour was considerably depleted on its return
to London by the exodus of players to the Philharmonia.[3]

Needless to say, there were things other than the splendours of
Switzerland, or who was next for 'the Phil', discussed at the lunch
or dinner table or on journeys. Some interesting stories of conditions
in the musical profession in the days before the First World War
were told by the senior members, none more interesting to me than
the anecdotes of the drummer, Frank Kennings. Frank, who for
many years was a member of the BBC Wireless Military Band (conductor B. Walton O'Donnell) was an ex-Royal Marine who had
served in China among other places, in the early part of the century.
His stories of the 'goings on' of the bandsmen, in some of the
decidedly remote areas in which the regiment was stationed, kept us
constantly entertained. In his gruff, though friendly voice, he told
us of how the patience of a sergeant-major in the Marines became
exhausted, not on the parade ground but at a church service. The
church was a small wooden hut used for the religious activity
connected with regimental duty, chiefly Sunday morning service –
not the most popular event in the curriculum of a detachment of
Marines on garrison duty, who had been given the freedom of the
mess on the previous evening. The musical accompaniment for the
church services was supplied on a harmonium, played by a young
ne'er-do-well, whose titled family (according to Frank) were delighted
that he was stationed where he was: on the coast of China. The
sergeant-major officiated as padre. He wore a surplice over his
uniform and conducted the service from an improvised lectern. The

[3] I received an offer to join the Philharmonia but declined (to Walter
Legge's perfect understanding) on the grounds of not wishing to disturb
my numerous activities.

young ne'er-do-well was a gifted musician with a flair for improvisation; a talent he expressed in a rather unusual manner during
divine service by filling in the holding notes in such hymns as 'O
God our help' with snatches of the recently-composed 'Alexander's
Ragtime Band'. For several weeks the 'padre' let these light diversions
go, but at last he could take no more of it, and after one particularly
clever 'frilling around' on the part of the ne'er-do-well, he banged
his hymn book on the lectern and roared, 'Look here, chaps. I'm as
big a b—— as anybody in the regiment, but when we're in church
let's be in church and cut out the s—— sky-larking.'

The last concert of the National Orchestra's tour was given in
Geneva. As always, we played to a packed house and a distinguished
audience, probably never more distinguished than at this final concert, which was attended by Richard Strauss. The whole orchestra
was presented to him after the concert, and despite the fact that he
was said to have supported the Nazis, we were honoured by the congratulations of this great composer, and especially that he made a
point of expressing his admiration of Alec Whittaker's oboe solo
in *Don Juan*. The journey from Geneva to London was uneventful with no problems at Dover, where the Customs accepted that
our 'presents' were really presents. Mine consisted of a music box
or two for the family, and a leather handbag for a certain young
lady oboist who I hoped would accept it and be pleased to see me
back in London. I had also bought a chromatic mouth harmonica,
which I knew better as a mouth-organ when a boy, and two second-
hand pocket watches for less than £5, one a Longines which is still
reminding me that time does not stand still. The customs officer
was of the opinion that I should pay duty on the mouth harmonica,
but I did not agree. When he said 'surely a mouth-organ is not used
in an orchestra' I replied (perhaps prophetically?), 'You never know
what you may be called upon to play these days.'

Back in England, despite a lack of luxuries, things were gradually
returning to normal. There was considerable activity in musical
circles with London fast becoming the musical centre of the world.
Glyndebourne was in full swing again with, for example, the first
performance of Britten's opera *The Rape of Lucretia* with Nancy
Evans and Kathleen Ferrier sharing the title role. Though I was
eventually to play this opera on many occasions and in many places,
I did not take part in those early performances, the percussionist
being Bert Wilson, who told me that at the first rehearsal he got so hope-
lessly lost in the percussion solo which occurs in the second act that
he ceased playing and apologised to the conductor, Ernest Ansermet,

who replied, 'My boy, you have beaten me by three bars'. I did, however, visit Glyndebourne in due course and on one occasion in a dual capacity as musician and 'guide'. As a musician I played the timpani in a Haydn symphony (at a concert given by the Boyd Neel Orchestra) and as a guide I showed an American gentleman round the Christie organ room, reeling out the information I had been given a few minutes earlier by an official who, on learning that this was my first visit to Glyndebourne and that I wished to 'see the place', gave me a conducted tour (gratis) around the chief places of interest. The American gentleman, mistaking me for a guide, enquired about the organ room, and after imparting to him what I had just learned almost word for word, he asked me to accept two pound notes.[4] As it would have taken too much time to explain matters I accepted the money but, after due consideration, my conscience pricked me and I put it in the Musicians' Union Benevolent collection box. It was easy money which I received for being a guide, but it was not so easy as the £12 I subsequently earned for crackling (in rumba rhythm) a crisp white £5 note in the palm of my hand for one of the early commercials ('jingles') which advertised a well-known brand of sausages frying in a pan !

Playing the timpani in such chamber orchestras, or concocting sounds for TV jingles, did not mean that I had forsaken the film studios or my connection with the world of light music. Though my days as a 'pukka' dance drummer were behind me I remained a member of such orchestras as Geraldo's Concert Orchestra; the Queen's Hall Light Orcestra; Peter Yorke's Concert Orchestra; the Robert Farnon Concert Orchestra and the Leighton Lucas Orchestra. Calls came from Harry Blech, Mantovani, Phil Green, Phil Cardew[5] and such novelty combinations as Troise and his Banjoliers. I continued to play for Charlie Kunz, as a deputy for my brother Tom. I also deputised for my brother in Wynford Reynolds' Orchestra in the BBC programme 'Marching and Waltzing' (known later as 'Marches and Waltzes'). This was a splendid date, for Wyn. Reynolds' orchestra always played the waltzes, but a different regimental band played the marches each week. I therefore not only had the pleasure of listening to one of my first loves – military music played traditionally – but as I took the opportunity of playing a few very discreet beats on my triangle during the forte passages in the

[4] My fee as a player was £3 10s. 0d.
[5] On an engagement in Wisbech with Phil Cardew and his Old Tyme Orchestra, I met my old friend and manager Mr. Harry Bancroft – still hale and hearty.

marches, I am able to claim (though I have not had cards printed to the effect) that I have broadcast with nearly every regimental band in the country. As a professional one sees and hears many things. I saw almost every major opera at Covent Garden whilst playing (as an extra or deputy) in the orchestra, or when playing on stage. My problem with the latter was to avoid losing my place in the music as I was tempted to watch and listen to the acting, for example, of Scarpia in *Tosca*, or peering to see if Tosca (after a private off-stage quarrel with Scarpia) deliberately placed the cross on the stomach of the corpse, instead of his heart, and gloated over the slight rise and fall. I also played many of Puccini's and Verdi's operas at the Cambridge Theatre with Alec Sherman's New London Orchestra under Erede. The seasons at the Cambridge were sponsored by Jay Pomeroy, and I remember surprising him on one occasion at a performance of *Rigoletto*. After the overture and introduction I was *tacet* for the remainder of the first act, and to get a better view of the stage I moved from the orchestra pit into a vacant front seat in the stalls. I applauded certain arias so heartily that a gentleman who had joined me in the next seat eventually remarked on my enthusiasm and also invited me to drink with him in the interval. As the bell went for our return to the theatre he said, 'We'll go back and enjoy the next act', to which I replied that I was required in the orchestra. My acquaintance, who was none other than Mr. Pomeroy, stopped abruptly and looking hard at me said, 'Well I'm damned! I'm paying you for playing and seeing the show and I've also bought you a drink.' I thanked him, even though he did not invite me out to supper.

I meet John Ireland

To most musicians, John Ireland is best remembered for his *A London Overture*, *These Things Shall Be* and his Piano Concerto. This fine British composer was also responsible for the epic score for the film *The Overlanders*, which described an arduous cattle drive in Australia. John Ireland was commissioned to write this score by Ernest Irving, who also commissioned such composers as John Addison, William Alwyn, and Vaughan Williams. The music for *The Overlanders* was recorded at H.M.V. Studios, Abbey Road. A fine orchestra was recruited with James Bradshaw as timpanist and I played second. To play alongside Jimmy was always an education, for his reputation of being 'the Daddy of them all' was no exaggeration. All went smoothly until Gideon Fagan (Ernest Irving's most

able assistant) came out of the box and said that Jimmy Bradshaw's
E flat timpano was sounding sharp. Now, to tell a timpanist of the
calibre of James Bradshaw that his drum was sharp was, to put it
mildly, asking for trouble. The studio became strangely silent, then
Jimmy barked, 'Sharp! – you're crazy', and giving his drum a hearty
thwack he said, 'That's my E flat and there it stays.' Gideon looked
at Ernest and Ernest looked at Gideon. Then Ernest looked at me
and said, 'What's it sound like up there, Jimmy?' I replied, 'To tell
you the truth, guv'nor, I've never had any ear for these things.' 'I
should have known – let us proceed,' came his reply. And the session
proceeded with Jimmy Bradshaw's 'E flat' staying put.[6]

The Overlanders was made in 1946, and it was in the early part
of that year that I became further acquainted with the music of Benjamin Britten, notably in performances of Louis MacNeice's The
Dark Tower. Ben was present at the rehearsals for the first broadcast
of this work (21st January 1946), and I must say that I found him
fastidious regarding his percussion score which portrayed the character of evil – in sharp contrast to the nobility of Roland's trumpet –
superbly played on this and subsequent occasions by Robert Walton.
The early performances of The Dark Tower were conducted by
Walter Goehr who, like all concerned, had nothing but admiration
for the musical skill of Britten. Another radio play that comes to
my mind is Shaw's The Adventures of a Black Girl in her Search for
God (broadcast on 19th June 1944). For this play I was asked to
provide the sound of jangling church bells as one of the characters
was supposedly carrying a church on his back. The producer (Peter
Cresswell), though most appreciative of my efforts to produce an
adequate representation, was not entirely convinced until I strapped
the set of tubular bells to my back and plodded round the studio.
Another sound which called for a great deal of experiment was the
background 'heart beat' effect for the film Hamlet (to intensify the
drama of the battlement scene). Laurence Olivier (the producer and
director) first let me hear a recording of a heart beat taken through
a stethoscope. This sounded like someone consuming thick soup with
a rhythmic intake, and was absolutely useless for our purpose.
What was required was a steady, gentle 'poom-poom – poom-poom'.
I made experiments with various kinds of drumsticks on muffled

---

[6] To my knowledge the only other occasion that Jimmy Bradshaw's
intonation was questioned was at a 'Philharmonia' rehearsal when Otto
Klemperer queried the pitch of the four solo drum notes (D) to open the
Beethoven Violin Concerto. This led, of course, to an interesting passage-
at-arms, with Jimmy eventually agreeing to lower the pitch one wave.

kettledrums, bass drums and tenor drums. The only sound which seemed in any way suitable to Sir Laurence was when I placed a blanket on the skin of my largest bass drum and prodded the rhythm with my fingertips. As it happened Vivien Leigh was an interested spectator, and I wondered if her fur coat would be better as a muffle. This was tried, and Olivier got the quiet 'shush' and the deep though light-sounding 'poom-poom' he wanted. A similar effect was required some time later for the prison scene in *Richard III*, but it was extremely difficult to repeat it.

Though my varied activities had kept me well occupied, I had found time to indulge a little in my favourite recreation: reading Dickens and 'messing about' on my Myford lathe, and also in enjoying the companionship of the young lady oboist whom my friend Wally Morris had so wisely suggested that I should take out for a meal. My friendship with Joan Goossens had ripened into a firm understanding between us which, unbeknown to me at that time, was to play an important part in re-shaping my career. It was in fact entirely due to her that I launched (or *was* launched) into my career of lectureship. This happened – as most things do – in a simple way. Joan was on the committee of the Sutton Music Club and, in a weak moment, I was persuaded to give a talk to the members on club night. 'Just a brief chat and demonstration on one or two percussion instruments during the second half,' I was told. So on 20th November 1947 I chatted to the members of the Sutton Music Club about what a professional percussionist does (or does not do), and, with 'J.G.' as my accompanist, played a few excerpts from the orchestral repertoire. The talk, or recital it might be called, was well received and before leaving the hall I was approached by a master at an Epsom school to give a similar demonstration to his boys. This I did, and over coffee was introduced to a few of the master's professional colleagues, who had been invited to hear the talk and who in turn invited me to their schools. The scholastic world is not without its 'bush telegraph', and in due course I was asked to address the young ladies of Roan School, Greenwich. And so it all started, and, due no doubt to my taking part in such broadcasts to schools as 'Adventures in Music' with delightful personalities like Dr. Reginald Jacques, and my own (first) spoken broadcast (in the Forces Programme, October 1947, at the invitation of the producer, Arthur Langford), and subsequently my work in North London schools with Archie and Joyce Camden, my recitals prospered sufficiently for one small boy – a real London urchin – to say to me after a talk in his school, 'Coo mate, that was smashing – I thought it was going to be all dry and mouldy – all opera.' In contrast (in another North London school) after J.G. and I had spent some time fixing up our equipment, a teacher asked: 'When do the musicians arrive?'

By 1948 Joan Goossens and I were convinced that we had sufficient in common to share our lives, and on 17th June (her birthday) we were quietly married in Weeke Church, Winchester, sufficiently early in the morning for the wedding breakfast to be a breakfast. Following a brief honeymoon in Switzerland we returned to our Ewell home, as I had already sold Dorset Drive, Edgware. My wife continued to play the oboe professionally and teach at, for example, Westminster School and St. Martin's High School, Tulse Hill. I remained busy in the film and recording studios and in the concert hall. My work in the film studios continued to interest and challenge me. For the film *Anna Karenina*, Dr. Hubert Clifford arranged for me to meet Constant ('Connie') Lambert to discuss the possibility of procuring three bells to sound as near as possible to the bells in St. Ivan's Church in the Kremlin in Moscow. Connie, a perfectionist, had carefully checked the pitch of these huge bells (the largest of which weighed nearly sixty tons) and had arranged a sequence in his score accordingly. Genuine church bells of the size of the Kremlin bells were out of the question, so Messrs. Boosey & Hawkes kindly experimented with bronze tubing, and tubular bells measuring up to fifteen feet in length proved satisfactory. They were suspended from a cross section in the roofing and a high platform erected to allow the percussionist to strike the tubes at the upper end. After the bell player nearly broke his neck in reaching the top of the platform, it was discovered that the bells sounded just the same when struck at the lower end.[7]

It may not be known that Constant Lambert, in addition to being a fine conductor, was an expert percussionist. It is said that on one occasion (at a party) he played the whole – or nearly the whole – of the percussion part in his *Rio Grande*. This led to me being challenged to play the percussion score (written for five players) on my own. To play everything in this involved score was, for me at least, quite impossible, but I edited a part for a single player and performed it at an afternoon and an evening performance at Dartington Hall. All went well as far as I was concerned, but at the afternoon performance certain members of the choir (and at least half the audience I was told) tended to watch my gymnastics rather than the conductor's beat, and so for the evening performance I played behind a large

[7] I subsequently used one of the bells in the film *The Beggar's Opera* at the request of Sir Arthur Bliss.

HALFWAY

screen. A memorable occasion for me, and to some extent for John
Amis who was singing in the choir, for at the evening performance
he was able to fulfil a life's ambition and play a stroke on my large
Chinese gong. Now John is a herculean figure (in stature as well as
musical scholarship) and I expected a great deal from him, but he
disappointed me, for whilst counting his bars' rest he developed a
touch of the palsy and when it came to his big moment his quivering
hand gave the gong a stroke that would have done justice to a
mouse striving to play *pp*.

Engagements involving a few days at pleasant places like Dartington proved a welcome break from the slog of London, which leads
me to the matter of holidays. All work and no play may seem a
strange adage for a musician to use, but the principle is applicable
as much to an instrumentalist as anyone else. My experience in
Switzerland with the National Orchestra, combined with happy
memories of this glorious country whilst honeymooning, resulted
in Switzerland or its near-neighbour Austria becoming our regular
holiday ground. If ever there was a place to relax and forget about
paradiddles and keeping the side drum roll trim with a spell of
'Daddy-Mammy',[8] it is Switzerland, and no better place I thought (in
1949) for a quiet holiday than Stalden – a delightful village on the
route from Visp to Zermatt and the Matterhorn. Following a splendid journey across France in my 1939 Rover 12, we found accommodation in a typical Gasthaus and after the day's drive I relaxed
before dinner by gazing at the not-too-distant ranges, and while doing
so said to my wife, 'We're a long way from crotchets and quavers
for a couple of weeks.' At that precise moment coming from the
distance I heard 'Mammy-Daddy-Mammy-Daddy' being beaten at
slow pace on a drum. So much for being away from crotchets and
quavers, I thought, and on investigation I found a group of Swiss
boys engaged in nightly practice as 'Basle drummers' (an illustrious
combination existing in Switzerland since 1332). The enthusiasm of
those young drummers thrilled me, and I may have startled some of
them, for after playing a jazz rhythm including a few 'rim shots'
one said, 'Herr ist ein Teufel.'

The Soldier's Tale

In my book *Percussion Instruments and Their History* I have described Stravinsky's *The Soldier's Tale* as a 'pearl' among percussion

[8] Mammy-Daddy RR-LL or LL-RR steadily accelerated produces a roll. A
paradiddle is LRLL-RLRR, or RLRR-LRLL.

scores. I shall always be grateful to my composer friend Clifton Parker for giving me a pocket score of the work and for his suggestion that I should study it – but not during the recording of his film score on which we were engaged at that time at Denham. I first performed *The Soldier's Tale* under the baton of Paul Sacher in December 1950. The solo violin on this occasion (a BBC broadcast) was played by Max Rostal. I subsequently took part in performances of this work under the batons of Stravinsky, Robert Craft and Harry Samuel, to name but a few. The orchestra directed by Harry Samuel included some young players who were climbing the ladder of fame. Among these were Colin Davis (clarinet), William Waterhouse (bassoon) and Philip Jones (trumpet). Performing the percussion score of *The Soldier's Tale* under Stravinsky in 1957 was an unforgettable experience, particularly as he explained to me his reasons for giving specific directions as to the placing of two drums in a vertical position and working the drumsticks back and forth between them: 'to give the utmost precision,' he said. (In certain rhythmic structures of a ragtime nature he complimented me by saying 'You must have played in a jazz band'.) The first performance of Stravinsky's *The Soldier's Tale* was given in Lausanne in 1918 conducted by Ernest Ansermet. In England the work was given its first performance in Newcastle in 1924 under Edward Clark (the husband of my dear friend Elisabeth Lutyens). The percussionist was William Bradshaw. It is not surprising that Edward Clark gave *The Soldier's Tale* its airing in Great Britain, since he was a pioneer in numerous directions.

I have had the privilege of taking part in many first performances including works by Benjamin Britten, Sir Arthur Bliss and Carl Nielsen. I could also say – not disrespectfully I trust – that I have taken part in first performances that have also proved to be 'last' performances: works by young and obscure composers who quite often produced creditable compositions that to their intense disappointment (and on occasions my own) failed to meet with any success. The memory of some first performances saddens me for other reasons, mainly that many of those taking part have played their last performances, as for instance that renowned and respected virtuoso Frederick (Jack) Thurston with whom I played the side drum obbligato in the first performance in England of Nielsen's Clarinet Concerto. This was at a concert given by the Haydn Orchestra conducted by Harry Newstone in the Wigmore Hall in February 1952. The programme included Mozart's *Serenata Notturna*, a work for strings and timpani which became my 'party piece' with the Max

Rostal Ensemble. Whenever I played this piece with that superb combination, Max would flick the D string of his violin near to the head
of my smaller kettledrum of a pair (tuned to D and A) to see if the D
rang in sympathy; and if it did not, he would wait whilst I adjusted
the pitch to ensure perfect unison.

Working with chamber ensembles such as the Max Rostal Ensemble and the Wigmore Ensemble, and larger orchestras, including
the Goldsbrough Orchestra and the London Symphony Orchestra,
playing in the Royal Choral Society's carol concerts under Sir
Malcolm Sargent, my annual Good Friday *Messiah* at the People's
Palace (under Dr. William Cole), and yearly visits to the Leith Hill
Festival, gave me great pleasure, as did my continued connection
with the film and recording studios. I spent much of my time at
Denham and the Gaumont Studios, Shepherd's Bush, recording with
Muir Mathieson and Louis Levy. I continued to meet interesting
composers including Georges Auric, Arthur Benjamin, Miklos Rosza,
William Alwyn, Matyas Seiber, Francis Chagrin, Antony Hopkins,
Elisabeth Lutyens, Priaulx Rainier, Mischa Spoliansky, Max ('Poppa')
Steiner, (Sir) Lennox Berkeley, Alan Rawsthorne, Kenneth V. Jones
and many others. Not unnaturally I was asked to provide numerous
percussion sounds, some orthodox, some otherwise: a 1925 Ford
car with a loose tappet, a gurgling brook, recording a short 'snippet'
on a glockenspiel with a clothes peg on my nose because the microphone was so close, or playing a Jew's harp in the BBC programme
'Just William' because the young hero had dreamed that he had
played a Jew's harp before Royalty in the Royal Albert Hall. Sounds
like these made the imitation of a ship's bell seem a simple matter.
Except in the case of a certain recording session for Antony Hopkins
who, when reeling out his percussion requirements to me over the
telephone, said that he must have a ship's bell to sound a pure F in
the treble register. This necessitated a visit to that Mecca of boating
enthusiasts, Beale's in Shaftesbury Avenue. My enquiry for a ship's
bell was received graciously, but the shop assistant's face fell when I
said that it must sound a pure F in the treble register. He did, however, allow me to rummage round the rear of the department and
after several customers had decided that they had entered the White-
chapel Bell Foundry in error, I found a medium-sized bell giving off
the required note. (I intend to will it to Tony in recognition of my
admiration for him, and also because he recommended me (in 1955)
to my first real plum of a club lecture: for the Leicester Music
Club.) Another effect I was obliged to produce for a nautical film
was a few calls on a bosun's pipe. To make certain that I did not

pipe the men up when I should have been piping them down, Louis Levy insisted that I 'got to know something about it' – so I took an hour's lesson with a semi-retired bosun who did relief work opening and closing Tower Bridge.

Due to the rapid progress in technique, I had little opportunity when recording at the Lime Grove Studios for a 'kip' in the five-shilling bed at the back of the screen (the bed I had purchased in 1930 in Shepherd's Bush market). It was there, however, and remained so until well after the BBC acquired the studios for TV purposes.[9] I well remember being called to provide some special percussion sounds for a TV film directed by Nesta Pain. On arrival a kindly commissionaire instructed a youth to show me where Studio 8 was, and on entering the studio I said to the youth, 'Is that the screen where they show the film?' On being told that it was, I told him that if he looked behind the screen he might find a bed there. He certainly found a bed there and taking a hasty glance at me he left the studio somewhat abruptly.

According to John Amis (in Vogue – Britannica Number, February 1953) my professional career to date had been spent in doing calculated violence to a variety of instruments. To this intriguing description of the professional side of an orchestral percussionist's vocation, could be added the task of calculating to a split second periods of silence, lengthy and otherwise; for strange as it may seem to some, it is at times far more difficult to do nothing than to do something. A count of 209 bars' rest instead of Wagner's prescribed 210 preceding the entry of the first mighty clash of cymbals in Die Meistersinger overture leads to 'being sent for'. I have been 'sent for' on many occasions, though not always for giving a mighty swipe in the wrong place. I was called on one occasion (somewhat hurriedly) to the Waldorf Hotel to a luncheon party organised by the Overseas Department of the BBC at which a number of overseas visitors were being entertained. The purpose of my presence was to reply to a certain American gentleman who had said that he considered the 'most heard percussionist in the world' to be Gene Krupa. Let me say immediately that as a drummer Gene Krupa was considered to have no peer as a player, and at that time was heard to a greater extend in person, on record and on the radio than any other percussionist. The BBC officials felt I had a fair claim to being heard more universally, and after explaining my part in the recording of the Rank film title (the gong strokes), the war-time V signal, and as a

[9] The first programme was transmitted from Lime Grove on 21st May 1950.

'slight extra' the sound of the town crier's hand bell in the corner of the Gaumont British newsreel, the American gentleman gave me best – and a large cigar. I could have added other examples of my 'calculated violence' that went round the world, but why expand on what is really just a job of work?

Playing before Royalty 1953

Over thirty years have passed since my pal Frank Hitchborn and I, following our escapade on the occasion the Prince of Wales opened Peterborough Agricultural Show, rushed to the stationer's shop in Peterborough to have cards printed 'Played before Royalty'. Little did I think at that time that one day I would be a member of the 1953 Coronation Orchestra in Westminster Abbey. This orchestra – one of the finest ever to be assembled in Britain – was conducted by William McKie (later Sir William) and Sir Adrian Boult. It was recruited, as was the 1937 Coronation Orchestra, by Eugene Cruft, M.V.O., O.B.E., the notable double bass player and musical authority, who for many years was principal bass in the BBC Symphony Orchestra. 'Gene' (founder of the Pro Arte Orchestra) will long be remembered as one of the best-known and respected of professional musicians. John Walton – Gene's successor in the BBC Orchestra – wittily assessed him by saying that he had spent the first six months in the orchestra erasing Gene's pencilled bowing marks and the following twelve months in replacing them. The invitation to play at the Coronation Service came from (Sir) William McKie. I took the invitation as stated, '. . . as an honour, carrying with it the obligation to do everything in your power to make the orchestra worthy of so great an occasion, and representative of the nation's finest orchestral playing'.

Much has been said and written about the Coronation of Queen Elizabeth II, and the presentation of the ceremony on the radio and television remains one of the highlights of the achievements of the BBC. Only those who threaded their way through the mass of cables of all kinds in the Abbey fully realise the skill involved in presenting the ceremony without a hitch. The smooth running of the several rehearsals was mainly due to the masterly direction of the Earl Marshal – the late Duke of Norfolk.[10] Apart from the difficulty

[10] A minor diversion which at least amused the members of the orchestra occurred when the Earl Marshal announced over the speaker that a telegram had been received for Mr. James Blades – my wife's only means of contacting me about a pressing engagement.

of seating sixty instrumentalists in the organ loft of the Abbey, everything went according to plan, with the exception of a minor hitch at the first rehearsal, when there was a slight delay at the start, due to George Eskdale and Harold Jackson taking some time to agree as to who was going to play first trumpet in certain items. Sir Adrian waited patiently until agreement had been reached and then said, 'Thank you gentlemen, may I now rehearse?' As he lifted his baton however, Jimmy Bradshaw stood up and in his deliberate and individual voice said, 'Sir Adrian – you are aware that I require four kettledrums and I have only room for three'. In dead silence (apart from stifled giggles) Sir Adrian rustled up his moustache and said, 'Mr. Bradshaw, under the circumstances I am certain that Her Majesty will forgive the omission of the fourth voice – may we proceed?' We proceeded, with Jimmy playing with his usual aplomb and accuracy and delighting Eric Pritchard and I, who were playing percussion immediately behind him. Jimmy was not unaware of our observance of his style, for when questioned by a friend some time after the Coronation about how he got on with his two colleagues, he replied that 'they both received a good lesson for which they got a medal and a matter of forty guineas' (four guineas Coronation expenses, plus various recording fees). The 'Day' was memorable and well typified by a newspaper caption: 'All this and Everest too' (the summit was reached for the first time, by Edmund Hillary and Sherpa Tensing, on 1st June). The expertise of those concerned with the 'mechanics' of that wonderful ceremony continues to amaze me, not the least the clever manner in which a noble knight 'fished' the white napkin which Sidonie Goossens had the misfortune to drop from the balcony just before the Queen entered the West door.[11]

As I made my way to Broadcasting House that evening to take part in an 'Empire Broadcast' with the L.S.O. (similar to the Christmas afternoon link-up before the King's speech) I thought sorrowfully of my late Uncle George and the fact that what to me were proud moments in my professional adventure could not now be shared with him or with my father, for only a few weeks earlier I had said a last goodbye to Dad.

[11] The orchestra assembled at 7.30 a.m. on the day of the Coronation and instructions were given to bring sandwiches wrapped in a white napkin.

13

I Join the English Opera Group

A telephone call from Basil Douglas, the manager of the English Opera Group (a few weeks before Coronation Day) had resulted in my making a quick trip to Wiesbaden in Germany to play in performances of Benjamin Britten's chamber opera *Albert Herring*. Meeting Britten again gave me intense pleasure, as did playing the percussion score of his fascinating opera. The stay in Wiesbaden remains in my memory for several reasons, not the least being when Dennis Brain invited me to be his car companion whilst he visited the famous horn manufacturers, Alexander's of Mainz. Whilst Alexander's premises were most interesting, what was even more enjoyable was talking with Dennis, who was as pleasant and interesting in conversation as he was thrilling on the concert platform.

There were other notable musicians in that orchestra of twelve players: Olive Zorian, leader; Suzanne Rosza, second violin; Cecil Aronowitz, viola; Terence Weil, 'cello; Francis Baines, double bass; John Francis, flute; Stephen Waters, clarinet; Joy Boughton, oboe; Jack Alexandra, bassoon; Enid Simon, harp; and Viola Tunnard, piano. At that time Britten on most occasions conducted his chamber operas. He was – though he would never admit to it – a magnificent conductor, being known to professional players, from the rank and file to the leader, as a 'musicians'' conductor. He always made a point politely but conclusively, as for example when I ventured to say to him at Wiesbaden that if another quaver had been included in a decidedly tricky passage for the side drum in *Albert Herring* it would have been simpler to play, he replied, 'Oh yes, but then it would have been ordinary, and I try not to be ordinary.'

My First Aldeburgh Festival

To take part in twenty Aldeburgh Festivals is not given to many, and I learned much of Aldeburgh and its folk, even from the first occasion when, breakfasting in the small dining room of The Railway Hotel, the proprietress, Mrs. Baker, told me of the goings on in Aldeburgh since 'the mad folk from London had invaded the place'. I was of course one of the 'mad folk', for she found it puzzling that I occasionally returned to London overnight or left Aldeburgh in the small hours to fulfil a London engagement on my clear days. Mrs. Baker made certain that I was well fortified internally and able to cope with the strenuous task of 'banging those drums for Benjamin Britten'. Like many others in Aldeburgh, she found B.B's music distinctly puzzling. More puzzling to me was fitting my equipment into the small corners allotted to me in the various rehearsal rooms such as The Working Men's Clubs in Aldeburgh or Thorpeness, a few square feet below the pulpit in the Parish Church, and finally into a corner of the Jubilee Hall, the orchestral pit being too small to accommodate my kettledrums and other percussion equipment.

To me that corner in the Jubilee Hall was hallowed ground, but not so to the dear lady who arranged the floral decorations and who refused to abandon her duty of constantly watering the large vase of flowers above my head, often to the detriment of my 'hair do' and occasionally of my drumheads. Before each evening performance in the small Jubilee Hall, I explained to those in a near and vulnerable position that, even though there were one or two surprises in the way of a sudden burst from my corner, there was no need to use earplugs. By this time Joy Boughton was usually sounding the A, and I secluded myself behind my screens awaiting Ben's entry and his downbeat which, if he stood on a small rostrum in the pit, I was just able to see without the use of a periscope. Looking back I marvel at what has been achieved in the Jubilee Hall, Aldeburgh – operas ranging from the gay abandon of *Albert Herring* to the tense drama of *The Turn of the Screw* have been staged to perfection, and for the very simple reason that there was always real co-operation on all sides. I made many friends in Aldeburgh and became well acquainted with its environs. One of my favourite walks was the half mile from the Moot Hall to the look-out post on the beach leading to Thorpeness. This post intrigued me. It seemed strangely familiar and eventually I realised why. I had seen it before: in 1936, on an Easter weekend trip during which my wife and son had camped in a nearby field, when the gale from the North Sea permitted (it was a shocking weekend), I took a snap of my small son on the post. My grandson has since been photographed on the same post. Another favourite spot of mine was Tunstall Forest. This became my retreat and an ideal place to browse over a percussion score, or plan material for a full-length adult lecture. Up to that time my lecture activities had been confined almost entirely to work in small schools, but I felt that presentations to music clubs and larger schools could be pleasant and profitable. This has proved to be the case.

Following the Aldeburgh Festival, the Group played *The Rape of Lucretia* in Schwetzingen in Germany, and *The Beggar's Opera* at the Taw and Torridge Festival in Barnstaple, but I do not know whether all who heard Britten's subtle arrangement of *The Beggar's Opera* fully understood its numerous subtleties. I feel also that my Barnstaple landlady (a Mrs. Adams of Sticklepath Hill) may not have fully approved of the workings of the English Opera Group, for when our first morning rehearsal ran over time, she telephoned the theatre to say that 'Mr. Blades must come home immediately as his dinner's getting cold'. I have pleasant memories of Barnstaple and Mrs. Adams' dinners, and of Devon cream teas. Over one of these I discussed my lecture activities with Charles and Beatrice Gregory who, in addition to controlling the interests of the Boyd Neel Orchestra, were then forming a concert agency. It was soon agreed that Charles and Beatrice should become my agents, and thus started a run of many happy and (I feel sure) mutually advantageous years. The Gregorys' 'right hand man' was a delightful lady in the person of Jo Slocombe. Jo had a happy knack of persuading me to accept dates in remote and distant places. On one occasion she almost convinced me that as Greenwich was only twenty miles from Watford I could do the journey by car in half-an-hour (at 5 p.m. on a weekday) and that Tenby could be considered an 'en route' date between Southend and Great Yarmouth.

From the autumn following my first Aldeburgh Festival, my adult recitals began to get under way, and by the end of 1953 James Blades and Joan Goossens were becoming known as recitalists; 1953 had been an eventful year, but not without its sadness. There was a vacant chair at the Christmas dinner table at 171 Star Road, Peter-borough – my father's. The Workington Conservative Men's Club was also short of an old member: my first wife's father 'the redoubtable C. E. Hewitt'. In addition, the musical profession was missing one of its greatest characters: Ernest Irving who had died in October.

That year closed with such activities as the Royal Choral Society's carol concerts under Sir Malcolm Sargent. Christmas Day was a holiday for me, but was immediately followed by various recording sessions with the London Symphony Orchestra and the English Opera Group. My diary for 1953 reminds me that I played percussion with Geoffrey Gilbert's Wigmore Ensemble, which must have included Marie Korchinska, a lady for whom I have a tremendous respect, both as an artist and as a person. On one occasion, after she had laboriously squeezed her harp into the only available space in the pit of the Royal Opera House, a famous conductor told her to change her position. She had the courage to tell him that if he did not want the harp there, he would not get it anywhere, and promptly set to work removing her instrument. Great people these lady harpists, as (for example) Marie and Sidonie Goossens, and Enid Simon. Enid was for many years the harpist to the Aldeburgh players and the English Opera Group, and I well remember her startling the male occupants in the staff canteen of the Staatsoper, Wiesbaden, by making her entry smoking a pipe. In Heidleberg she made a similar entry but added a pull on the rabbit's tail which hung in the doorway of the canteen. This, unfortunately for Enid, rang a bell, and according to tradition cost her 'beer all round'.

The Turn of the Screw

Quite a lot of my professional life has been spent in turning screws, as before the general use in England of pedal-tuning drums it was necessary for an orchestral timpanist to be a nimble screw-turner. For instance, in Coleridge Taylor's *Hiawatha*, there are 122 changes of tuning. In many symphonic works there are numerous changes, giving rise to the remark of a lady, who said of the timpanist after a Prom that 'he never seemed satisfied with his drums as he was turning the little taps first one way then another all through the concert'. However, this section does not relate to changes of pitch on orchestral timpani, but to Benjamin Britten's chamber opera *The Turn of the Screw* which, of all Britten's works, remains my favourite piece to play. For some months before the première of this opera (at the Teatro Fenice, Venice, September 1954), Ben (through Imogen Holst) had kept me 'posted' as to his requirements, and in fact 'Imo' sent me the percussion score a few pages at a time as they were completed. From time to time Ben discussed certain details with me, such as making, in the workshop/garage of my new bungalow home in Cheam, a special set of chimes for the 'mad bells' in the church scene (2nd act). For the opening scene, B.B. typified the nervous beating of the heart of the governess as her coach approached Bly with a motif on four kettledrums. He told me that he felt certain this would work as he had tried the pattern on the kitchen table. To this I ventured to ask, 'But Ben, did you try it out on four tables?' After a prior rehearsal in London, the company flew to Venice, where rehearsals continued for several days. At the world première performance, which was broadcast, Ben relieved any possible tension on the part of the instrumentalists by giving each of us as we entered the orchestra pit a small silver brooch in the shape of a gondola.

Whilst in Venice I acquired – quite by chance – a private gondolier. My hotel, the Pension Seguso, was situated on the Zatterie, and to reach the centre of Venice it was convenient and pleasant to walk by the side of the Giudecca Canal and the Church of the Salute, and then cross the Grand Canal to St. Mark's Square in a 'public' gondola.[1] No strict charge was made by the gondolier, who merely collected tips in his straw hat as his customers left the boat. On my first trip I obviously tipped him so liberally that on each occasion thereafter he arranged that I had the gondola to myself. Crossing the Grand Canal in my 'private' gondola is but one of the pleasant and interesting recollections of Venice in 1954. Among other memories were seeing in the *New York Times* a rather flattering reference by Cynthia Jolly to my performance of Britten's percussion score; sitting below one of the gaily-coloured sunshades outside the Pension Seguso and watching idly the constant activity on the Giudecca; working on the script of my first lengthy entrance into literature (an article for The Fountain Press entitled 'How to Choose an Instrument'), and my encounter with a Venetian shopkeeper when purchasing a batch of postcard reproductions of famous composers. I spent a long time in this unusual but delightful shop collecting a picture of every composer on display. I took them to the proprietress who sat ogre-like behind a desk at the doorway of the shop. She counted them deliberately, and on reaching the last one she banged it on her desk, eyed me fiercely and said, 'What! No Verdi?' to which I replied, 'Madame, there is no Verdi in the shop.' Still eyeing me suspiciously she looked at her stock, and then from a cupboard produced 'some Verdis'. I bought two – one for luck! A satisfying moment for me, and nearly as satisfying as collecting odd scraps from the well-stocked table at Pension Seguso and feeding the emaciated cats in the nearby square who seemed to exist only by keeping down the fly population of Venice, or my search for a wedding present for my son and Doreen Christian, his bride-to-be.

1954 ended as had 1953, with school and other recitals, a spate of carol concerts, broadcasts with the Boyd Neel Orchestra, Trevor Harvey's St. Cecilia's Orchestra and the Kalmar Orchestra, plus a variety of film sessions – and (as a reminder of old times) playing the New Year in at an Old Year's Night Ball held in a rather exclusive establishment in Golders Green. Any cobwebs from the crowded

---

[1] I had an ideal room-mate at Pension Seguso: Terence Weil (the 'cellist), who invariably 'came home with the milk' about the time I was rising.

ballroom at Golders Green were blown off on New Year's Day at
Eastbourne during the break between the rehearsal and performance
with Geraldo and his Concert Orchestra. Reading my 1955 diary I
find that on the day following my engagement with Geraldo I played
for another personality in the entertainment world: Vic Oliver.
Vic, like Geraldo, was a splendid master, more full of fun than
Geraldo, but equally cool, even when Jimmy Clubb (his favourite
percussionist) gave a terrific clash on the cymbals at the end of
Bizet's *Farandole* after the orchestra had finished, and excused himself by shouting (to the delight of the audience) 'I won't charge
you for that one Vic!'

Under the Gregory banner my lecture activities were rapidly
expanding. As Charles exercised no 'sole rights', I continued to do
odd dates for my friends the Camdens, and a rather special ('shop
window') recital at the Royal Festival Hall for the Orpheus Society,
whose artistic director was John Francis. Taking part in the recording
of Britten's *Ode to St. Nicholas* in Aldeburgh in mid-April made a
welcome break.[2] In May the Orpheus Society invited me to give an
evening talk in the recital room of the Royal Festival Hall. This was
followed by a delightful couple of weeks in Schwetzingen with the
English Opera Group. The stage director for the opera (*The Turn of
the Screw*) was a young man with a foot well placed in the theatrical
ladder of fame: that ace producer Colin Graham, whom I had first met
as assistant stage manager at Barnstaple. Schwetzingen was followed
by the Aldeburgh Festival and the Holland Festival. Performances
were given in Amsterdam and The Hague of the same opera. In both
cities Britten's superb chamber opera was received with the greatest
of enthusiasm. My own contribution did not escape attention and
in the Amsterdam *Telegraph*, H. J. M. Muller wrote: '. . . More
eloquent we did never hear this instrument, and the artist who
plays it is, briefly, a great master.' The press were unanimous in
their approval of Britten's skill as a composer and as a conductor,
which made the remark of the wife of an eminent British personage
puzzling, for at a dinner at The Hague, in speaking approvingly to
Ben of his opera she said, 'Please tell me Mr. Britten, have you written
other works?' (Possibly as difficult to reply to as was the remark
made to Owen Brannigan by a lady who, after a performance of
Britten's *A Midsummer Night's Dream* said – from a distance in a
crowded restaurant – 'Oh, Mr. Brannigan, I did enjoy seeing your
"Bottom" last night'.) A further memorable performance of *The
Turn of the Screw* was given at Llangollen – in a tent! It was a wet

[2] My brother Tom was the other percussionist.

night I remember, but the pitter-patter of the raindrops had its compensation: it helped to drown the sound of the several and varied competitions being held alongside. That engagement in Holland was, for me, full of splendid occasions such as meeting the timpanist of the Concertgebouw Orchestra. Jan Labordus remains a good friend of mine, and has honoured me by including me among his children's god-parents. He was most complimentary of my work in the Opera House, and I became fully acquainted with his own skill when invited to hear him play Beethoven's 7th Symphony at a memorable performance under Van Beinum. To strengthen his argument that only 'practice makes perfect', Jan showed me a practice pad that his father had made for him and that he had used from childhood. It consisted of a block of wood which strapped on his knee. The wood, which was nearly one inch in thickness, was almost worn through in the centre – an example of diligence that I have quoted to my students on many occasions.

Jan Labordus also introduced me to many off-beat nooks and crannies in Amsterdam. Others I discovered in my own ramblings, including a second-hand bookshop in a back street where I purchased – in almost a decrepit a condition as the shop and its proprietor – an early edition of Naumann's *History of Music*. The bookseller, though it was late afternoon, was robed in an old dressing gown, and though not of Jewish persuasion reminded me of Fagin as he is frequently portrayed in *Oliver Twist*. He had however (as far as I could judge) none of Fagin's doubtful habits. On learning that I was a professional musician performing in Amsterdam he almost gave me the book. He told me (in excellent English) much about himself and how during the 1939–45 war he had 'worked for Britain'. On learning that my wartime activities included making the 'V for Victory' signal he proffered his hand and said, 'Come into my home'. His 'home' was a small unkempt bed-sitting room at the rear of the shop. Here, from a somewhat secret-looking desk he produced two 2½ Dutch guilder pieces (dated 1932 and 1933). These he gave to me 'for making the poom, poom, poom signal', the rhythm of which he tapped many times on the table with one of the coins.[3] On my return to England

---

[3] I have often been reminded of the impact of the BBC signal at my lecture-recitals where I demonstrate the use of my African drum on which the original beats were recorded. On an occasion in Bath (1954) I addressed the members of the Savage Club, my invitation following a visit by Winston Churchill. At the conclusion of my talk a gentleman in a wheelchair asked if he could touch the drum on which the V signal was recorded. He said that he had often been cheered by the sound of it during the years spent in Stalag IX.

I used those coins on the timpani in Variation 13 of Elgar's Enigma Variations where the effect of the ship's engine is required. In Elgar's day it was produced by the timpanist executing a tremolo on the drum with two pennies – in the fifties it was *infra dig.* to use anything less than half crowns, and today, of course with inflation, 50 penny pieces are necessary. I used those Dutch guilders many times before the close of 1955 and, as my lecture-recitals were becoming more numerous, in music clubs and public schools, including amongst others Liverpool Philharmonic Arts Club, Leicester Arts Club, Leicester Music Club, Wellingborough School for Robert Britten (Ben's brother), Radley College, Cranleigh School, and Aberdeen Music Club and the High School for Girls – a school with one of the most forward-looking curricula in the country, for the City Music Adviser was John Dalby. Intermingled with these recitals were recording dates with Yehudi Menuhin and with Sinfonia of London, a break-away from the L.S.O. The Sinfonia of London was managed by Gordon Walker, with his son Eddie as artistic director. It quickly became, and remained for many years, one of the best-known orchestras in film music, its chief conductor being Muir Mathieson.

I notice that my diary for 1955 shows 343 working days. Some may say how did I do it? – others of course why did I do it?

Man Proposes

Lecture-recitals at the Cambridge University Music Faculty, the Composers' Concourse, and the Royal Academy of Music gave a good start to 1956. I cannot remember, however, whether my New Year's resolution for this year was to keep up the pace of 1955, but if so it received an unpleasant shock before the year was halfway through, for on Sunday 27th May, during a rehearsal with the Robert Farnon Concert Orchestra, I fell from a rostrum at the BBC Lime Grove TV Studios, and left the building – from which I had so often rushed by taxi or other means to the Piccadilly Hotel – in an ambulance bound for Hammersmith Hospital, with a knee injury which laid me up for the following six months. I spent most of my first night in hospital in a coma, watched over by my brother Tom, who had taken my place so hurriedly and efficiently with Bob Farnon, and who kept my wife (somewhat discreetly) advised of my condition. The following day a major operation – the first of three – was performed. As I 'came to' I had a fleeting glance in the haze of a face peering into mine. It was none other than dear Jennifer Vyvyan, who had made a tedious journey to wish me well. In due course, during another short spell of consciousness, I recognised my wife, who had waited at my bedside for hours. She was armed with titbits for me, and a spray of flowers which had come from 'Ben and Peter'.

My condition at this time and for some months to follow was serious. Of my six weeks in hospital and the lengthy period of convalescence I prefer to say little. I have been extremely fortunate in my recovery, due in the main to the help of the Lord, a remarkably expert surgeon and a cheery private physiotherapist and, according to my surgeon, my own determination to get well. My recovery was a surprise to some, particularly one of the ward sisters who was convinced that I would die if I did not eat meat. I astounded this lady by amply supplying my bodily needs with no help from animal flesh. Despite the lack of exercise, my muscles were kept in fair trim, for some weeks those in my left leg being stimulated by the application of Faradism to the thigh muscles. I meet the surgeon each Christmas and he remains delighted with the knee joint he so skilfully pieced together, and over a convivial 'dram' we remind each other of the fact that, when I lay hung in a gantry, a member of my family circle informed me that 'if I had faith I could get up and walk home'. Though at the time I felt little like doing this and the hospital staff had their own views on the outcome, it remains the contention of Mrs. X that it would have been worth a go!

The BBC decided to contest my claim for damages, and so, aided by the legal department of the Musicians' Union, I instituted proceedings. A miserable and drawn-out law suit followed, ending in the Queen's Bench Division of the High Court in December 1961, where after five days of legal wrangling, judgment was given in my favour and I was awarded damages. It was felt by some that, in suing the BBC, my position with the Corporation would be jeopardised. Others felt that if my engagements were reduced in number I had a clear case for intimidation. No one need have worried: the most friendly relations have continued and remain between the BBC and myself. I am happy to say that I was able to play for Sir Malcolm Sargent at the Royal Choral Society's 1956 Christmas carol concerts, and this time I did not blot my copybook, as on a previous occasion when I gave a terrific whack on a pair of cymbals to open (as I thought) 'The First Nowell', but which proved to be an encore of 'Silent Night'. I was 'sent for', of course, and excused myself by saying that I was carried away by the occasion, to which Sir Malcolm replied that it was indeed a splendid evening. So much for 1956, not the best of years, but bearing in mind the nature of my injury and the extent of my recovery I can truthfully say that 'things could have been worse'.

As far as the following year was concerned, in many ways things could not have been better, professionally – and otherwise, for I had a grandson, John Malcolm Blades. Sinfonia of London continued busy, as did Louis Levy, who was now musical director for ABPC at Elstree. The English Opera Group's activities included performances of *Albert Herring*, Lennox Berkeley's new one-act opera *Ruth* at the Aldeburgh Festival, and *The Turn of the Screw* at the Berlin Festival. I also spent an interesting week lecturing at the Dartington Summer School of Music (directed then by William Glock), playing the *Sonata for Three Unaccompanied Kettledrums* by Daniel Jones (a work I subsequently recorded for the BBC), taking part in a performance of Constant Lambert's *Rio Grande* conducted by Raymond Leppard, and playing percussion with the Wigmore Ensemble in two performances of Stravinsky's *The Soldier's Tale*, the first conducted by Robert Craft and the repeat performance by the composer himself as I have already described.

It may Lead to Something

There used to be a saying in the dance band world that an audition or a 'ribby' date might lead to something. The most strenuous efforts, however, often led to nothing. This did not happen on the occasion I first lectured at Charterhouse School, in February 1957. Over the splendid meal following the recital, John Wilson, the Director of Music, asked my wife and me if we would consider repeating our presentation at the Music Masters' Association Summer Conference to be held at Charterhouse in the coming July. To address an audience of public school boys is one thing, but to entertain a gathering of music masters following a lecture of the calibre given by Thurston Dart is another. Mr. Wilson convinced us, however, that the music masters would be delighted with us, and indeed they were, with the result that the lecture 'led to something': the 'something' being that nearly every member of the audience asked for a brochure or the name of my agent. The Gregory Concert Agency lost no time in filling our vacant dates with public school talks, and our winter engagements included visits to Felsted, Wellington College, Uppingham and Stonyhurst. On the evening before the visit to Stonyhurst we were in Cleethorpes, and at 9.30 a.m. on the morning following Stonyhurst we were due to start our first of three talks in Junior

Schools in Haslemere. As we drove past the railway station in Wigan my wife observed (through the November mist), that the dimly-lighted clock registered 10 minutes past eleven. Though she did not say it, her thoughts could well have been similar to those expressed to me once by Leon Goossens who, at 11 p.m. as we neared the fourth three-hour film session and looked like running into the fifth, said, 'Jimmy, there comes a time when even the money isn't attractive'.

Long journeys such as those from Cleethorpes to Stonyhurst and thence to Surrey, followed by little more than two hours sleep, had their compensations, particularly the manner in which our recitals were invariably received and also when reading such press notices as the one in a Nottingham newspaper in which 'R.P.L.' wrote: 'From a forest of percussion instruments assembled on the platform of the Queen's Hall, Nottingham, last night there emerged a Pucklike figure with a grin as wide as a glockenspiel and a confidential manner which would have done credit to a Cabinet minister. He is, however, neither sprite nor statesman, but a musician – a musician with a mission.' Such pleasurable moments are occasionally tinged with disappointment, however, as for example that my colleague Bill Bradshaw and I after many years were now no longer invited to play at the Royal Choral Society's carol concerts. We were given no explanation, neither did we discover any reason for the break. I suffered no pecuniary loss, as I was asked to join the music ensemble which Frederick Haggis used for the Goldsmith Choir carol concerts. Here I partnered Dr. O. H. Peasgood, Hubert Dawkes and Edwin Benbow, and was also given a solo percussion spot.

Meeting Young People

I have met a few young people in my time, some extremely young, my least mature observer (and participant) being a child who, on her first birthday, was brought to the music room of the Birmingham Chest Hospital and who surprised the audience of sick children by giving my bass drum one or two healthy strokes. In contrast I have met young gentlemen in their 'teens, as for instance those in the crowded Great Hall at Eton (in February 1958) for a recital which coincidentally was followed by another on the next day at Harrow School. These engagements were followed by autumn visits to many other schools. All were pleasant experiences and full of interest and amusing incidents. At Allhallows (Lyme Regis) for example, at question time a young man asked me which instrument he should now study as he had 'mastered the piano'; I felt obliged to reply, 'the piano, my boy'. At Bishop's Stortford (a public recital in Big School) I was presented with something of a poser by a prep. school boy who asked 'If a member of an orchestra played a wrong note would some members of the audience go round after the concert and ask the conductor for their money back?' When the mirth had subsided I replied to the effect that the profession had not, as yet, reached a crisis of this description.

No single work has involved my meeting groups of young people more than Britten's *Noyes Fludde*, which had its première (directed by Colin Graham) at the Aldeburgh Festival of 1958. Included in the large instrumental ensemble is a percussion group of six performers, presided over in most cases by a professional timpanist who, in the case of the Aldeburgh première, the recording for Decca and BBC TV, and numerous subsequent performances (including coaching the percussion group) in many parts of the country, was myself. The incidents surrounding these performances of 'The Fludde' are legion. All are pleasant, even if tinged with pathos, for there is rarely a dry eye at the conclusion of the performance (or run of performances) when, on coming 'back to earth' the participants realise that it is over until the next time. One important soloist is the player of the slung mugs which typify the rain drops heralding the storm, a sound Britten devised with the cooperation of Imogen Holst. Earthenware mugs, however, have a nasty habit of breaking at an embarrassing moment, and as part of my task in training the percussion squad has been to equip them, I have never lost an opportunity to acquire mugs or cups with a clear ringing sound and of different pitch. Trying out these elusive vessels has led to interesting situations such as at Ashby-de-la-Zouch, when on a certain Saturday morning some years ago I spent a long time testing a job lot of mugs and cups in the doorway of a hardware shop. After finding six beauties, I took them to the owner, who, on my saying, 'I'll have these six, please', replied, 'Oh you will, will you? Well if you don't mind my saying so, you're mighty particular at tuppence a time.'

In addition to meeting children concerned with various productions of *Noyes Fludde* I have met many thousands in schools. I have also met many who are not so fortunate as others, for I have become concerned with those who are physically handicapped by giving talks in such schools as the Vale Road School for Physically Handicapped Children in Harringay. Later I became President of the Poplar branch of the Wingfield Music Club for the handicapped, founded by Herbert Lyon. In contrast I spoke at the Sixty-First Annual Conference of the Incorporated Society of Musicians[4] on the last day of 1958.

A Mad Chase

If I were to set down in detail the whole of my professional activities for the years of 1959 and 1960 I feel that some people would, correctly or otherwise, say that I should have had my brain tested. Suffice to say that my diaries for these two years record one mad rush from studio to studio, or school to school. It may of course be considered that I was 'chasing cash'. I think that in fact I was chasing the clock, due in several cases to invitations from public school music masters who had attended my Charterhouse lecture, and Jo Slocombe getting me to agree that Aberystwyth was not all that out-of-the-way if I fitted it in between Sedburgh and Ipswich. A Scottish trip included a visit to a recently-opened school on Loch Rannoch. All Rannoch was invited to the recital, and I recollect that after my somewhat spirited rendition of *The British Grenadiers* a small girl was found to be sitting in a pool, and the proceedings were halted whilst she was cleaned up. I also remember that whilst tea and large rich tea biscuits were being consumed after the lecture, I saw an elderly gentleman (a retired minister from Skye) endeavouring to imitate my demonstration of the thumb roll on my tambourine. Such incidents, and an encounter with a young gentleman at Rugby who, during questions, said, 'Sir, they tell me that all your instruments were unloaded from a private car', and my replying that I could prove it to him by having his assistance in re-loading them, made the 20,000 to 25,000 miles a year on my car clock seem like a run to Brighton and back.

Work in the film and other studios moved along in much the same way. There were changes of course, and certain names ceased to appear in my diary, as for example, the indomitable Richard Crean whose maxim was that an orchestra is known by its last performance, and who had now ceased to give a piece 'another coat of paint'; and my old friend Louis Levy, who, shortly before his death, called me to him at the end of a film session at Elstree and said, 'Jim, how long is it now?' to which I replied, 'It is twenty-seven-and-a-half years, Mr. Levy.' Shaking me by the hand he said, 'and Jim, we've never had a wrong word, have we?', and we never had.

There were changes at Aldeburgh also. The orchestral arrangements were now controlled by the English Chamber Orchestra

[4] Of which my wife and I are members.

led by Emmanuel (Manny) Hurwitz and effectively managed by Ursula Strebi, and the Jubilee Hall pit had been slightly enlarged to accommodate my equipment. I was no longer known as 'the mole' to my landlady as Mrs. Baker had left Aldeburgh, but I was still capably managed domestically: by her successor at 'The Railway', Mrs. E. A. Kirby, who had taken me along with her to 'The Mill Inn'.

Among several friends in Aldeburgh were the Outerbridges, whose friendship I gained when young Richard Outerbridge became my Suffolk barber. A barber's shop is an ideal place for local gossip, and I heard as much about the mad folk from London and others whilst having a hair cut as I had done at breakfast in 'The Railway Hotel'. On one occasion a notable Aldeburgh resident (Arthur Burrell, whose son 'Billy', a fisherman like himself, was known to Benjamin Britten and was in Ben's mind when he and E. M. Forster were beginning to work on the libretto for *Billy Budd*[5]) informed me that he had told Mr. Britten ('Benjy' he said) that 'his music reminded him of his old winch when it wanted oiling', a remark I am certain Ben received graciously. Some comments by those who are not entirely aware of a musician's craft are often highly amusing, as are the comments of schoolchildren. A small boy in a Tottenham school, whilst admiring my array of instruments, asked me if they were all mine. On being told that they were he said, 'Coo mate, are they all paid for?' In the same area a small girl told my wife that she also played the piano, and on being asked if she did her scale practice each day replied, 'Oh, I left the scales behind a long time ago.'

It was just as well that I had not entirely disregarded my scales, for I had some exacting passages to perform at the '59 Aldeburgh Festival and later in Britten's Nocturne for tenor voice, seven obbligato instruments and string orchestra. I first performed this work, the timpani part of which is one of the most searching I have ever encountered, on a rather sad occasion, namely the memorial concert for Erwin Stein, who had been a pupil of Schoenberg and editor for Boosey & Hawkes, and a gentleman who never failed to chat with me at Aldeburgh and elsewhere. Another sad occasion was taking part in the memorial concert for that remarkable musician Matyas Seiber who, in addition to being a true friend of mine, had greatly influenced me musically. I must record two further entries for 1960. First I was approached by Faber & Faber to write a lengthy book on the history of percussion instruments, an invitation I accepted – encouraged to a great extent by my wife and my dear friend Arthur

[5] Ben and E. M. Forster became god-parents to Billy's first child.

Langford – and, second, I appeared in a programme commemorating V Day on Nederland Television on 5th May. My part in the Dutch programme was to demonstrate the recording of the V signal. The transmission went out 'live' from Scheveningen. Before leaving Amsterdam on the following day I called to see my friend Jan Labordus at a rehearsal in the Concertgebouw where I received an unexpected ovation from the orchestra. I was also recognised at the airport, and was obliged to let one or two officials have a tap on my 'V signal drum'.

🎝 14 🎝

The Sixties

I am by no means alone in feeling that, as I grow older, time slips by more quickly. I now seem to find myself at the Christmas dinner table before I have digested the previous New Year's morning breakfast, over which I have made so many good resolutions. One resolution I never fail to make on New Year's morning is to lessen my labours, but the sixties found me still very much of a mole and burrowing as deeply as ever. In addition to my normal orchestral and lecture activities, I was busy at my desk on a contribution for the Pelican *Musical Instruments Through the Ages*, a symposium edited by Anthony Baines. This was a commission 'handed' to me by Robert Thurston Dart, known to his friends as Bob Dart – hence his unique signature

I was also working on the early chapters of my *Percussion Instruments and Their History*, during the writing of which I wore out much shoe leather up and down the stone steps leading into the British Museum, where I searched among the mass of information on music and its history. It encouraged and pleased me to find my recently-published O.U.P. *Orchestral Percussion Technique* and my contribution to *How to Choose an Instrument* (Fountain Press) in the main catalogue of the British Museum, and that in addition to my entries in *Encyclopaedia Britannica* I was listed in the music catalogue as a composer: an obbligato for the side drum in Stanley Taylor's realisation (for recorder sextet) of The Earle of Oxford's Marche; a percussion part for two players in Tippett's *Crown of the Year*, and as editor of Boosey & Hawkes' *Tonal Perspective Series for Tuned Percussion*. In contrast, I was busy for the BBC on a script for *Music to Remember*, a programme presented in early March.

My work in schools continued, adding quite often to my postbag. In many of the letters from schoolchildren, my wife and I were told of matters not strictly connected with music, such as 'my

Auntie Mabel's linnet died yesterday'. On the other hand one letter read, 'I do not play an instrument, but the boy next door has a cousin who plays the guitar'. In some cases questions were asked that needed careful consideration. One eleven-year-old girl from Sussex wrote '. . . I hardly ever see an orchestra so I hope you will pardon my ignorance in asking this question. When a conductor waves his baton does he have to wave it in any special way? If so, can you tell me some of the signs he makes? – Love from Josie Goring.' Young as she was, I sent this child a valuable guide as to what a conductor does – Sir Adrian Boult's *Handbook on the Technique of Conducting.* In addition to charming compliments in letters, I have often been complimented in person. One small boy in a London school told me that he thought I was nearly as good as Ringo Starr. Another that I was 'as good as Dave Clark'. One boy (David – aged 8) said that I was very clever and that if he had a face like me he would 'go on TV and make people laugh'. Adults have also made interesting observations. One elderly gentleman told my wife as we were packing up at a club recital that 'Mr. Blades ought to take it up as he is nearly good enough to be a professional', and asked, 'What does he do in the daytime?' Comments from school teachers have been equally illuminating. One headmaster in a Cotswold village asked me to hold up the talk for a few minutes as he had made an error in placing some big boys in the front row, but then suddenly said, 'Oh, carry on please, from what I know of what is inside those boys' heads, those at the back will see all right.' Another headmaster introduced me quite neatly, I thought, by saying, 'Mr. Blades is one person I do not mind going on strike', whilst another announced me by saying, 'We've had the scrapers and the blowers, now we're going to have the bangers' – a strange conception of orchestral percussion I thought, but excusable, as was the remark by a caretaker at the Town Hall, Greenwich, who, in reply to my wife saying that the hall was a fine one but it was difficult to hear oneself, said, 'It's not you what wants to 'ear yourself – you've 'eard yourself thousands of times – it's them out there what wants to 'ear you.' Letters from parents to headmasters explaining the absences of their offspring are most revealing, none more so than two shown to us by the head of a secondary modern school in Norwich. One parent explained that her son was absent due to 'having diarrhoea through a hole in his sock', and another that 'John was late because he had to take his father's wooden leg to be mended'.

Observations by professionals can also be interesting, as for instance, the quiet remark of a famous singer to the somewhat lusty brass, 'I trust I am not singing too loudly for you gentlemen', or the reply by Anthony Collins to my colleague Jack Simpson who, ruffled by Anthony questioning the quality of a certain percussion instrument, said that he had 'two thousand pounds' worth of equipment in the studio' only to receive Tony's shattering reply, 'Break the orchestra for tea – I'll hear every pen'oth of it.' To cross swords with a man like Anthony Collins was dangerous. Tony, who had risen from the ranks (he was for some years principal viola in the London Symphony Orchestra) was a master in repartee as well as in composition. His wit could be friendly, though it was more often icy. He had his favourites and I was one of them; a fact which might have placed me in jeopardy with one or two of my drummer friends, when at a session at Watford Town Hall where two or three of my associates were battling manfully against great odds with instruments placed in almost inaccessible positions, Tony yelled, 'Sack the lot and send for Jimmy Blades'. Quite unfair of Tony of course, but I hope I deserved his more serious approbation. I feel that I did over the matter of a theatre production featuring Orson Welles in (among other items) a scene from *Moby Dick*. My instructions from Tony were to meet him at the Shaftesbury Theatre, together with my brother Tommy, and record some percussion motifs to back Orson Welles' narrative. 'I'll write for such things as timps, cymbals, gongs, and possibly side and tenor drums', Tony told me. Tommy and I were in readiness at the appointed time and place, but no sign of Tony. In due course (at closing time) Tony arrived, and with him Orson Welles. Both were a little the worse for wear. After lengthy felicitations I asked for the music. 'I've been too busy to write any', Tony explained, adding that he was certain the Blades Brothers could invent something in the way of the required incidental sounds. This we did and quite successfully, for our 'inventions' were used throughout the production. (Some considerable time after this incident I was approached by the Music Department of the BBC who required the 'Moby Dick music' for a broadcast production. I was told that every effort had been made to trace the original score. I explained the position as tactfully as I could, and was engaged to repeat as much of the mixture as I could remember.)

All's Well That Ends Well

To lose a treasured instrument is like losing a good friend. Imagine my horror, on striking my famous J. Arthur Rank gong before a talk at Charterhouse, to find its tone impaired. On investigation I discovered a small crack near the centre of the gong, and after much thought concluded that I had done a foolish thing once too often – closed my car door with a bang which could have pressed the instrument tightly on to the handle of a kettledrum. With a little humouring of the damaged instrument and the indulgence of the Carthusian audience I 'got by'. My orchestral gong was used until my friends the Paiste Brothers (who are famous as makers of cymbals and 'China' gongs) made me – in their Rendsburg factory – a tam-tam (a large gong) the tone of which corresponded to the original sound of my Chinese gong. The instrument they made for me (it is still in use) proved so superb that I immediately asked for another like it! To date, though the Paiste craftsmen have made many experiments for me, and supplied me with some excellent tam-tams and tuned gongs – including some for certain of Britten's operas – they have failed to produce the exact timbre of their initial attempt.

Gongs, like bells, have always fascinated me, and I rarely lose an opportunity to examine these instruments wherever they may be, and to increase my stock of them. I have not been able to indulge my fancy and search the temples of the Far East, or for that matter to see, as I have so often wished, Mount Everest at close quarters. But I have seen many places and had pleasant experiences, such as drifting down the Grand Canal in Venice in my private gondola, or swimming in the Adriatic. Both relaxations I enjoyed in company with other members of the Melos Ensemble, whilst battling with an avant garde composition during the 1961 Venice Festival of Contemporary Music, organised by Bruno Maderna.

The work with which I was concerned was *Improvisation 7*, a young composer's conception (a brilliant one) of a small ensemble improvising. It was a fierce piece, and to help myself in reading I re-wrote the part to lengthen each bar: from 2/4 into 4/2. After the second rehearsal Gervase de Peyer said he thought that I was 'the nearest yet' as I always did two heavy 'plonk-plonks' at about the same time. He also begged of me not to miss the 'plonk-plonks', as on hearing them he jumped to a given place in his part. After the first run-through at the dress rehearsal in the Teatro Fenice, Venice, I was kissed by the composer who said, 'Magnificent – never before has the percussion been played so well. How do you do it?' I explained by showing him my music, which he admired. After the second run-through which followed a convivial meeting in an adjacent wine bar, due to a misunderstanding over the starting place I played from the beginning of the piece, whilst the rest of the ensemble started halfway through. Eventually, noticing Gervase's look of anxiety, I decided to play my 'plonk-plonks' and we finished in great style. I was again greeted with, 'Wonderful – never before. . . .' *Improvisation 7* was repeated some months later to enthusiastic audiences in Warsaw.

Warsaw made a strong impression on me. I witnessed affluence, as for example the smart dinner parties that took place in our hotel, and I also saw poverty – one bicycle between several families, and so on. The swarms of schoolchildren in the book shops fascinated me, as I judged many of them were having a sly read of what they did not intend or were unable to purchase. Watching the re-building of Warsaw – the centre as it was originally – was also pleasant and a sharp contrast to my visit to the Ghetto. For reasons of exchange of finance we were paid 'on the nail' with instructions that it must all be spent in Poland. I bought cut glass and spent my last schlottis on a taxi ride round the city. Whether Terry Weil was too busy practising the 'cello to spend any money I do not remember, but I recollect that he showed me a handful of cash and said, 'Never before have I had too much money'. Another thing I remember is that on our departure David Mason, our trumpeter, was reminded that he had left his overcoat in his bedroom, and he replied 'I won't take it back to England – it might help that starved-looking liftman to keep warm in the winter'. He then changed the subject to who was the nearest or the furthest out at the previous performance – and did I start in the right place.

I hope I started in the right place in my pieces at the Aldeburgh, King's Lynn and Bath Festivals, and also at my recitals throughout 1961. These included a lecture-demonstration in my home town to a disappointingly-small audience. Compensation came a few days later with a bumper audience at the London University and a unique experience in Liverpool – a lecture in the canteen of Messrs. Bibby's. In addition to the comings and goings of the audience, my talk was frequently interrupted by the hissing of steam from a faulty heating sytem, though this may have added reality of my imitation of an old-fashioned 'puffer' train. The audience at Bibby's proved a grand one, and so did the lunch that followed, over which Mrs. Bibby kindly arranged that I should lecture at a small music club in Neston. Due to a trifling misunderstanding I was billed as 'James Blake' and my presentation as 'a rhythmic evening of beat and rhythm through the years.' A few changes in my routine covered the situation, as they did at a small club in Wales where, on arrival at the village hall, a lady requested her partner to put on the kettle as 'the concert party has arrived'. Over tea we were told how lucky the club had been the previous month, as two gentlemen from London who were going to sing 'from Schoenberg and Britten' were unable to appear, and that an audience sing-song concert took place instead. Our revised programme went down very well and my wife made no complaint about the grand piano being minus the pedals! Other memorable occasions include delivering my presentation from a boxing ring at Wrekin College, and one evening at Grendon Hall, Northants, where we christened a piece given us by Malcolm Arnold: *Concert Piece for Percussion and Piano*. This work continues to be a favourite with us and with our audiences, as does Benjamin Britten's *Timpani Piece for Jimmy*, the sketch of which Ben discussed with me on a train journey between Munich and Venice.

My 1961 Christmas dinner was eaten with a lighter heart than those since 1955, for my lawsuit was behind me, judgment having been given in early December, and I may have reflected on the judge's summing-up, during which he said that the case had been a difficult one, but that he felt the plaintiff had spoken the truth as he had remembered it. I certainly had, considerably aided by having before me a Biblical quotation (given me by my wife): '. . . when they deliver you up, take no thought how or what ye shall speak: for it shall be given you in that same hour what ye shall speak.' (Matthew 10: 19.)

Meeting the Great

In my professional adventure I have met many famous people and been in many famous places. The Great Hall at Eton, for instance. Here, on a return visit – June 1962 – to quote Kenneth Malcolmson the Director of Music, I more than kept awake 700 tired schoolboys. The concert halls at Uppingham, Harrow and Rugby (among others) are also treasured memories, particularly as I had so longed to see inside a public school when I was a boy, and had imagined myself in the quad, or dormitories of Rugby or Blundell's after reading *Tom Brown's Schooldays* or *Lorna Doone* – 'dreams' that have now been realised. Another thing that I little thought, as I watched (from the 4d's) the early Charlie Chaplin comedies, or as an apprentice engineer singing 'For the Moon shines bright on Charlie Chaplin' after winning the Bun and Lemon Competition, was that I should ever meet this great man. But I did meet him, and I have also had the pleasure of working with and for him, the first occasion being in a trade viewing theatre in Wardour Street where his silent film *The Champ* was shown to Louis Levy and me so that Louis could arrange a musical background and I had a chance to judge the requirements in the way of sound effects. Mr. Levy and I had the assistance of the maestro himself, who was as anxious as we were that the presentation of the film should be perfect at a forthcoming Royal Command Performance. The most important effect for me to 'catch' was to give a mighty crash at the point where Charlie (whose boxing glove was loaded with a horseshoe) gave his heavyweight opponent the knock-out blow. This he did after a terrific swing with his right hand had missed, causing Charlie to execute a series of spins which gave impetus to the final blow. The fact that I caught the effect on the first rehearsal caused Mr. Chaplin to say that he was certain I had done this sort of thing before. Over coffee I told him that at the run-through I had counted the number of pirouettes before the impact, and how my first manager had impressed on me the value of taking no notice of my music but to watch the screen! My subsequent meetings with C.C. were in the film studios. At Sound City, Shepperton, Charlie supervised the background music 'dubbed' to many of his silent films. The musical sequences were, in the majority of cases, composed by himself. They were orchestrated and conducted by Eric Spear from sketches taken down by Eric James, a fine pianist and arranger who spent many weeks with Mr. Chaplin in his Swiss home – Manoir de Ban – and who told me that Charlie was a martinet of a worker, and kept him hard at it from early morning until late evening, $5\frac{1}{2}$ days a week – so much so that instead of joining the constant convivial parties that were part of the routine in the Swiss mansion, he spent his off-time in bed recuperating in preparation for the next onslaught. I am sure, however, that he enjoyed his grilling as I so often did, for on most evenings at Shepperton at Charlie's request I worked overtime with both of us creating percussion effects. For one film (*Shoulder Arms* I think) Charlie required a 'tick tock' effect to dramatise the situation where an officer was intently watching the second hand of his wrist watch awaiting zero hour – the signal to attack.[1] 'Not wood blocks – something really sinister', I was told. The sound that most pleased C.C. was when I placed a small cymbal on a small kettledrum and a larger cymbal

[1] Zero hour in the film studios, though tense, was less dramatic. It occurred at the concluding time of a session when another 'take' meant running into a further session, and a full fee for possibly only a few minutes work. Many a hopeful or perhaps I should say expectant glance has been cast at the percussion section awaiting the drop of a triangle beater or collapse of a cymbal stand – accidentally of course.

on a large kettledrum, and struck the cymbals gently with coins. The difference in the size of my cymbals and the resonance of the drums produced a rather uncanny tick-tock. 'I'll have thirty seconds of that,' said the maestro, adding that he would hold the studio clock for me. I asked if I could try a 'take' without the clock (which moved silently in seconds), to which he agreed. By singing (mentally) the tune 'Colonel Bogey' in march time at $\quarternote = 120$ I was 'spot on' at the end of thirty seconds. I must add that Mr. Chaplin stopped the clock at the end of the thirty seconds and said, 'James, you are an artist', to which I replied, 'Sir, coming from you I will accept it.' A splendid occasion for me, when I experienced the magnetism of this great man, as I did some years later at Denham in 1966, when working on the film A Countess from Hong Kong. On this occasion Charlie (now Sir Charles Chaplin) inscribed my copy of his autobiography, and at the same time advised me that if ever I contemplated writing my life story, to do as he had done: 'Never be afraid to talk about yourself and recall your earlier life.' Advice from such a master has not gone unheeded, and I hope my acquaintances have forgiven my frequent reminiscing.

In musical circles 1962 could be called 'Stravinsky's Year' for there were many celebrations to commemorate his 80th birthday. One event in which I participated was a Musicale consisting of a new production by Michael Flanders and Kitty Black of The Soldier's Tale in honour of Stravinsky's birthday (broadcast from the Birmingham Studios of the BBC Midland Region). I recollect the vivid performances of Deryck Guyler, Ronald Shiner and Marius Goring, and the fine playing of the Delphos Ensemble conducted by Norman Del Mar. Norman, who is at home with scores of every description, was in tremendous form; a little too tremendous for me, for he noticed that one beat on my deep military side drum (a rope-tensioned drum that Stravinsky had admired) was slightly out of context due to a loose snare. As far as I remember, Stravinsky conducted several of his compositions in Britain during the sixties including a performance of Agon at the BBC Maida Vale Studios. I met him there, and he mentioned my playing The Soldier's Tale for him. I said, 'You are certainly conducting an anxious piece in Agon, sir,' to which he replied, 'and no one is more anxious than the conductor.'

I Deputise for Moiseiwitsch

A call from Ibbs and Tillett (now my agents) for me to deputise for Moiseiwitsch at Edinburgh on the Sunday eight days before

Christmas of 1962, meant a hurried change in my normal arrangements. Due to the sudden illness of Moiseiwitsch, the Edinburgh
Festival Guild felt that a complete change in their programme might
be acceptable to their patrons, so my wife and I and our 4 cwts of
equipment were rushed to King's Cross in a hired vehicle and thence
by train to Edinburgh – or to be precise trundled to Edinburgh in a
slow-moving 'express' delayed by fog and repair work. We arrived
at Waverley Station at 6.30 p.m. (two hours late) where we were met
by a contingent of anxious members of the Guild who had taxis
ready to take us to the Guildhall. I tipped my taxi driver £1 and
asked him to collect me at 9.45 p.m. as it was imperative we caught
the sleeper train for King's Cross. I was assured in a delightful Scots
brogue that nothing but a call from Royalty would forbid him
assisting me. The recital was to start at 8 p.m. At three minutes to
the hour we were 'set up'. As I had declined refreshment ('No time
to eat', I said) I was duly introduced as a hero who had refused all
hospitality in order to be 'on the dot'. Following a terrific ovation I
opened my talk by saying, 'What need is there of refreshment when
one is filled with the warmth of an Edinburgh welcome?' Maybe
my remark made up in some way for the disappointing absence of
Moiseiwitsch. We had a splendid reception and with the help of
my taxi driver, who had not received a call from Royalty, the last
portion of my equipment was put in the brake van of the '22.30' as
the guard prepared to blow his whistle. We slept the sleep of the
just until reaching King's Cross. Here the hire car awaited us, and
we were back in Cheam in time to change the equipment into my
car and get to Broadcasting House to join the English Chamber Orchestra and catch the down beat at 10 a.m.

My 'Voice' Goes Round the World

To say that my voice has gone round the world may sound boastful.
I hasten therefore to add that I merely refer to having made (in
addition to the Decca records of *Organ and Chimes* with Charles
Smart) three short films in the World Mirror series *We Make Music*
and played a small part in the BBC TV series for schools, *Making
Music*. The three short World Mirror films (20 minutes each) were
based on my lecture-demonstrations dealing with the history, de-
velopment and present-day use of orchestral percussion. My wife as
usual acted as my accompanist and assistant. The films received many
good notices. In two cases my presentation was criticised, in one
case that I did not spend more time in demonstrating *how* to play

the instruments, and in the other that my examples were in some cases too simple. I do not ignore criticism and have profited by studying it, but I must say that in the case of the World Mirror films, these were not intended to be didactic, and that as far as simplicity is concerned there are many different opinions as to what is simple. For my part I find 'simple' music often difficult to play. My part in the BBC *Making Music* series (in which I worked under the direction of John Hosier) was to show young children how to make and use simple instruments. The first story in the series was Ian Serralier's 'The Midnight Thief', with music by Richard Rodney Bennett. The work was performed on TV in weekly parts and subsequently played in schools in many parts of the world: my own fan mail included letters from Australia. Later programmes included 'Ahmer the Woodseller' with music by Gordon Crosse, and 'The Turtle Drum' with music by Malcolm Arnold. In some cases my experiments to obtain simple sounds from simple objects led to amusing incidents. For the wedding scene in 'The Midnight Thief' I made some tubular bells from ½-inch aluminium tubing. A few days after the televising of this episode I needed a further supply of tubing. On enquiring for this material at a shop in Shepherd's Bush the assistant said, 'Aluminium tubing? – we haven't got an inch left in stock, we've been besieged by kids wanting to buy special lengths of the damn stuff.' I said, 'How extraordinary' – a reply I also made one lunch time to a Gloucester tobacconist from whom I had made a small purchase and asked if by chance he had an empty cigar box. I did not tell him that during the morning I had (in the nearby Town Hall) shown an audience of 350 children that, if they had no such thing as an orchestral wood block, they could imitate galloping horses on a cigar box. The tobacconist's reply to my modest request was, 'Please don't mention cigar boxes to me, my trade has suffered enough during the last hour with children trooping in for cigar boxes.' I did not tell him that he might have a further batch of 'customers' during the afternoon as I had no intention of deleting the horses' hooves demonstration at my afternoon talk. At that performance I remember that a small girl I called to the stage to play a tambourine whispered in my ear that she had got 'butterflies' in her tummy.[2] As a contrast to horses' hooves on cigar boxes and

[2] Over lunch on this occasion the City Music Adviser for Gloucester (Mr. Harold Briggs) told us that he had recently been criticised in the local press for exercising class distinction in suggesting that a certain secondary school should have a brass band, whereas the grammar school had an orchestra.

wedding bells on different lengths of aluminium tubing, I was also instructing 'older children' in the art of percussion playing, having accepted Sir Thomas Armstrong's invitation to become Professor of Timpani and Percussion at the Royal Academy of Music. My orchestral duties in 1964 took me to Milan (with the Melos Ensemble) where Britten's *War Requiem* was performed in La Scala, conducted by David Willcocks.[3] Another particularly memorable occasion that year was my lecture-recital at the farewell party given for the choristers and choir school of Westminster by Sir William McKie. A recital given to open the season of the Faversam Subscription Concert Society also remains in my memory. I hope I justified the billing:

RE PERCUSSION

Repercussion?
Re Percussion . . .
Don't cut Blades!
What Blades?
Not Blades. Blades!
What are they?
They aren't. He is
He is what?
He is giving a lecture-recital
Who is he?
Jimmy Blades, who bangs the
Gong on those films

That all?
No, he's funny too
More than this is!
What else?
Come and see!
Blades – don't cut him!

I Return to Jarrow

Jarrow in 1964 was a very different place from the town I had known in 1924, and so was the reason for my visit. On this occasion my purpose was to meet several hundred small school children, and to tell them about orchestral percussion instruments and how ancient people made their music by clapping hands, beating on chest and stamping the ground, and that a clever one invented a rattle from

[3] I subsequently played this work under (Sir) Charles Groves and Meredith Davies.

the pod of a plant. I also told them, as I have told thousands of others, that men who once lived in forests found that a drum could be made by covering the end of a hollow tree trunk with the skin of the animal that had been killed for food. At the end of my first day in the Tyneside schools I made my way to the Jarrow Empire. It looked much the same as I had known it forty years earlier: a trifle sprucer maybe. The lady in the paybox replied to my enquiry as to whether I could see the manager by informing me that he would be back in 'two ticks'. During the 'two ticks' I learned from her that the theatre just managed to carry on as business was up and down, and that the picture that week was particularly duff and not worth seeing. The manager duly arrived and I asked if I could have a glance at the corner in which I played as a youth. To this he agreed, adding that the flea pit I had known had been converted into a floral display. I learned from this genial man that many people had re-visited Jarrow Empire and had signed an autograph book. I was asked to sign this book – a rather insignificant signature, I fear, when compared with the entry of Charlie Chaplin.

My Jarrow engagement on this occasion was not followed by a journey to the west and a 'trot down street' with John Henry Wright, Percy Pegleg and the barrow to 'T'Oxford, Wukkin'ton'. My impending engagements called for a considerably longer 'trot' and travel of varied descriptions. Somebody once wrote that travel pays a big dividend, for 'a well-travelled man can sit in an easy chair and in a matter of seconds transport himself to all corners of the globe'. This is certainly the case with me, and at this moment, though not in an easy chair, I have mental pictures of Holland and Switzerland. The picture of Holland is of the Opera House, Amsterdam, and searching the theatre for a stand tall enough to suspend the long tubular bell (low G sharp) required in the finale of Britten's A Midsummer Night's Dream. Charles Fletcher (my fellow percussionist on this occasion) and I failed in our search, but we found a suitable stand in a nearby street: on a rag-and-bone barrow. It took us some time to convince the owner of the barrow that we really wanted to purchase the odd-looking piece of furniture. After some strange bartering which I am sure resulted in our paying for the entire contents of the barrow, we got the stand, though our efforts seemed to attract the curiosity of the entire population of Amsterdam (it was rush hour). That night our 'mast' gave the percussion end of the orchestral pit of the Amsterdam Opera House the appearance of a battleship, but all went well.

My professional time in Switzerland was completely taken up

with the concerts given by the English Chamber Orchestra. My private time in Lucerne was almost entirely confined to studying the railroad system of Switzerland (past and present) at the Swiss Transport Museum, a short distance from the centre of the city, and to watching at the Hauptbahnhof the arrival and departure of the smooth gliding trains exactly on the *second* on the platform clock (and my pocket Longines). Trains and boats have always fascinated me, and if time permits I prefer to see the countryside or smell the sea instead of being flown from one mass of skyscrapers to another, for to me all cities look alike today.

One of my most pleasant journeys must have been one of my shortest – the ride across the River Yare on the ferry boat at Reedham Ferry. It could have been a unique experience for the ferryman also, as he expressed astonishment at the contents of my car – my lecture equipment. He was not as astonished, however, as the gentleman who drew up in a Rolls on the river bridge at Fountains Abbey and found me dangling my African drum in the swift-running water below. On explaining to him that I was thoroughly soaking the drumskin, and that I intended to let the head dry slowly in the sun so that the true tone of the instrument be restored he exclaimed 'Well I'm damned!' The ride across Reedham Ferry was as placid as I feel sure was the crossing of the *Curlew River*, a journey which is so faithfully typified in Britten's church parable opera of the same name. In this work, first performed in Orford Church in 1964, the small orchestra (six performers) are virtually part of the cast and are robed as monks. In the processions they join in the singing of the plainsong, some of them, like myself, mumbling the Latin text but shouting out any familiar words. It was this 'chorus' work that caused Ben to remark to me at the conclusion of the recording session in which the processionals were 'put in the can', 'as a Latin scholar and a vocalist you are an excellent percussion player'. I think I did well for him as a percussionist on the recording of *Albert Herring* (April '64) and as an 'engineer', in reply to his request for the sound of a ferryboat bell – to sound the note C for the opera *Curlew River*. 'Not a bell or a gong – you know what I want', he said. Now, when a composer of the calibre of Britten makes such a comment there is no point in arguing. If you cannot purchase the instrument you make it or get it made, and that is just what I did. With the help of the Mitcham Foundry, a bronze plate was cast and machined to sound the required pitch. I sent it to 'The Red House' and received an immediate reply from Ben, 'Splendid, please get another as a spare'.

In addition to the performance of *Curlew River* at the 1964 Aldeburgh Festival, Britten's *War Requiem* was performed at Cambridge and Ely. On the morning following the performance in King's Chapel, Cambridge, I bought some cigars for a friend – I am a non-smoker. The genial Cambridge tobacconist followed his observations on the weather by asking if I was on holiday, to which I replied, 'Not exactly – I feel that playing the solo percussion part in Britten's *War Requiem* is by no means a holiday.' The shopkeeper then said that he had attended the performance at King's on the previous evening and had greatly enjoyed the work, 'but', he added, 'I must confess that it is not my favourite work by Benjamin Britten'. 'And what is your favourite work by Britten?' I asked. '*Merrie England*', he replied; which comment made me hastily revert to our conversation about the weather. I left the shop quickly as I was shortly due at Ely but – I hasten to add – not to perform *Merrie England*. The Aldeburgh Festival was followed by the Edinburgh Festival, where I took part in a performance of Bartók's Sonata for Pianos and Percussion. My percussion colleague was my friend Steve Whittaker who, like myself, never played the Bartók work without thinking of our late friend Sammy Geldard, and of Bill Bradshaw, the latter sadly having been obliged to retire much too early – a loss to the profession in every respect.

A Trip to Russia

Vivid as the above events remain in my memory, my most vivid recollections of 1964 are my experiences in Russia with the English Opera Group and the circumstances surrounding the performances in Leningrad, Riga and Moscow of the operas *The Rape of Lucretia*, *Albert Herring* and *The Turn of the Screw*. The Group first flew to Moscow, where we changed to an internal flight for Leningrad. En route to Moscow our manager Keith Grant gave us the Russian for the three most important words in any language – 'please', 'thank you', and 'toilet'. On arrival at Moscow airport we were greeted by an enthusiastic crowd of well-wishers headed by Rostropovich. Each member of the company was given flowers and an embrace. Our welcome at Leningrad was on a par with that in Moscow. We were given an enormous supper (at 1 a.m.) at which Keith Grant explained – in perfect Russian – that I was a vegetarian. To make matters easy, I was henceforth given a private table, the finest of spa waters, fruit, nuts, and the best from the soil of Russia, plus the 'honour' of being addressed as 'Professor'. Breakfast on the following morning delayed the rehearsal, for the simple reason that we were not aware then that if a boiled, poached or fried egg is ordered in Russia, it arrives in a matter of two hours. The rehearsal got under way eventually, and during it and at all subsequent performances we were overwhelmed with the reception. On most occasions dinner followed the evening performance – opera commences early in Russia. At Leningrad we dined to the accompaniment of music from an excellent, though the loudest, dance band I have ever heard. To compete with the musicians, a lady vocalist, whose voice could have filled the stadium at Wembley without amplification, sang as close as she could to a microphone which had been adjusted to full volume. In honour of the occasion Ben and Peter were given a table directly in front of the band, a situation that Keith Grant most diplomatically eased by suggesting that this special table be taken by the Group in turns.

When I was asked to broadcast from the Leningrad studios, it was not a dissertation on the history of percussion instruments, or my boyhood wish to be a professional. It was merely a short interview for relay to Britain and elsewhere, during which I spoke of my impressions of Russia. It may be asked why was I chosen to represent the orchestra. Admittedly I was the senior member, although there may have a been better reason. I had constantly told my room mate, a young violinist named Peter Poole, how understanding I had found the Russian people, and of their kindness to me. For instance, the lady who was in charge of the orchestral pit arrangements, when tidying the pit, never failed to dust my equipment and polish the bowls of my kettledrums. I also remember frequently remarking on the excellence of my meatless cuisine and how friendly the Leningrad percussionists had made themselves. Maybe these bedroom conversations were the real reasons for my broadcasting my impressions of Russia.

My Leningrad percussion friends included Mischa Vofsi (one of Leningrad's recording angels) and Popoff – the timpanist at the Opera House. With Vofsi as guide (he spoke good English) and Popoff as guard, I saw much of Leningrad, including the Hermitage, the Conservatoire and its museum, the ship *Potemkin*, the house where Tchaikovsky died (where I stood with my friends in silent recognition of the Master), and the interior of several Russian homes. Vofsi's flat was one of hundreds which were so identical, he explained to me, that he had remained sober at night for the first six months of living there, in case he had found himself getting into bed with a stranger.

From Leningrad the Group flew west to Riga – incidentally the birthplace of Gustav Holst's forbears. Here the Group again received a magnificent reception and unstinted hospitality. From Riga we flew to Moscow. At every performance (often two operas in one day) the reception was tremendous, with the audience stamping for encores and coming to the pit rail to greet us. Many would count the thirteen instrumentalists as they were astounded at the wealth of sound that Britten conjured from such a small orchestra. Our domestic wants were well catered for, though there were minor incidents which caused us to think, such as when one of the cast took her camera into the shop at the base of our hotel for a film to be developed and the assistant on opening it showed her the empty interior and said, 'Ha Ha! you have been taking a picture of the Red Square from your bedroom window'. My own films were not confiscated, which pleased me greatly, as apart from being given the privilege of in-specting some famous military kettledrums in the Kremlin Armoury Museum, I was allowed (as with similar instruments in Leningrad) to photograph these for inclusion in my literature.

No visit to Moscow would be complete without a visit to the Red Square to see Lenin's tomb and the Tsarine Kolokol bell. This huge bell, which weighs 193 tons (Big Ben weighs 13½ tons), stands as a monument to Russian craftsmanship. It was unfortunately damaged by fire, which caused the suspension structure to collapse soon after the bell was cast. There is now an aperture in the bell large enough for use as a doorway. I went inside the bell and tested with my voice (as thousands of others have done) the glorious resonance of the chamber. Emerging from the bell I observed Benjamin Britten and Peter Pears showing a keen interest in the monster. Imagine my feeling of apprehension, bearing in mind the recently completed special bell for use in *Curlew River*. I thought, surely not another on the lines of the Tsarine bell? On the day before leaving Moscow, I was asked to accompany our young harpist, Hilary Wilson, on a visit to the home of a remarkable Russian lady, Madame Erdely, who, though quite elderly, was still Russia's principal teacher of the harp.[4] This fine old lady, the widow of a Russian officer, was, according to our interpreter from the British Embassy, one of the few persons allowed to live in the style of a White Russian. In addition to listening to her fine harp playing and also that of her three most gifted pupils, we were permitted a sight of her treasures which included auto-graphs and photographs of famous musicians dating from the end

[4] Madame Erdely was Marie Korchinska's early teacher at the Moscow Conservatoire. Marie was subsequently awarded the Conservatoire's first gold medal for the harp.

of the nineteenth century. The visit ended with tea served in real Russian style with tea poured from a gleaming silver samovar. There was rich fruit cake followed by sweetmeats. During tea Madame spoke highly of Britten's operas (she had seen all three, though ordinary folk were permitted only one – and that by ballot) and was complimentary about my work, saying she 'knew' me already from my sounds on the H.M.V. records *Instruments of the Orchestra* with commentary by Yehudi Menuhin. With the sweetmeats came the wine, and on asking to be excused the wine, as in addition to being abstemious I had to play an opera that evening she said, 'It is a comic opera *Albert Herring* – you can play it even with wine inside you.' How could I resist her charm or that of her lady companion who said that she had been a ballet dancer, but had been injured in the 1940 siege of Moscow and was now forced into domesticity? Her recovery, she told me, was nothing short of a miracle, for on 'coming to' she found herself lying on a cold slab in a mortuary. I had much to think about as I returned to the theatre, but helped perhaps by the wine I survived the evening and awoke the next day in good trim ready for the return journey to England.

Back in England I met another Russian friend, Dmitri Tiomkin, the eminent composer whose film music is legendary, as for example his scores for *The Guns of Navarone* and *The Fall of the Roman Empire*. To those who know him, Dmitri is a lovable character and a most friendly man. He fears no one, however, and I must say that he can at times be particularly exasperating. On more than one occasion he has made me play a single note on a timpano at least twenty times, but finally noticing an unusual glint in my eye he would approve and say, 'Jimmy, I love you.' I was not alone in having to play a single note time and time again. Whilst working on the music for *The Guns of Navarone*, Dmitri questioned the sound of a chord on the piano. Now, the pianist Robert Docker is a pianist who can play a thousand chords in succession and every one a 'pearl'. This Dmitri knew well, so he said, 'It is the piano – get in another one'. When the producer said that to get another one would cost nearly £500. Dmitri barked, '£500, what is £500? – this film will make a million'. How right he was, and how right this grand musician was when, excusing a group of six percussionists their difficulty in getting their strokes absolutely together, he said, 'One sometimes makes the mistake of putting too many plonking instruments together'.

To be told by a person like Dmitri Tiomkin that 'I love you' is a nice thought. It is also a nice thought to be told by children that they like you. One small girl told me that she wished I would come and live in her house, and another that she wished I could be her grandad. The post has brought me hundreds of letters from school children, and the remarkable drawings of myself at work (all of which I have kept) would stretch from Land's End to John O'Groat's. The poems I have received are also typical of the creative minds of many of the young children, and I for one am not critical of their efforts, even if they clashed the tom-tom instead of beating it, as in this poem from the children at a Sussex Primary School.

> We've clashed the tom-tom, played the drum;
> Our cymbals cleaved the air.
> But as well as beating time for us
> We found some magic there.
>
> Bells and blocks, sticks and claves,
> They all can play their part;
> Especially when, with Mr. Blades,
> They echo from the heart.
>
> The instruments are nothing
> Without your magic touch,
> So, sir, please come to us again,
> We've loved you very much.

Some children of course express their appreciation differently. One boy, after I had demonstrated a ride on a 'space ship' in which I play a crescendo roll on my huge gong reaching near ear-splitting point[5] shouted, 'Do it again – louder!' A question I am frequently asked by adults is how I get my mass of equipment (4 cwts – requiring a stage width of at least 30 feet) into a private car. One questioner at Coventry was eventually only convinced by seeing my whole kit comfortably stowed in an Austin Westminster. On a return visit to Coventry the next year I was interviewed and photographed for an article in the *Austin Magazine*. For this service I asked no fee, neither did I receive a new Austin in recognition for 'services rendered'. (I did 140,000 miles in that 1958 Westminster – without a 'decoke'. Before disposing of it I sat quietly in the driving seat and thanked God for the many safe journeys in it. As I did so, though I was alone, I felt as if two arms gently embraced me.)

My varied activities at this time took me to Aldeburgh, Darting-

[5] In the region of 120 decibels.

ton, Edinburgh, France (Tours) and Italy (Perugia). Due to the ever-increasing interest in percussion playing, my 'class' at the Royal Academy of Music was growing. I also taught on one or two occasions at Kneller Hall in the absence of that stalwart of percussionists Denis Brady, whose daughter Pat was for some years co-principal timpanist (with Eric Pritchard) in the BBC Symphony Orchestra. I made further appearances on TV in *Making Music* and similar programmes for young school children, and in contrast played in many classical programmes with the English Chamber Orchestra, including a Haydn programme directed by H. Robbins Landon. This great scholar discussed certain aspects of timpani playing with me and gave me the benefit of his research into the matter of drums and drumsticks used in Haydn's time. I have always felt justified in seeking information from those better informed than myself. In extenuation, once when apologising to Benjamin Britten for picking his brains, he replied, 'There are plenty, including myself, who have picked yours'. My few appearances at the 1965 Proms included a concert at which Steve Whittaker and I played percussion with the Virtuoso Ensemble in Roberto Gerhard's *Hymnody*. As always, Roberto's percussion parts required the numerous instruments to be conveniently placed. So whilst awaiting the down beat Steve and I spent a little time accustoming ourselves to the position of the equipment by gently tapping instruments. Afterwards a friend of Steve's told him that he liked Gerhard's work, especially the percussion solo at the start.

Roberto Gerhard was my friend and I learned much from this amazing musician. He visited my home on occasions: never without his tape recorder with which he recorded every percussion instrument in my collection that appealed to him. He once found a miniature 4-note xylophone (sounding above the normal high C), which I had made in 1936 to enable me to complete on my 5-octave marimba-xylophone[6] the effect of Jack Hulbert running down a long spiral staircase. Roberto included these high-sounding notes in his next score, and on being told by Gilbert Webster, the principal percussionist in the BBC Symphony Orchestra, that there was no xylophone that went up into that register, he immediately replied, 'Oh, yes there is – I have seen it in Jimmy Blades' loft.' One could never win with Roberto. On one occasion he booked me for a film session (a cartoon) saying that he would provide a special percussion instrument. On arrival at the studio he presented me with a bottle of gin! 'But Roberto,' I said, 'it is empty.' 'Yes, I know it is empty,'

[6] This type of instrument is now styled a 'xylo-rimba'.

242

he replied. 'It makes the note F sharp when it is empty and that is the note I want.' Whether I took him to my nearby club (the Savile) for a gin I cannot remember. I always found the atmosphere of the 'sandpit' at the Savile most relaxing, and nothing was more pleasant on a winter's afternoon than to take tea there and later sit back comfortably in an armchair until suddenly remembering one of those duties such as polishing my tubular bells because the Christmas Carol Concerts were at hand.

✤ 15 ✤

A Rung Higher: '66 Onwards

If playing with some of our most illustrious orchestral combinations; teaching at the Royal Academy of Music; lecturing in establishments ranging from infant schools to the faculties of famous universities; broadcasting and televising, and being commissioned to write about percussion instruments is indicative of 'getting on', then I can say truthfully that I was making headway up the professional ladder. One of my most cherished connections is my several years as the timpanist of the English Chamber Orchestra, an orchestra which has brought me in contact with so many expert musicians and taken me to many interesting places, some extremely warm and others intensely cold; none colder than Sweden in the January of 1968. Here, in Stockholm and Mälmo, the programme included Britten's *Symphony for 'Cello and Orchestra* with Rostropovich as soloist.[1] I enjoyed the concert in Stockholm, due largely to the cooperation of the Swedish percussionists who loaned me some really fine timpani. Of my performance in Mälmo I can only say that it was a disaster, as due to the fierce central heating it was impossible to change pitch on the kettledrums loaned to me. I left Sweden with mixed feelings as well as a cold in the head. I had no trouble with unmanageable drumheads or fierce central heating in Windsor Royal Chapel, where on Palm Sunday 1968 I took part in a performance of shortened version Handel's *Messiah*. This was indeed a splendid occasion, at the conclusion of which the soloists and the members of the orchestra (and wives) were presented to Her Majesty.

The 1968 Aldeburgh Festival found me in a dual capacity: as a musician and as a mechanic, for following my success with the ferryboat bell for *Curlew River*, I had become 'engineer-in-chief' to Benjamin Britten. My commissions for his parable opera *The Burning Fiery Furnace* (the second of the trilogy) were: a bass drum – portable though fairly large, to sound if possible low D in the 'cello register and to look Babylonian; an anvil effect; a four-toned whip for the crackling of the flames; two tuned woodblocks to sound A

---

[1] Due to the sudden indisposition of Benjamin Britten, these concerts were conducted by Alexander Gibson.

and E (but not to sound like Chinese woodblocks); a pair of small cymbals; and a form of glockenspiel or dulcimer, so portable as to allow it to be played in Nebuchadnezzar's orchestra in the march round the church. (See Plate 31.) For the bass drum I felt that an illustration of a Sumerian drum dated 2500 B.C. would be a good guide, and I started to work on the lines of a large single-headed drum with a narrow shell. A friendly drum-maker gave me a sizeable shell. It was not altogether Babylonian, being in fact emblazoned with the insignia of the Grenadier Guards. For the skin I went to my friend Len Hunt's world renowned shop in Central London. Len ('Doc') Hunt obliged me with a tough vellum that had seen the weather on the roof of his shop for at least twenty-five years. It was by no means a hide from a fat bull of Basan, for as far as I could gather it had once belonged to a cow in Kent. After four days of soaking I managed to fix the skin to the shell, and with the aid of concealed screw mechanism got the required tension to produce a reasonable low D in the 'cello register. A coat of bronze (fiery) paint and a few ornamental knobs gave the drum, if not a Babylonian appearance, at least a look 'of the past'. For the anvil effect the genuine implement was out of the question (lack of space and airport weight regulations, etc.), so I submitted various steel plates and lengths of railway line, as are used in the orchestra to imitate the ring of an anvil. 'Hardly strident enough,' said Ben after the first rehearsal in Orford Church. So I went along to a nearby garage (Friend's) to enlist the help of Bill Smith, one of the finest car mechanics I have ever met. 'Bill,' I said, 'I want something to make a real clanging sound. What have you got?' He ruminated for a time and then took me to a heap of car springs. These seemed possible. I said, 'Nip this one in half – no, better still, make it different lengths then I'll have a choice of two notes.' With the acetylene flame the job was quickly done. I strung up the longer piece and quite remarkably it gave the desired note (C). On hearing it Ben said, 'Marvellous'. I replied, 'It should be, the spring came from a Rolls-Royce!'[2]

Making the four-tone whip for the 'crackling of the flames' was quite a problem. Ben confessed to me that Peter Pears and he had

* When the opera was performed in New York I was asked to provide illustrations of the percussion instruments for guidance. After the performances a letter came saying that it was felt that Mr. Britten would have been satisfied with the results, and that the only instrument not faithfully repeated was the Rolls-Royce car spring, but, as a substitute, they had used one from a Bentley.

tried every piece of wood on the Aldeburgh estate and all seemed to sound the same! This was not surprising as slabs of wood clapped together (which form the foundation of the orchestral whip effect) have little respect for musical pitch. After much trial and error with wooden slabs of varying density, length and thickness, and being thrown out of several 'Do-It-Yourself' shops, I arrived at four distinct tones, and with the help of my brother Chris, who is more skilled in woodwork than myself, a 'multiple whip' was made with spring-controlled slabs that rendered manageable the written 'flippidy-flap' for the crackle of the flames in the fiery furnace. The two woodblocks to sound A and E 'but not to sound like Chinese woodblocks' proved a more simple task. By mounting two tuned lengths of rosewood in the manner of xylophone bars, and slightly off-setting the insulation positions away from the nodal points, a 'choked' tone was produced which was quite different from the sound of Chinese woodblocks or, for that matter, a xylophone. For the small cymbals I consulted a treatise in the British Museum. Among the 'cymbals of the ancients' were cup-shaped cymbals, so I coaxed the management of the Mitcham Foundry to experiment with vessel-shaped castings. The chosen instruments had a delightful sound, possibly echoing the loud, high-sounding or well-tuned cymbals mentioned in the Old Testament.

My instructions regarding the 'portative glockenspiel' were precise. Something in the form of a glockenspiel or dulcimer, with the performer, incidentally, to be myself. An authentic dulcimer was ruled out as there was to be a stringed instrument in the procession in the form of a small harp, and I had no wish to compete with Osian Ellis. From all accounts, frontal harps or similar instruments were used in processions in Nebuchadnezzar's time, so I decided on a portable instrument constructed of a single row of metal bars arranged in a lyre-shaped frame with a carrying handle. The part that Britten had written for this instrument was just as much as I could manage with a single beater. (See Plate 31). Other problems arose, particularly because I was virtually playing on a small pianoforte keyboard, consisting only of the white notes, which were arranged vertically. There was the difficulty of marching round the church enveloped in a monk's habit and trying to keep up with (and in step with) some of the tallest men in the profession. Whilst thus trotting along there was the problem of counting bars' rest and coming in at the right moment, which always seemed to coincide with the point when I reached the darkest area in the church, so that I had to put a piece of luminous tape on my starting note and play thereafter with the aid of that second sense that one seems to develop

246

in difficult circumstances. I was also confronted with the problem of deportment during the march, and the fact that a certain lady in a responsible position in the English Opera Group (Myra Thomas) was diligent about Nebuchadnezzar's little band marching in time, and being discreetly clad in soft slippers. The wearing of socks was taboo to all but myself, as even Myra agreed that I was a little taller in socks, and that any addition to my height might help to reduce my occasional gallops to a discreet shuffle. Ben was delighted with the glockenspiel, and so was a lady in Versailles who, at a reception following a performance in the Royal Chapel, said that I had made a beautiful instrument for Mr. Britten 'and what is even more remarkable', she said, 'it makes different sounds when you strike it in different places' – a fact which I considered not so remarkable for an instrument consisting of a series of graduated metal bars. My 'Babylonian' instruments aroused considerable interest at Aldeburgh, King's Lynn, Ripon, a Prom concert and the Flanders Festival. So did the march round the 'church'. At one of the performances in Ripon Cathedral, the herald who led the procession missed a turning in the aisle which resulted in a few of us marching into the graveyard. This, however, did not lead to the great disorder which occurred when I wheeled to the left instead of the right at a performance in Sydney some three years later.

I Fight a Duel in the Royal Albert Hall

Few professional musicians have been stripped to the waist in the Royal Albert Hall, and after having been 'weighed in', face an opponent similarly scantily clad, and at the sound of the bell fight five rounds in true professional ring style. I can claim this distinction by having fought (in boxing garb) a five-round contest with Allan Wicks,[3] he as an organist and myself as percussionist in the first performance of Alan Ridout's *L'Orgue Concrète* ('*Il combattimento d'organo a Batteria*'). The occasion was the 'Organ in Sanity and Madness' concert organised for the benefit of the centenary appeal of the Royal College of Organists. Allan Wicks and I were given a tremendous welcome from the huge audience. We each had a second who 'towelled' us between rounds. In the fourth round I claimed a foul which was granted by the referee. Odds remained even throughout. The final chord, in which Allan opened almost every stop on the Royal Albert Hall organ, and I played a tre-

[3] Organist of Canterbury Cathedral.

mendous crescendo roll on my huge gong, gave the referee a problem in deciding who was the loudest, but a draw was announced and Allan and I, each supported by our second, retired dishevelled but not disheartened. Soon after this I took part in a completely different concert, the memorial concert in memory of dear Olive Zorian, a violinist who will be long remembered for her expertise and charming personality. My part at this concert was a simple one: merely to play the three bells in Bach's *Schlage doch, gewünschte Stunde*. I had rather more to do a few days later when my wife and I recorded a 30-minute programme in the BBC 'Studio Portrait' series. My book was also keeping me busy. Perhaps a little too busy, for I remember Peter du Sautoy (of Faber & Faber) saying when glancing through a page or two of my script, 'everybody will learn from this book', to which I replied, 'I have already learned never to write another'!

Dreams Realised

The twentieth Aldeburgh Festival saw one of my dreams realised: to play at the first concert in The Maltings, Snape. I must confess that I played the solo drum roll to open the National Anthem (before Royalty – the Queen was present) with a catch in my throat. Another dream that was realised (without a catch in my throat) was riding in a Canadian Pacific Express train, and boating on a Canadian lake. These experiences I enjoyed whilst with the English Chamber Orchestra at Expo '67. Though the schedule was heavy (performing Walton's *The Bear*, and Britten's *A Midsummer Night's Dream* and his church parable operas), there was time to see much and to meet people. When in Montreal I met a player I had long admired – Professor Richard Hochrainer, the timpanist of the Vienna Philharmonic Orchestra and Professor at the Vienna Conservatoire. Not surprisingly we had much in common and, often over breakfast, we discussed the respective qualities of flesh and plastic kettledrum heads, and how great are the opportunities given to students of today when compared with our own ways of entering the profession. As for the Expo itself, one of my greatest thrills was to learn that a British regimental band had proved the star attraction. It was certainly the 'tops' with me, with the Sun Life Centenary Carillon a close second. This carillon was said to be the largest glockenspiel in existence. It consists of 671 small bars of bell metal electronically amplified, the lowest note being equivalent to that produced by a 22-ton cast bell.

I left Canada with memories of the beauty of the fall, a visit to Brockville to see my wife's cousins and crossing the border into America at The Thousand Islands with them. I also remember that, not having a visa with me, I got back on Canadian soil by imitating my hosts' 'from Brarkville' in reply to the official question, 'Where are you from?' Back in England, I continued to burrow and furrow over a wide area, ranging from Eton (my third visit); Bishop's Stortford, where a young man told me that he was the boy who, on my first visit to the club (in 1958), had asked if some people wanted their money back if an orchestral player played a wrong note; Truro, where in 1959 our lecture had been given in the showrooms of the Gas Company – making my reference to the kitchen department of the orchestra no exaggeration; and a club which shall be nameless where, on being shown an upright piano my wife was told 'the club only go to the expense of a grand piano if a real pianist is coming'. Abroad I was reminded of the futility of war when taking part in a performance of Britten's *War Requiem* in St. Maarten's Kathedral, Ypres. This performance was to commemorate the dreadful Passchendaele offensive of November 1917 where so many thousands of lives were lost in the 'war to end wars'. In addition to the memories evoked by the solemnity of this occasion, I have dismal recollections of this particular evening, for due to the shocking atmospheric conditions prevailing in the Cathedral on this dank November night, my performance was not the one I most wish to remember. Conditions in the Parish Church of St. Andrew's, Holborn, were better and I felt happier with my timpani solos in Bach's *Christmas Oratorio*. When exchanging seasonal greetings, Ben, who had conducted the work, hinted that he had one or two ideas in his head for some rather unusual instruments for the last of his church parable operas (*The Prodigal Son*), and a work for the Save the Children Fund – *Children's Crusade*. So there seemed every prospect that 1968 would find me occasionally quitting the concert hall for the bench.

My commission for *Children's Crusade* – in addition to helping to assemble a battery of normal percussion instruments – was to produce a bass drum with variable pitch and an instrument to imitate the sound of a dog's bark, first when in good trim, and second the same dog when suffering (as did the children) from privation. For the dog's bark it was agreed that, of the various sounds I submitted, the most realistic for the specific purpose was the sound of a *reso-reso* (a notched bamboo scraper as used in Latin-American orchestras). Placed with the open end on a desk or a drum and 'rasped' with a steel rod, this 'primitive' instrument produced a healthy bark. When scraped gently with a pencil or the slender shaft of a xylophone beater a fainter 'woof' was produced. The additional resonance obtained from the desk or drum produced an overall effect with the curious carrying power of a dog's bark. So the dog's bark presented no problem. To produce a bass drum with variable pitch was quite a different matter. As economy was a consideration, a foot-pedal-operated instrument on the lines of a pedal timpano was out of the question. I tried several ways of producing the variable pitch (a glissando) on a normal orchestral bass drum – all with negative results. I finally threaded a cord through the centre of a single-headed drum[4] and applied the tension by pulling the cord. An appreciable rise and fall was produced, leading me to secure the end of the gut string to an upright post fixed to the side of the drum, and applying variable pressure to the string in the manner the pitch is changed on the double bass.

Bass drum
variable pitch

When used in the orchestra one player varies the pressure on the gut string whilst simultaneously bowing it with a 'cello bow, while another performer plays a tremolo on the drumhead with two soft-headed drumsticks.

So much for the *Children's Crusade*. For the final parable opera *The Prodigal Son* I received a request for the following: 5 drums – *passim*; medium cymbal; tuned gong (F); wooden blocks (A and D sharp); high-pitched wood block and a rattle; and for the acolytes: small drums; tambourine; small cymbals; sistrum and a small bell-lyra. The instruments for the acolytes were to look Biblical of course.

---

[4] In shape not unlike the Babylonian drum made for *The Burning Fiery Furnace* (the parable operas were televised, directed by John Culshaw).

I had no difficulty with this batch with the exception of the rattle, the sound of which was to illustrate the plodding feet (in sand, gravel, rough earth, etc.) of the prodigal son on his long journeys. I made a few experiments with gourd rattles such as maracas, and in answer to an invitation from Mr. Britten went to the Red House with a sizeable case of shakers of several descriptions. After lunch, over which we discussed the entire percussion requirements for the opera, we started work on the rattle. Ben seemed most interested in the sound of a cabaca: a gourd with an exterior mesh of beads which, when spun in the palm of the hand, produced a distinct 'shush'. 'A very good sound, Jim', said Ben, 'but what else have you?' I said, 'Can we try a Latin-American chocolo?' This is a tube rattle which when tilted from side to side causes the interior rattling pieces (seeds or similar) to strike alternately the small vellum at each end of the tube. 'Very good – we are getting near,' said Ben. Then, after a pause he added 'but what I really had in mind was a left and a right foot'. A *left and a right foot!* It seemed to me that the rattling pieces had to strike either differently tensioned skins or different sized skins. So back to the 'Blades factory' and, from a sheet of fibre, I made a conical 'gourd rattle' which gave a high and low 'shush' as well as a tiny thump. In due course I demonstrated this to B.B., who said, 'Marvellous, but could you mute it in the quiet parts?' *Mute it in the quiet parts!* After a little experimenting, the 'muted' effect was produced by placing the gourd in a cardboard 'jacket' and covering part of each vellum with a handkerchief and using my fingers to adjust the tone further.

The conical gourd rattle caused considerable interest at Aldeburgh. Quite often whilst taking my stroll along the sea front I was asked, 'What makes the effect of the boy trudging on his journey?' On one occasion I was hailed (in no uncertain way) by an acquaintance – a military man – who said, 'James, a word with you'. I thought, 'Hello, the walking machine', but no, something quite different – a complaint. The booking office had told this Aldeburgh patron of many years standing that he could not purchase a seat for the première of a 'certain' opera (a somewhat avant-garde one). After passing censure on the booking clerk, my informant told me that he received a ticket with an apology that it was not a good seat. 'It turned out to be the best seat in the house', my friend continued, 'it was right next to the door!' This particular opera is said to have had some noisy moments. My friend should have given his ticket to a boy from Burgess Hill who wrote me as follows:

Dear Mr. Blades,

Thank you very much for coming to our school and talking to us about percussion instruments, I liked the gong and the side drum best because of the noise. I cannot play anything and like football best. My mum can play the piano but that is all.

Yours sincerely,

P. Ladd.

I am sorry that young Ladd's mother could only play the piano, and that my performance at this school might have suggested that I was one of the pair of professionals (bosom friends) who were referred to as 'Thud and Blunder'. (It was also said of them that because of their *tour de force* they were 'forced to tour'.) My own 'thudding' however has made me many friends and brought friendly invitations, as for instance the one from a boy in Birmingham who made certain that I would know where to find him – and I did. I included his school in answer to his request which read:

Dear Mr. Blades

On your percussion program on Monday Nov. 4th you said you would be visiting some of the schools in Birmingham. Could you please visit Northfield Manor Junior and Infant school although the sign only says Northfield Manor Infant School. My class is Junior 2 H. By the way, my brother (who is Infant 5) liked your program. My brother is James Borcherds. Our headmaster is Mr Mackmillan.

From Richard Borcherds

(The boy enclosed a map of the district showing his house)

I Conduct at the Royal Festival Hall

My début as conductor at the Royal Festival Hall (incidentally my first and last appearance as such) was not wielding the baton in front of one of our major orchestras, but as guest conductor at a concert of music given by the combined orchestras of the branches of the Wingfield Music Club. With the exception of only one or two tutors, the orchestra was comprised of physically handicapped children who had met each week for many months to rehearse their Festival Hall programme – simple and not-so-simple arrangements of musical items of various descriptions. To see and hear these young people overcoming and temporarily forgetting their handicap, severe in many cases, was an inspiration. What mattered if there was an occasional wrong note or faulty intonation? Under the baton of their founder and leader Herbert Lyon, or one of his noble band of young helpers, this orchestra of over fifty performers made music and enjoyed and profited by making it. My main occupation at this concert (I merely conducted the final item: the 'Wingfielders Theme Song') was to turn the handles for a change of pitch on the pair of timpani that Barbara Cook, the Club's secretary, played. Barbara, who is my 'pin-up' girl, has been in a wheelchair for many years. This does not prevent her from holding a kettledrum stick between her two frail hands, and playing the tonic and dominant notes exactly as they are written, or, from the wheelchair, playing a solo on a xylophone or a set of tubular bells. Some people ask, 'How can afflicted people achieve perfection in music?' My reply is, 'Who has?' I made this reply to a certain lady who ventured the opinion that music with the handicapped should not be encouraged for reason of the poor quality of the end product. I left her with no reply when I said that despite my years of playing with and for some of the greatest, I had not always heard perfection; and I gave her a Wingfield brochure and list of patrons. I also sent one to a famous politician who, in an evening broadcast, deplored the fact that the British had entirely lost their sense of responsibility to others. The club did not receive a donation, neither did I receive a reply.

Fire at The Maltings

I could write much about my activities in 1969; performing *The Soldier's Tale* in Dublin in January, followed by a tour of Germany and Switzerland with the English Chamber Orchestra with Daniel Barenboim as soloist and conductor, and an appearance on 'Jackanory' with Raymond Leppard narrating a script by Susan Hill about a drummer who became a professor; but my most vivid recollection of 1969 is hearing on the 8 a.m. news on Sunday 8th June that a disastrous fire had occurred at The Maltings, Snape. Within a few minutes of hearing this news I received a telephone call to say that the instruments destroyed included my kettledrums, which had been housed in the hall for rehearsals and subsequent performances of Mozart's *Idomeneo*.[5] I took the first train to Saxmundham as my Austin was garaged at The Maltings. (It had been saved by the prompt action of Neville Bromage, the young landlord of the nearby Ye Plough and Sail Inn.) At Snape I found a grim situation with

[5] I had returned to London by train to take full advantage of a day's break in rehearsals.

damage that reminded me of some of the wartime blitz incidents. What little remained of my drums was buried beneath tangled metal girders and shattered masonry. My second pair of drums (for use with the trumpets in the off-stage music), though damaged, were repairable. My best pair were 'written off'. A sad loss those drums, but even worse was the complete destruction of a case of drumsticks which included two pairs of timpani sticks that had been made and used by the late James Bradshaw, and of my own home-made 'Mozart' sticks that 'Wilkie', Decca's senior recording engineer, had made certain I used whenever practicable, and particularly when recording such works as Mozart's *Serenata Notturna*, which, with Mozart's Symphony No. 40 in G minor, was the first disc to be recorded in The Maltings. Benjamin Britten[6] conducted the E.C.O.

My insurers agreed that I should buy a new pair of drums, but whatever else I may have done in 1969, or for that matter in 1970, I could not replace those drumsticks. I used other drumsticks in the newly-constructed 'Maltings' and other places in Britain and abroad: places considerably more than a stone's throw from Big Ben which, with the Royal Albert Hall, 'Dickens Land' and the many places where I have worked so pleasurably, remains 'my London'.

1970

Other than for a broadcast, it is not often that a lecturer is asked to time his presentation to one hour exactly, but such is the case at the Friday evening Discourses at The Royal Institution of Great Britain. Having been invited to speak at this illustrious establishment, my wife and I got to work 'tailoring' our ninety-minute recital to sixty so that we complied to the strict instructions of the eminent nineteenth-century lecturer Michael Faraday, who said 'One hour is enough for anyone and they should not be allowed to exceed that time'. (Michael Faraday lectured at The Royal Institution from 1835 to 1862.) After dinner with Sir George Porter, the Director, and Lady Porter, we entered the Lecture Theatre as the clock 'pinged' once – 9 p.m. precisely – having been gently advised by Sir George that it was the custom for lecturers to commence their talk without preliminaries – not even 'Good evening ladies and gentlemen' – and that not a word must be uttered after the clock had 'pinged' at 10 p.m. Of the lecture itself I will only say that we addressed a capacity audience who were 'with us' from the word go.

[6] Benjamin Britten was made Life Peer in the Birthday Honours List, 1976. His death in December 1976 caused worldwide sorrow.

Due to the brilliant spot lighting I could not see the theatre clock, but at 9.57 on my Longines (placed discreetly on my xylophone) we rattled off our final xylophone duet: an hilarious galop lasting 2 minutes 15 seconds and then, referring to 'the passage of time' I drew my talk to a close by striking the four quarters of Big Ben on my tubular bells. Some call me 'Lucky Jim': as I paused before striking the 'hour bell', the Lecture Theatre clock struck, and Joan and I retired with a standing ovation.

An invitation to spend six weeks with the English Opera Group in Australia in the autumn of that year was not to be sneezed at. I did sneeze a little, however, as I left England in a fierce early March snowstorm and again when landing at Calcutta some hours later. The journeys outward and inward, allowed brief but interesting glimpses of such places as Rome, Damascus, the glare of the Arabian oil fields, the Ganges – the holy river which at first sight seems to be a very dirty river – Kuala Lumpur, Singapore, and, an unforgettable sight, the tremendous ball of sun, heralding the dawn, rising over the far Pacific. We set foot in Australia at 2 a.m. in Darwin, the hottest and clammiest place I have ever been to, even hotter than Athens in July, where the heat of the sun as it approaches its meridian is such that rehearsals in open air places such as Herodias Attikus Theatre are held before normal breakfast time. At Darwin the whole company was fumigated in the Customs shed by walking, or endeavouring to lift our feet from, a long length of sorbo-rubber matting impregnated with disinfectant. The next port of call (en route for Adelaide) was Sydney. It was a trifle cooler at Sydney, particularly on the airfield, where I paused to admire our plane and the purr of the Rolls Royce engines which had run virtually non-stop for 14,000 miles and, by the sound, were waiting to get going on the return trip. In Adelaide the company was given two whole days to recuperate and acclimatise and, speaking for myself, I needed every minute of it. My instruments (the parable opera equipment) were also in need of acclimatisation and some repairs, for crossing the equator in a cargo boat (they travelled with the small circular stage and other props) had put a severe strain on the pigskin heads of the five Chinese drums used in every opera and the cowhide on the Babylonian drum. The Chinese drums were undamaged and settled down to their new surroundings like the seasoned travellers they were, but the strain on the cowhide of the big drum had proved too much. The wood shell had a nasty crack. With the exception of an occasional disappointingly small audience, the operas went well. The local percussionists, in addition to being the most friendly people, were extremely interested in the products of my workshop. Speaking musically, I was given the 'freedom' of Adelaide with Richard Smith, Professor of Percussion at the Adelaide University, loaning me instruments (and his students as porters) to enable me to lecture at the University for Professor David Galliver, two training colleges, and one or two schools.[7] In the schools I was treated as an old friend as I was known (through the BBC TV *Music Time* series) as 'the man who shows you how to make and play percussion instruments'. I found the Australian children exactly as our own. One or two little girls may have had butterflies in their tummies when helping me to play the tambourine, but such things had happened elsewhere of course.

Melbourne, Canberra and Sydney were equally pleasant. In Australia I renewed acquaintance with an English timpanist, Albert Setty, who was with the A.B.C. Symphony Orchestra, one of Australia's finest orchestras. At the invitation of Professor Donald Peart, another prominent English musician, I lectured at the University of Sydney.

Whilst in Australia I learned much of the life of the aboriginal, and how clap sticks and the didjeridoo remain in many cases their sole musical instruments. I also had the privilege of 'sitting in' with the orchestra of a Balinese troupe of dancers, where I heard techniques on the xylophone that made me want to get back to the xylophone in my practice room and start all over again. With the rest of the company I saw the beauty of the Blue Mountains. The short tour was conducted by a guide, who though he told us little about the Blue Mountains, gave us on the outward and return journeys a lengthy running commentary on the history of nearly every 'bottle' shop in the suburbs of the city,[8] and who owned the shops next door. I left Australia thoroughly enlightened and with memories of great kindness. Numerous presents included two new fifty cent coins which the delightful Director of Music (Nancy Tuck) at the Presbyterian Ladies College, Pymble, had, whilst I was taking tea after a talk given to the school, made a special journey to the bank and persuaded the manager to release, a day before they were due over the counter, as an Englishman wanted them for playing a roll on the drum in Elgar's *Enigma* Variations. I found it no easy

---

[7] David Galliver was well known in England as a concert and oratorio singer. On his staff (also from Britain) were Tom Whiteman (one-time principal bassoon of the London Symphony Orchestra) and Jimmy Whitehead, 'cello.

[8] Bottle shop: off-licence.

matter getting acclimatised to Europe after that trip to Australia. There was plenty to 'acclimatise' me however: the Leeds Festival, the Aldeburgh Festival, performances of the parable operas in Aix en Provence, Flanders Festival, and Decca recordings of *The Rape of Lucretia* and *The Fairy Queen*, among others, in the re-built 'Maltings'. It was during the recording of *The Rape of Lucretia* that I dropped a lovely brick as, failing to recognise a lady who entered the hall whilst I was preparing my instruments, I quietly mentioned that permission to enter the Maltings Concert Hall was given only to those concerned with proceedings. The lady was one of the founders of the Aldeburgh Festival – the Countess of Cranbrook!

The Best Laid Plans

My schedule for the autumn of 1970 was, according to my diary, a heavy one. Preparations were in hand for the tele-recording of B.B's *Owen Wingrave*. This alone had compressed my lecture and teaching activities, added to which I was too often feeling under the weather. Even my doctor's famous bottle of tonic failed to make me feel myself, and for the first time in my career it was only with a great effort that I was able to give what was expected of me. I had of course been doing what many others have done before me: burning the candle at both ends. On 22nd October after a lecture at Bognor I realised that my plans for the next few months were beyond me, and, though I loathed to do it, I took to my bed and kept my wife busy as a nurse and cancelled my forward engagements. Everyone was most understanding and kind, doing much to help my recovery. As soon as I was able I visited a specialist friend who, after the most exacting tests, agreed with my own doctor's opinion that I had been driving myself too hard and an overhaul was necessary. The overhaul included taking stock of myself and – a secret from my wife – making plans for a spurt in the coming year, if all went well.

On the whole 1970 had not been a bad year. I had seen much and learned much. The close of the year saw the publication of my 210,000-word book: *Percussion Instruments and Their History* from which, according to most critics, much could be learned. I learned much from writing it for I was reminded of the fallibility of man; there were certain errors which I trust I have corrected in the second edition. I had also found time (whilst convalescing) to prove that the author who wrote that travel pays a dividend, was correct, for in a flash I had in mind pictures of the Ganges, or the snow-covered

Alps, and had seen a picture of Geza Anda (one of my favourite pianists and conductors) playing a Mozart concerto in a famous Swiss concert hall. I reflected on what to me were interesting incidents. How on one occasion during the tea break prior to a performance in The Royal Festival Hall I had walked along to The Cut near the Old Vic to see a slice of London life, whilst having a cup of tea in a real London café. A blind man entered, also to have a cup of tea. This blind old gentleman, after housing his white walking stick, settled himself comfortably in a corner and removed his blue glasses. He then pulled out a newspaper from the breast pocket of his overcoat. After reading the paper for some time he collected a cup of tea from the counter and returned to his corner. Keeping a watchful eye on the proprietor he drew from an outside pocket of his overcoat an empty tobacco tin which he stealthily filled with sugar. After pocketing the tin he resumed his perusal of the news of the day whilst sipping his tea. His tea break over he put on his blue spectacles, paid for his tea and left the café.

Quaint stories that had been recounted to me by my professional colleagues came to mind. How for example Charlie Donaldson, a contemporary of mine, had told me that as a young man he was once persuaded to go on the stage as 'The Great Donaldi' the 'wizard xylophonist', and that his wife, who attended the first performance, was asked by a gentleman in the next seat, 'Who is that little squirt up there trying to play the xylophone?' Charlie's success as a symphonic percussionist proved the gentleman wrong about 'The Great Donaldi'. A great pity that Charlie Donaldson did not write his life story: he was full of Irish wit and good humour.[8] The same could be said of Freddy Harmer, one of the great percussionists of this century. I was always curious as to how Freddy became a professional and why a percussionist, and he told me his history one lunch time in the smokeroom of a King's Lynn hotel over a double gin. To be brief: as a boy in the Hibernian School, Freddy was given the choice of playing the fife or the drum. To use his own words, 'On entering the band room I noticed that the fifers were standing up to practice and that the drummer boys were doing their "Daddy-Mammy" sitting down – so I became a drummer!' Freddy Harmer and Charlie Donaldson were never without an apt reply even to a conductor. On one occasion Sir Malcolm Sargent expressed his disapproval of the way Charlie was playing a tubular bell. Charles eventually asked Sir Malcolm to demonstrate what he had in mind. 'I most certainly will,' said Sir Malcolm and forthwith struck the bell in

[8] His son John is one of our best known percussionists.

a rather strange manner. 'I think that sounds bloody awful, Sir Malcolm', said Charlie, to which Sir Malcolm retorted, 'It may sound that way to you my man, but that's the sound I want'. A risky business crossing swords with conductors like Sir Malcolm or, of course, Sir Thomas Beecham, or being confronted with the gentler but none the less penetrating wit of Sir John Barbirolli who, on one occasion at King's Lynn Festival, told the members of the Pro Arte Orchestra (myself included) that though he was no ornament, they should glance his way now and again! The 'Beecham' stories are well known and have been faithfully related, none more delight-fully than the 'plum' told to me over coffee in the London Orchestral Association by the late George Orrell (a well-known viola player) who, prior to his many years as the secretary of the L.O.A., was the orchestral manager the Royal Philharmonic Orchestra; a full-time occupation George told me as it embraced coping with the vagaries of both Sir Thomas and Lady Beecham. George had collected a fund of orchestral anecdotes, many of course concerning Sir Thomas and perhaps none more typical than the one concerning 'Tommy's' visit to an auction room in a Northern town. Sir Thomas (like most of us) could not resist the attraction of an auction room and on this particular afternoon as he was being driven to his hotel following a rehearsal, he passed the rear (open) entrance of a sale room. He told his chauffeur to stop and they both quietly entered the room. As it happened the auctioneer was preparing to call for bids for a set of four of those interesting articles of bedroom equipment that (in those days) had an honoured position under the bed for a specific purpose. 'What am I bid for these poes, jerries, piddlepots – call them what you will', said the auctioneer. Despite the auctioneer's coaxing and enlarging on the usefulness of the articles, the bidding was slow. At last Sir Thomas called out, 'Half-a-crown.' 'Half-a-crown – half-a-crown – going at half-a-crown', said the auctioneer. 'Two gentlemen at the back – names please?' 'Chambers and Philpot', replied Sir Thomas as he flicked a half-a-crown from his thumb and made an immediate getaway (without the pots) in the conveniently placed Rolls-Royce.

Only rarely was Sir Thomas placed at a disadvantage, as on the occasion when a well-known oboist pierced this famous conductor's armour. The oboist (James MacDonagh, father of the eminent Terence) had replied with his customary Irish wit to a thrust from Sir Thomas. 'Ah!' said Sir Thomas, 'we have a fool at the end of the oboe.' 'Which end Sir Thomas?' replied 'Mac', as he pointed the bell of his instrument towards the rostrum. These minor passages at arms between conductors and players are in most cases thoroughly relished by both sides. It is not often, however, that a concert audience is given the pleasure of experiencing a shaft of orchestral wit, as at a performance of Berlioz's *Symphonie Fantastique* in a certain northern city during which the bell player got adrift. The timpanist of the orchestra managed, with the help of a second violinist, to get a message to the bell player who was mounted on a ladder off stage. 'Mr. X says you are to stop playing the bells', shouted the violinist to the perspiring campanologist. Unfortunately the message was conveyed to the entire audience by the system amplifying the bells, as was the undaunted bell player's reply, 'Tell Mr. X to go and . . . himself!'

✵ 16 ✵

Fifty Years of 'Percussing'

On 1st January 1921, if I made a New Year resolution, it could have been to become a 'professional'. On 1st January 1971 I was within a few months of having been a 'pro' for fifty years and my New Year resolution may have been to curtail my professional activities and be much less of a 'mole'. If I *did* make a resolution it was very fragile, and my excuse for commencing to 'burrow' once more was that two months of enforced idleness had convinced me that my mother was right when saying that one could rust out more quickly than wear out. I succumbed to the urge to get under way – but took heed of good advice, and restricted my professional activities to a more comfortable working day, thus saving wear and tear on myself and on the engine of my car. Gossip of course had it that I had retired, but my answer to that was, 'Yes, I've retired, I work only eighteen hours a day now, and it's a wonderful feeling not to be forced to rise before five in the morning.'

The year that marked my fifty years as a professional sped along, and with the coming of summer I mentally compared leaving my Cheam home with my brief case bound for the Royal Academy, or taking the boat train from Victoria en route to Ath to tutor the percussion section of the Youth and Music World Orchestra, or loading my car with my extensive and unique equipment in preparation for a lecture-recital at the Aldeburgh Festival, with leaving my Peterborough home with my 'precious equipment' and with my pal Frank Hitchborn's help, trundling the 'horse muckin'' barrow to the station en route for Henley-on-Thames, to take up my job as a circus drummer at £3 5s. od. a week, uniform and tent. Like my experience in the circus the whole of those fifty years has been an adventure, a professional adventure. I have reached the concert hall and I trust the concert hall feels as happy in my reaching it as I do in getting there. Have I any regrets? It would be foolish to say that I have none, for example, I would like to have another crack at the performances in which I may have gone a trifle astray for I have never been able to say of the drum as the young man at the public school said of the piano, 'I have mastered my instrument!'

Then and Now

To reach three-score-and-ten feeling hale and hearty as I did on 9th September 1971 is comforting. I had a lot to look back on and a lot to be thankful for. It was also gratifying to know that many people wished to hear about my professional adventure, prompting me to give an alternative lecture to my established 'Recipes from the Orchestral Kitchen' and my 'A World of Percussion'. This talk I christened 'Then and Now – on becoming a professional – James Blades reminisces whilst discussing fifty years of percussing.' I could of course add four years to the fifty and if I were permitted, add a chapter to this story. Instead I will set my calendar at 9th September 1971 and take a look into a crystal. If I had been in the possession of the power of foresight what would I have seen? Among other things: our lecture-recital 'A World of Percussion' televised on BBC 2 (in Studio I: the largest TV studio in the world); my two appearances on BBC TV in the *Times Remembered* programme; appearing as guest in *Face the Music* (BBC 2) and meeting the young (or they meeting me) when telling them stories in TV *Play School*;[1] giving my 'Then and Now' talk at the Royal Institution and again finishing as the Lecture Theatre clock pinged 10 p.m. – my timing helped by using the relentless 'swish-shush' of *The Prodigal Son* gourd as a fade away; attending an investiture at Buckingham Palace to receive the O.B.E. from the Queen; quite a number of my R.A.M. students installed in our major orchestras; an interesting sketch of myself on the jacket of my LP *Blades on Percussion*; the typescript of my 62 entries for the Sixth Edition Groves Dictionary; addressing an audience from the altar of a small chapel in Sark (not my first lecture in a House of God as I had already given my recital in Ashwell Parish Church and in Chelmsford Cathedral); playing the timpani in the Bach Choir carol concert given in Wormwood Scrubs, and telling a few stories to the men (after being tactfully advised not to open by saying, as had a recent speaker, how delighted he was to see so many people there); meeting and chatting to Duke Ellington in Westminster

[1] A group of small children at a Sussex Primary School found one of my appearances on *Play School* (a tele-recording) distinctly puzzling for it coincided with my visiting the school in person. Quite a number of the infants begged to touch me to see if it was 'really me'.

Abbey on United Nations Day 1973; being elected to *The Percussive Arts Society's* (U.S.A.) *Hall of Fame*; being invited to receive an award of Honorary Degree of Master of Music of the University of Surrey; and the journey to satisfy my urge to renew my acquaintance with a theatre that had so helped to shape my career: 'T'Oxford', Workington. Like most other places, Workington in half a century has seen many changes and my arrival there in 1974 was a totally different experience from being greeted in 1924 by John Henry Wright, Percy Pegleg and the barrow. My first port of call was of course The Oxford Picture House, and what a change I found in 'Brown's Palace'! The final spit and polish was being applied to what was to me an almost unrecognisable structure. 'T'Oxford' was about to be opened as a 'Super Nighterie' ('The Rendezvous') with the lower ground floor as a beer hall, the ground floor as a cabaret theatre, and the upper gallery a dance salon. I asked a gentleman at the front of the house if I could have a look round the place where fifty years ago I had played the drums. After eyeing me carefully he said, 'Certainly, and what is more you can have your job back if you wish, they need a drummer and an organist.' If I had not given a firm date regarding the submission of this autobiography I might have had another spell as 'T'all Oxford' drummer.

And so ends my story. I can claim to have reached the concert hall and that I started on the bottom rung of the ladder in my professional climb. Have I reached the top rung? It would be unwise to claim this distinction, though following a performance at the King's Lynn Festival it was said of me, 'Even now this modest little man lays no claim to having reached the top rung of the professional ladder. But there seems little doubt that he has done so.' (A.J.H., *Eastern Evening News*, 30th June 1974.) It may be asked, would I like to experience my climb all over again? Yes, I most certainly would. I would like to take the *da capo* sign; but that cannot be, and as it is not possible for me to put back the clock I will venture to put it forward and take the coda, trusting that in the years that remain I will continue to have those dear to me around as I grow older: my wife Joan continuing to look and feel as young as ever; my son and his wife Doreen watching young J.M.B. forging ahead; and my brothers Tom and Chris continuing to enjoy their retirement (this year God called Cecil, the youngest). I hope also to thank in person wherever they may be, everyone who has helped me to put pen to paper, and possibly find the time if I feel so inclined, to read a newspaper (I cancelled my order for daily papers in 1945).

And if I never become the Methuselah that so many small children think I am already because I am supposed to know all about Stone Age men, I would like to see the turn of the century and, if not too painful, to listen to the music of A.D. 2000. Yes, I would like to live until I am a hundred, if only for the reason that I have enough to do to keep me busy for another quarter of a century!

Index

Forster, E. M., 222
Fountainbridge Palais, Edinburgh, 108
Francis, John, 209, 214
Frankel, Benny, 130, and *n.*, 133, 151

Gainsborough Studios, Islington, 131, 139
Gale, Herbert, 96: 'Gale's Jazz Band', 96; 'Gale's Jazz Loonies', 96–8, 100
Galliver, Professor David, 256 and *n.*
Gaumont British Studios, 139, 142, 154, 164, 205; Orchestra, 141
Geldard, Sammy, 120, 124, 127–8, 182, 183, 237
General Film Distributors, 151
General Post Office Studios, Blackheath, 152
George V, King, 152; death of, 152
George VI, King, 167, 187–8
Geraldo's Concert Orchestra, 198, 214
Gerhard, Roberto, 242; Works, *Hymnody*, 242
Gezink, William, 120 and *n.*
Gibbons, Carroll, 141
Gibilaro, 'Fof', pianist, 132*n.*
Gibson, Alexander, 244*n.*
Gibson, Kenny, 104
Gielgud, Sir John, 160
Gilbert, Geoffrey, 211
Ginnett's Circus, 66, 68, 72–3
Gish, Lillian, 77
Gleghorn, Arthur, 155, 194*n.*
Glock, Sir William, 218
Glyndebourne, 198
Goddard, Alf, 159
Goehr, Alexander, 187
Goehr, Walter, 161, 186–7, 200
Goldsborough Orchestra, 205
Goldsmith Choir, 219
Gooding, Arthur, 26
Goodley, Matty, 17, 35, 39, 165
Goossens, Joan, 193, 201, 211, 263; marriage to James Blades, 193, 202
Goossens, Leon, 219
Goossens, Marie, 158, 212

Goossens, Sidonie, 208, 212
Goring, Marius, 231
Graham, Colin, 214, 220
Grand Hotel, Eastbourne, 108
Grant, Keith, 237–8
Gray, Alan, 186
Great Yarmouth, 27–8, 37
Green, Phil, 198
Gregory, Beatrice, 211
Gregory, Charles, 211
Gregory Concert Agency, 218
Grey Street Picture House, Newcastle-upon-Tyne, 104
Grimshaw, Ernest, 124–7
Grossman, Sam, 141
Groves, Sir Charles, 234*n.*
Guitry, Sacha, 160
Guyler, Deryck, 231

Haggis, Frederick, 219
Hallé Orchestra, 119–20, 120*n.*, 124
Hamilton, Victor, 106
Handel, George Frideric, 26, 184–5, 189, 244: Works, *Messiah*, 185, 244; *The Harmonious Blacksmith*, 184
Harmer, Freddy, 258
Hartley, Fred, 106, 121, 125; Sextet, 106*n.*
Harty, Sir Hamilton, 119, 124
Hawkes & Son, music publishers, 58, 80–1
Haydn, Franz Joseph, 140; Works, Trumpet Concerto, 140*n.*
Haydn Orchestra, 204
Haydn, Walford, Café Collette Band, 161
Haymarket Theatre, London, 146
Henley-on-Thames, 66–7, 69, 188, 261
Henson, Leslie, 169
Hewitt, Charles E., 98, 163, 165, 211
Hewitt, Mabel, 165, 176
Hewitt, Olive, 98, 107, 109, 116, 133, 176: marriage to James Blades, 100; death, 191
Hibberd, Stuart, 152
Hicks, Sir Seymour, 160, 166–8, 170–2
High Wycombe, 70

Taw and Torridge Festival, 211
Taylor, Alan, 174
Taylor, Coleridge, 212; Works,
Hiawatha, 212
Taylor, Harry, 174
Taylor, Stanley, 224; Works, The
Erle of Oxford's Marche, 224
Tchaikovsky, Peter Ilyich, 238;
Works, Overture 1812, 174
Teddington Film Studios, 165
Terris, Ellaline (Lady Hicks), 167
Theatre Royal, Drury Lane, 166
Thomas, Myra, 247
Thorburn, Bill, 132
Three Choirs Festival, 140
Thurston, Frederick (Jack), 204
Tiomkin, Dmitri, 240
Tippett, Sir Michael, 224; Works,
Crown of the Year, 224
Tivoli Cinema, Strand, London, 111
Toscanini, Arturo, 124, 187
Total Abstinence League, 18
Troise and his Banjoliers, 198
Tuck, Nancy, 256

'V' Committee, V signal, 177, 178,
179, 180, 215 and n.
Valentino, Rudolph, 77
Van Beinum, Edward, 215
Van Dam, Alfred, 126-7
Vaughan Williams, Ralph, 188,
199
Venice Festival of Contemporary
Music, 227
Verdi, Guiseppe, 20; Works,
Requiem, 20
Vere, Vera, 62
Vienna Philharmonic Orchestra,
248
Villa Marina, Douglas, 121, 123,
127
Vinter, Gilbert, 154
Virtuoso Ensemble, 242
Vofsi, Mischa, 238
Vyvyan, Jennifer, 216-17

Walker, Eddie, 149, 216
Walker, Gordon, 139, 149, 173n.,
216
Walker, William, 166-7
Waller, Sims, 107-8

Walton, Freddy, 64, 65-6, 78-9,
80
Walton, John, 207
Walton, Robert, 200
Walton, Sir William, 158, 188,
248: Works, Facade, 158n.; The
Bear, 248
Ward, Dorothy, 169
Warsaw, 228
Waterhouse, William, 204
Waters, Stephen, 209
Watford Town Hall, 226
Way, George H., 105, 108
Webster, Gilbert, 242
Webster, Tom (cartoonist), 166-7,
170-1
Weil, Terence, 209, 213n., 228
Welbeck Abbey, 172
Weldon, George, 174
Welles, Orson, 226
Wells, Bombardier Billy, 152
Westminster Abbey, 207, 262
Whelan, Tim, 159
White, Albert, 105
Whitehead, Jimmy, 256n.
Whiteman, Paul, 123
Whiteman, Tom, 256n.
Whittaker, Alec, 194-5, 197
Whittaker, Steve, 119, 124, 127-8,
182, 237, 242
Wicks, Allan, 247-8
Wigmore Ensemble, 205, 211, 218
Wigmore Hall, 183, 204
Wild, Albert, 141
Wild, Harry, 141
Wilkinson, K. E., 135n.
Willcocks, Dr. David, 234
Williams, Bransby, 84-5
Williams, Charles, 131-2, 185
Williams, Gerry (Geraint), 139,
178n., 187, 192n., 196
Wilson, Bert, 197
Wilson, Hilary, 239
Wilson, John, 218
Wilton, Robb, 191
Windsor Castle, 187, 188
Windsor Royal Chapel, 244
Wingfield Music Club, 220, 252-3
Wisbech, 73
Wood, Freddy,142-3
Wood, Harry,124, 127

INDEX

Wood, Haydn, 124
Wood, Sir Henry, 141–2, 174, 181
Woodgate, Leslie, 115 and n.
Woolf, C. M., 151
Workington, 91, 93, 94, 96, 97, 98, 99, 100, 103, 263
World Mirror series, 232–3
Wragg, Urban, 54
Wright, John Henry, 91–5, 100, 142, 235, 263

Yarholm, Mr., choirmaster, 13, 17–18
Yates, George, 181
Yorke, Peter: Concert Orchestra, 175, 198; 'Sweet and Lovely' Players, 161
Youth and Music World Orchestra, 261

Zildjian, Robert, 33
Zorian, Olive, 209, 248